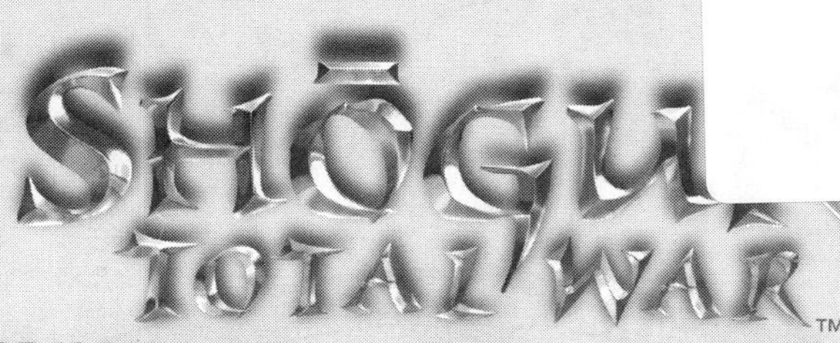

PRIMA'S OFFICIAL STRATEGY GUIDE

WRITTEN BY DEAN EVANS

Created by PRIMA GAMES UK
Published by PRIMA GAMES
A Division of PRIMA COMMUNICATIONS, INC.
3000 Lava Ridge Court
Roseville, CA 95661
916-787-7000

PRIMA GAMES UK
Licensing Director: **Steve Faragher**
Publishing Director: **Maryanne Booth**
Product Manager: **Ashley Young**
Assistant Project Editor: **Michelle Trujillo**
Sub Editor: **Helen Woodey**
Senior Designer: **Sue Huntley**
Project Designer: **Josephine Jeffery**
Additional Design: **Larraine Lawrence and Kieran Holden**

Developed by CREATIVE ASSEMBLY

Printed in the United States of America
ISBN: 0-7615-2779-6

Library of Congress 00-101556

WELCOME

It is foreknowledge that enables
A brilliant ruler and an excellent leader
To triumph over others wherever they move

Sun Tzu (translated by R.L. Wing in "The Art of Strategy")

INTRODUCTION

When I first saw **Shogun: Total War** it was a design document describing a game of humongous proportions—something that was huge and intriguing, vast and epic in scale and deeply atmospheric. I saw a game with great potential and endless possibilities. Simply put, it was aiming to blast the hordes of top-down RTS "point-and-build" games out of existence.

Two years later, as we are adding the finishing touches to the game, I am delighted to see that we have achieved everything that was outlined in the original design brief. I still feel a sense of awe and surprise when I look at **Shogun: Total War** in comparison to games that have gone before.

Instead of focusing on specific policies to use in order to beat the game, **Shogun: Total War** makes me think like a real general. Having built my army from scratch, trained them, paid for them and fed them, I now find that I really do care about their health. Not only that, but I have begun making plans for them, I know that as soon as I have a legendary swordsman he will be used to train other higher-honour swordsmen. With each individual samurai having his own artificial intelligence, I also know that they have plans for me—some who are of low honour may be planning to run away at the first sign of deadly combat. Other more experienced troops are going to prove that they are willing to die for me.

"Seek victory before you seek battle," wrote Sun Tzu in his definitive book on war tactics, probably not imagining that "The Art of War" would still be read by army generals today. Certainly he could not have foreseen that we'd steal his rules and use them in our Artificial Intelligence. But since we put the enemy through school, you should probably do a little reading yourself before taking on this immense game.

Jason Fitzgerald
Studio Marketing Manager

CONTENTS

PREPARATION

Getting Started 7

Game Options 8

The Tutorial 12

ANALYSIS

Knowledge is Power 21

The Basic Unit Types 22

Terrain 33

Weather 37

CONFRONTATION

Prepare for Battle 41

The Battle Screen 42

Formations 43

Battlefield Calculations 45

Battlefield Strategies 52

KNOWLEDGE

Learn from the Past .57

Anegwa 58

Nagakute 62

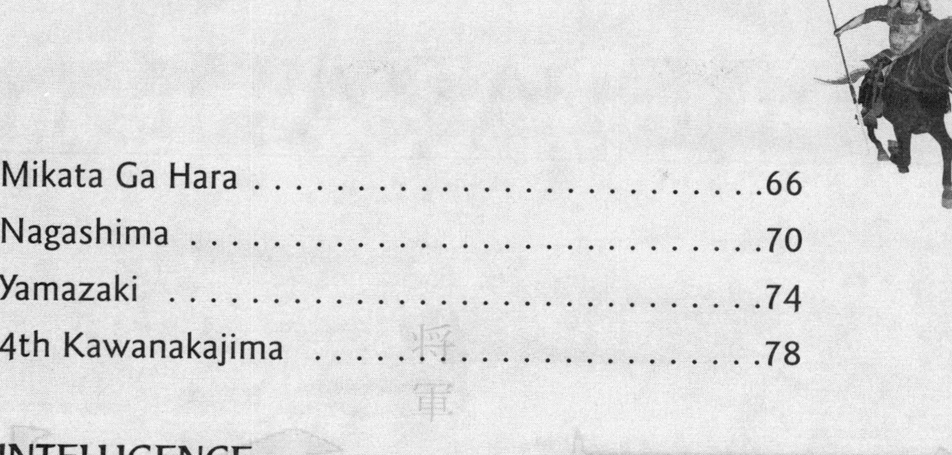

Mikata Ga Hara .66
Nagashima .70
Yamazaki .74
4th Kawanakajima .78

INTELLIGENCE

The Five Strategic Arts .83
The Seven Clans .84
Rebels and Bandits .98
Building Types .100
Building Development .116
Special Unit Types .121
Campaign Map .124
Campaign Provinces .126
Strategies .187
General Campaign Strategies .195

TRIUMPH

Build Your Own Battles .203
Multiplayer .208

PREPARATION

将軍

将軍

支配

将軍

Those who triumph,
Compute at their headquarters
A great number of factors
Prior to a challenge.

Those who are defeated,
Compute at their headquarters
A small number of factors
Prior to a challenge.

Sun Tzu (translated by R.L. Wing in "The Art Of Strategy")

GETTING STARTED

More than just another strategy wargame, *Shogun: Total War* is an exhaustively researched slice of interactive history. Alongside the point-n-click clash of continually warring armies, this game lifts the lid on life in 16th Century Japan. From the personalities and heraldry of this epic age, to the weaponry, battles and ancient tradition, Creative Assembly has created a wargame with extraordinary depth, detail and realism. Fighting with samurai swords, spears, even early gunpowder weapons, *Shogun: Total War* invites you to battle for control of Japan and to recreate history on famous battlefields. You can even design new confrontations of your own. In this strategy game, war can be as "Total" as you want it to be.

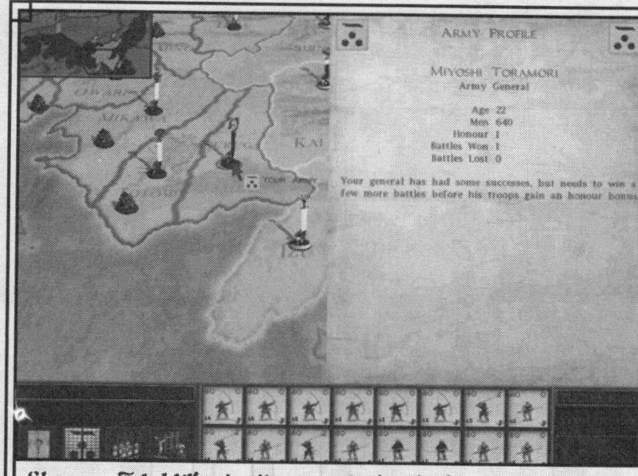

Shogun: Total War invites you to battle for control of Japan or recreate history on famous battlefields.

Shogun: Total War is nothing if not flexible. As such, the game has been designed to be played in several different ways. After familiarising yourself with the basic controls and features in the Tutorial section, three distinct gaming modes await the Oriental armchair general. Six Historical Battles invite you to replay and recreate some of the bloodier moments in Japanese history. In addition, a Multiplayer option enables you to fight with up to seven other players on any of the provinces featured in the game. Custom Battles, meanwhile, invites players to construct and play out their own skirmishes with the full range of units and battlegrounds that the Japanese war machine has to offer. Lastly, and most impressively, the giant Campaign mode offers to satisfy your expansionist bloodlust with an ongoing strategic challenge. Construct buildings, recruit new troops, mastermind a long-term plan that will see your family clan rise from rural obscurity to ruling elite.

Every good Daimyo in ancient Japan had a trusted and loyal advisor. Consider Prima's Official Strategy Guide to be yours.

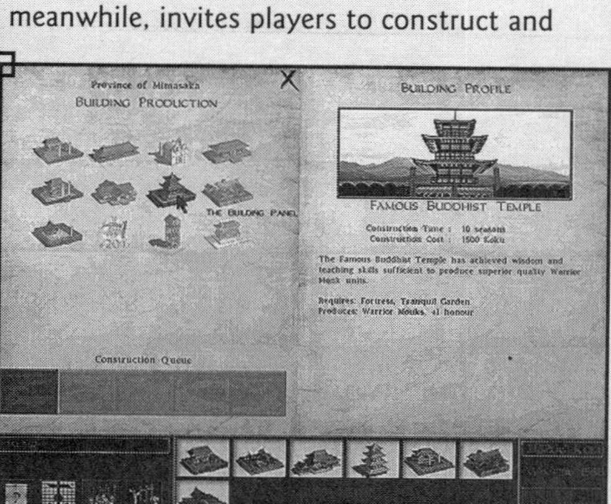

Build temples and Dojos and you can develop a family clan into a mighty Imperial army.

Master politics, diplomacy, resource management and strategy on the battlefield.

GAME OPTIONS

So much more than just a Japanese-themed expansionist wargame, this game offers a variety of different options for the would-be Daimyo (translated as "big name"). All of the game's Campaign and single-mission modes are accessed via the Main Menu. This screen gives you the opportunity to select either New Game, Load Game, Multiplayer, Tutorial, Options or Quit. Before starting any new game, take the time to set your preferred game options. To do this, click on the Options heading near the bottom of the Main Menu listing.

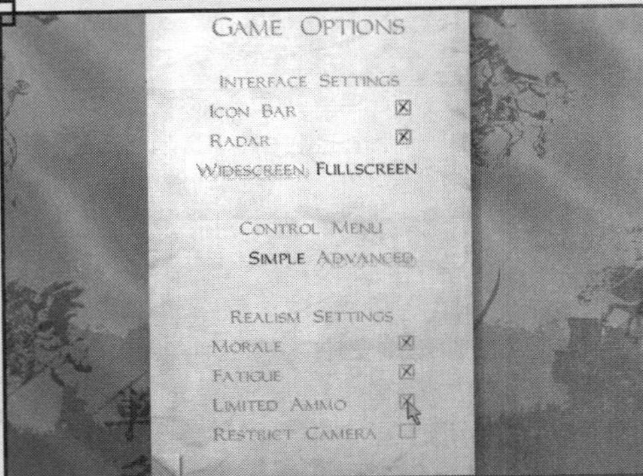

Customise *Shogun: Total War* just the way you like it. Infinite ammunition? No problem.

OPTIONS

When *Shogun: Total War* is installed, it automatically configures itself to take advantage of the specification of your PC. If you want to change the default setup, the options available to you on this screen include:

VIDEO

Adjust whether the game renders its graphics using software or with a little hardware-accelerated help (if applicable). You can also increase or decrease the resolution of the Strategy Map and the Battlemap here, plus adjust the Gamma Correction level.

AUDIO

Choose the level of the game's sound effects and music in the Audio sub-menu. Sound can even be turned off completely via the Mute button, allowing covert office play when the boss isn't looking...

GRAPHICS

You can adjust various graphical elements depending on your PC's specifications. Detailed visuals such as smoke and dust can be switched on or off, while the basic unit size (max 120) and the number of soldiers permitted on the battlefield (max 16,000) can be tweaked.

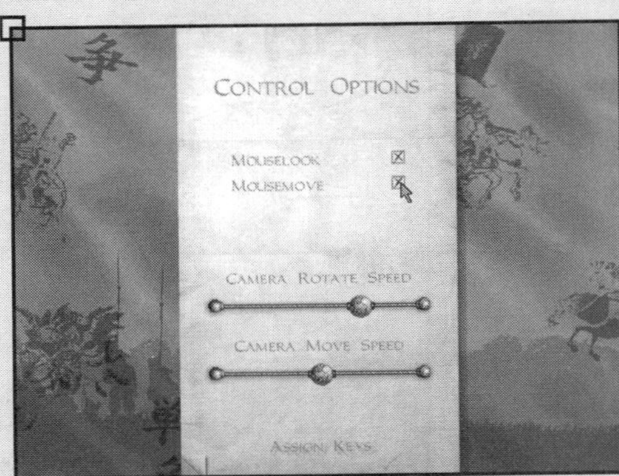

How you control the game, and how quick the responses are can be altered here.

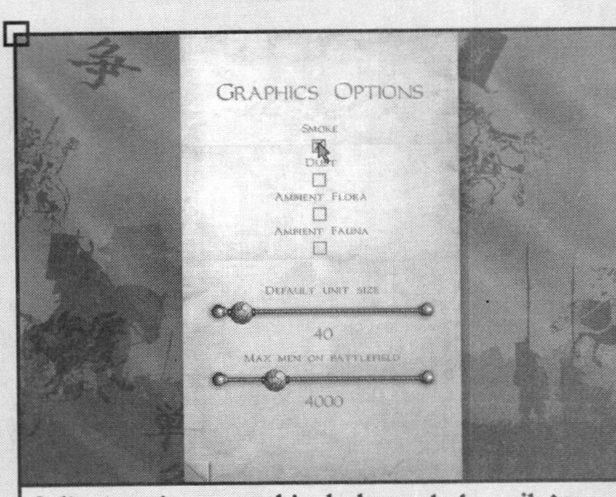

Adjust various graphical elements to suit your PC's processing power.

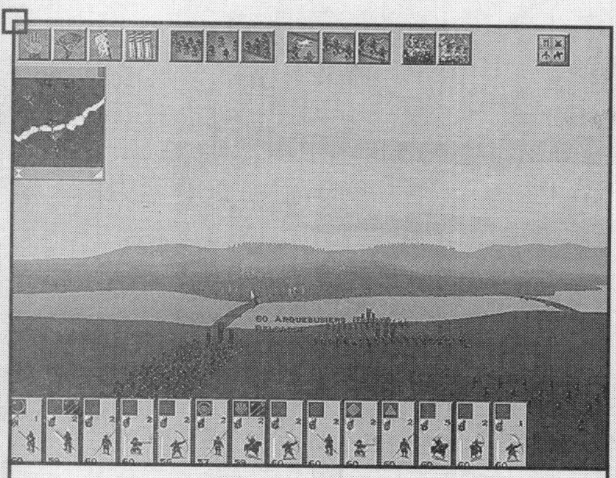
There are six Historical Battles to play, including the battle at Anegawa in 1568.

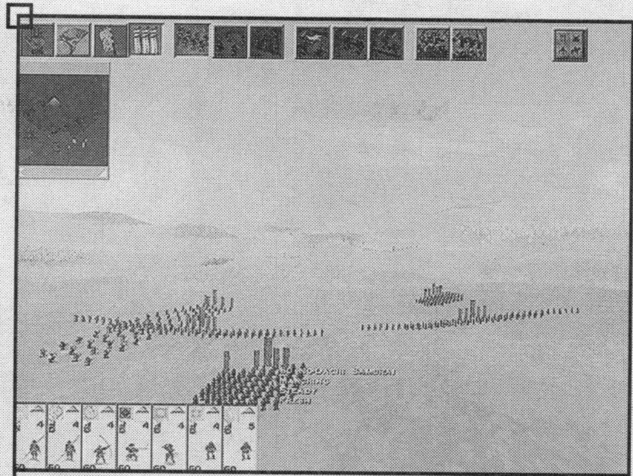
At Mikata Ga Hara in 1572, your force will be outnumbered by a factor of 2:1.

CONTROLS

Here, players can meddle with the speed of mouse movement, redefine the keyboard commands, and decide whether the mouse or the cursor keys should be used to rotate and move the camera during battles.

GAME

Finally, adjust the way the game looks and how realistic it plays on the Game sub-menu.

NEW GAME

Set the game options to your liking, then select New Game. At this point, if you haven't already tackled the Tutorial section, do so now—it provides a valuable insight into how *Shogun: Total War* works. Once you have mastered the five training sections (see page 12), the New Game menu gives you the option of choosing from Historical Battles, Full Campaign or Custom Battles.

HISTORICAL BATTLES

The Historical Battles section challenges you to recreate medieval Japanese history by fighting in one of six legendary face-offs. Where the other options give you a choice of the units you can use and the battlefield you fight on, in these Historical Battles you fight with what you're given on a pre-defined killing ground.

Extensively researched and simulated in extraordinary detail, the Historical Battles simulated include:

ANEGWA (1568)

A battle fought between the celebrated general Oda Nobunaga and an alliance of forces led by Asai Nagamasa and the renegade Shogun, Asakura Yoshikage.

NAGAKUTE (1584)

A clash between two giant armies led by Tokugawa Ieyasu and Toyotomi Hideyoshi.

MIKATA GA HARA (1572)

Outnumbered by a factor of three-to-one, Tokugawa Ieyasu faced a mighty invading army commanded by Takeda Shingen.

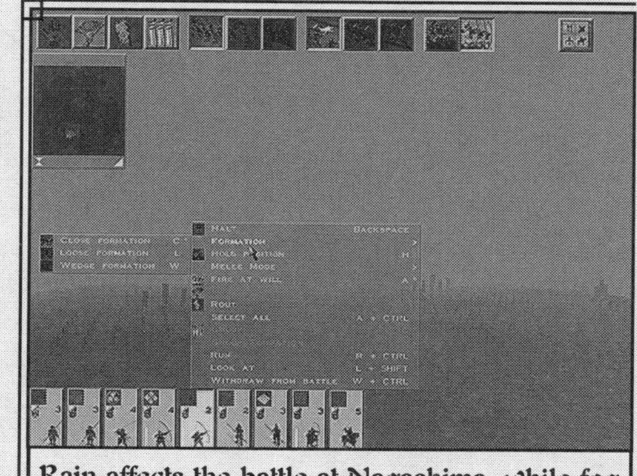
Rain affects the battle at Nagashima, while fog wrecks tactics at Kawanakajima.

NAGASHIMA (1573)

After a disastrous attack against the fanatical Ikko-Ikki Warrior Monks in 1571, Oda Nobunga took personal control for the second siege of Nagashima two years later.

YAMAZAKI (1582)

After the death of Oda Nobunga, Toyotomi Hideyoshi swore revenge and led an army to crush the forces of Akechi Mitsuhide who had murdered Nobunga's only son and heir.

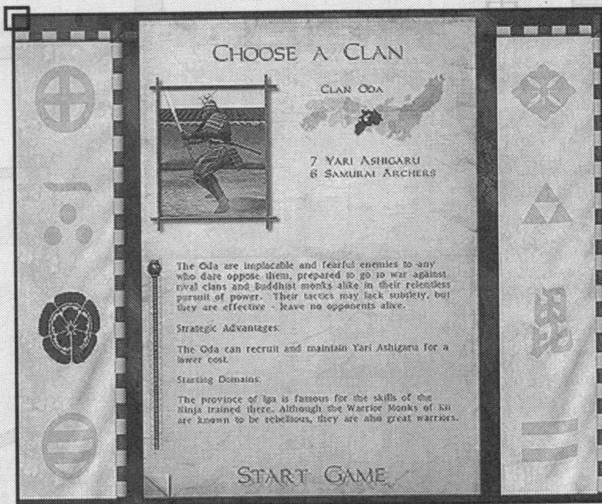

Take command of an ancient Japanese clan and strive for dominance over six rivals.

4TH KAWANAKAJIMA (1561)

This was the fourth battle to be fought on this desolate stretch of land between the Takeda and Uesugi clans. It is deemed to be the bloodiest confrontation of this Sengoku period.

FULL CAMPAIGN

Playable on one of four difficulty levels (Easy, Normal, Hard and Expert), the Full Campaign is a tough challenge. Taking command of one of seven clans, you ruthlessly confront, fight and conquer your empire-building rivals. Starting with a small standing army, you need to learn how to juggle your clan's resources so you can fund your lust for power. New buildings must be constructed to develop new troop types, while your clan's homelands need to be protected with border forts and irrigated to improve the annual harvest. The more Koku you can produce, the greater the army your clan can support. Each one of the seven clans in the Campaign mode has its own particular strength. Choose to become Daimyo of the Shimazu family (famous for their No-Dachi samurai), or head up the Mori clan (renowned for the fanaticism of its Warrior Monks). The Oda family (a big hit with the peasants) sits threatened on all sides by potential enemies,

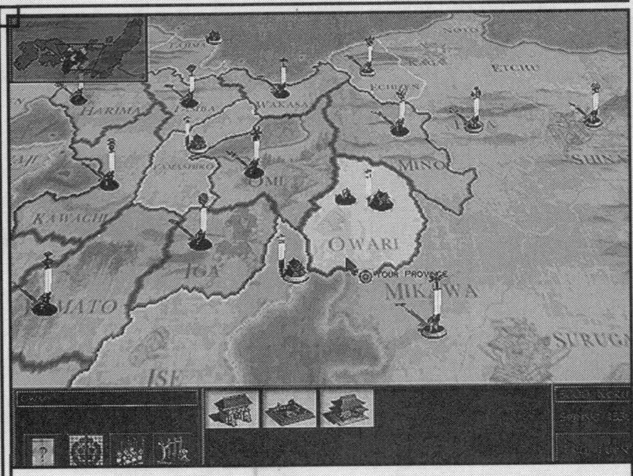

Starting with a small empire, you must develop and expand to conquer Japan.

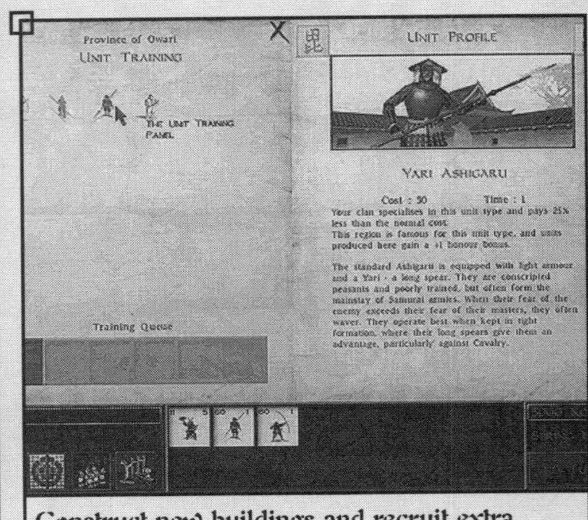

Construct new buildings and recruit extra troops as you aim to become Shogun.

while the Imagawa lands are rumoured to be the training ground for elite spies and Ninja. The Takeda clan brags long and loud about its legendary Cavalry units; the Uesugi family write epic poetry about the enduring accuracy of its Archers. Which leaves the Hojo who, rumour has it, can build Castles so strong not even the mightiest army can breach their walls. Add to all this political instability the appearance of Portuguese traders (bearing gunpowder weapons like the Arquebus) and the menace of bandits, and the Full Campaign mode offers an enticing challenge. With 60 individual provinces to invade, 11 different troop types, plus numerous special units (spies, emissaries, Ninja assassins), the Campaign mode puts your strategic skill to the ultimate test.

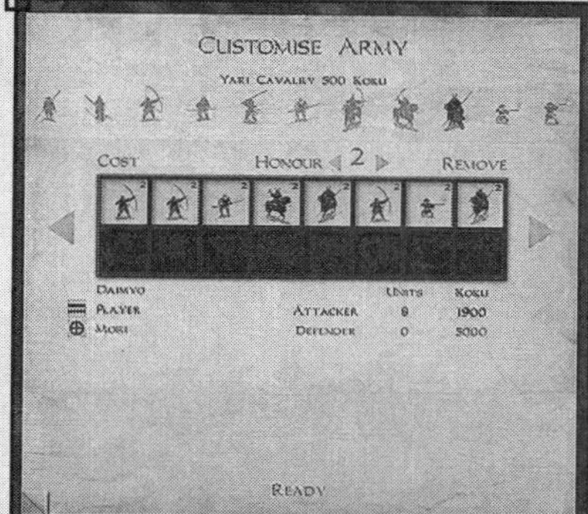

Design your own clashes with the Custom Battle option.

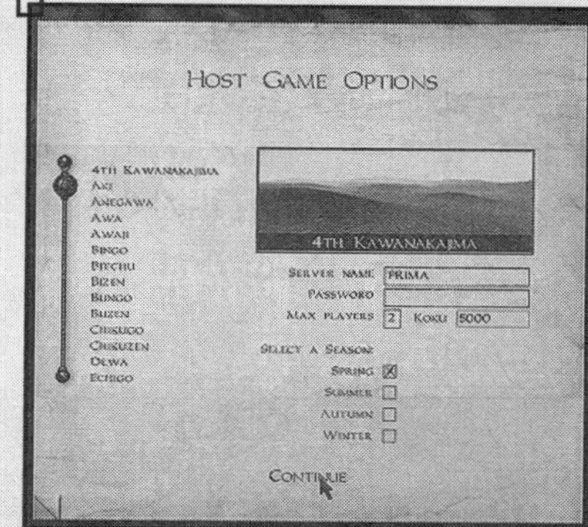

Play alone or against other players over the Internet or LAN.

CUSTOM BATTLE

Should you best the six Historical Battles or dominate old Japan in the Full Campaign, *Shogun: Total War* also gives its players the opportunity to design and fight their own skirmishes in the Custom Battle mode. Here, players can choose not only where they fight but the sort of troops they want to use. All of the battlefields and basic unit types featured can be accessed, allowing DIY scenarios to be built pitting peasant soldiers (Ashigaru) against Warrior Monks in a Castle siege, or samurai against Cavalry Archers in a battle for a strategic bridge.

LOAD GAME

As the Campaign mode could take weeks, if not months to complete, you can take a break from your Shogun-ing by saving your game. Use the Load Game option when you want to continue where you left off.

MULTIPLAYER

Pit your wits and tactical know-how against other human players in the Multiplayer option. On the Multiplayer menu, you can connect to the *Shogun* world via EA Net, or host/join a game on a Local Area Network. There also options here to connect to the official *Shogun: Total War* website and news server. Note: You need to specify a Dial Up Adapter in this menu so that the game can access the Internet-related features and content.

TUTORIAL

Familiarise yourself with *Shogun: Total War's* 3D battle interface, troop types and basic tactics in a series of easy-on-the-brain training missions. You can read more about this section on the Tutorial pages overleaf.

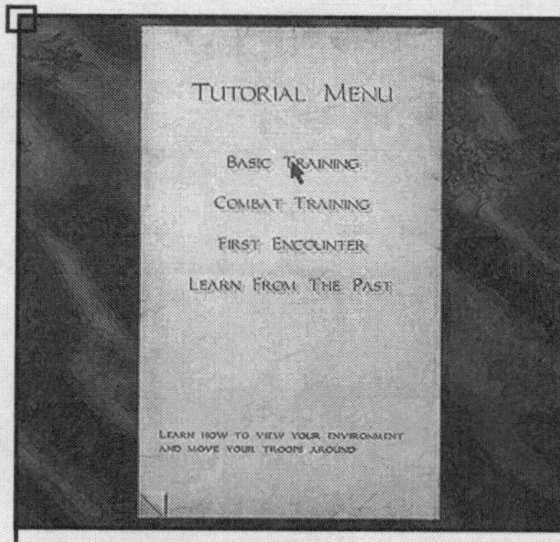

The best way to ease yourself into the game is to complete the built-in Tutorial section.

THE TUTORIAL

Much of the game's design and balance has been inspired by the ancient teachings of Chinese strategist Sun Tzu. His work, referred to as *The Art of War* or *The Art of Strategy*, is believed to have been written sometime between 480 and 221 BC, in the period of Chinese history known as the "Warring States". In essence, Sun Tzu developed a set of philosophical principles that were designed to achieve victory over an enemy. Throughout his work, emphasis is given to the planning and analysis *before* a confrontation as much as the tactics required required to achieve victory. Sun Tzu taught that a successful strategy is not just a case of studying how your target functions, but how your own troops and resources can be used to best effect.

The Tutorial offers four basic modules that are crash courses in battlefield leadership.

Although Sun Tzu's original treatise was developed as a consequence of political and social chaos in China, it's equally relevant to feudal Japan. Similar to the Chinese Warring States period, a sprawling conflict that lasted over 150 years, *Shogun: Total War* simulates a dangerous age of small wars and big ambition. In the game's Campaign mode, definitely its biggest challenge, players must amass not only battlefield experience, but the tactical knowledge that must sit alongside it. What good do the past deeds of 200 samurai do them if they face an army three times their size?

In this section you will learn everything from formations to battle strategies.

Basic Training aims to familiarise you with the basic control system.

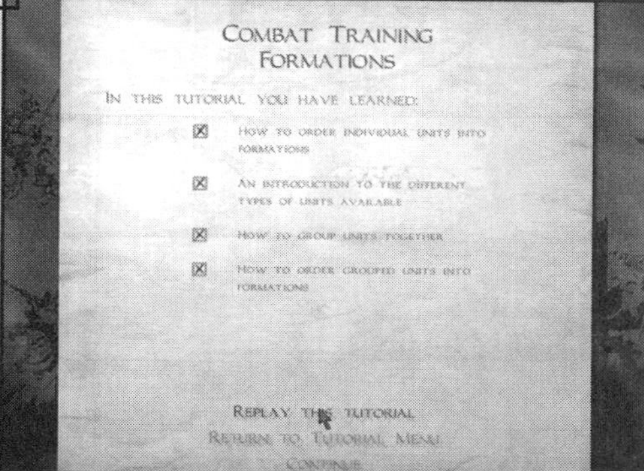

Complete every section and you will be able to tackle the Campaign and Historical Battles.

Anybody can learn "how" to attack or "where" to strike at an enemy to cause maximum damage and destruction. A good general must also know "when" to fight, and equally "when" to withdraw.

First, let's examine the "how". *Shogun* school begins in the excellent Tutorial section, an essential crash-course in Japanese battlefield etiquette that should be completed before you embark on any Historical or Campaign conflicts. While the strategies, tactics and other information featured within this guide are designed to help you overcome the enemies you will face, they are almost useless without a grasp of the game's basic functions. Thus, the Tutorial section not only instructs you on the most efficient ways to move your troops but shows you how to use the camera to view them. It also shows how to group units together for combat, how to manage different military elements and what basic combat tactics are required to survive, let alone succeed in battle.

The Tutorial section teaches the basic functions and tactics in the following training modules:

- Basic Training—Movement
- Combat Training—Formations
- First Encounter—The Advantage of Height
- First Encounter—The Advantage of Cover
- Learn from the Past—The First Encounter

Master these five basic arts and you will have the basic knowledge to tackle the greater challenges that lie ahead in the Historical Battles and Campaign modes.

The Tutorial's lessons are spoken by an instructor and displayed onscreen.

The first Tutorial will teach you how to move a unit of Yari samurai and use the camera to view them.

BASIC TRAINING—MOVEMENT

In this opening lesson, a patient general seeks to teach you the basic mouse controls that will enable you to move and direct a unit of soldiers on the battlefield. While these controls are extremely straightforward, their use needs to become fast and instinctive. The Basic Training section teaches the following:

- How to use the arrow keys to move the camera about.
- How to focus the camera with the right mouse button.
- How to select a unit with the mouse.
- How to move your troops in a march and charge.

There are no enemies to face in this opening training session. Get used to the camera controls (using the mouse or cursor keys), and use the unrestricted view to tour the landscape. In later battles and Campaign conflicts, the roving nature of the camera view is limited to the area immediately surrounding your troops.

As in all of the training missions, you are guided through the basics by helpful onscreen text. If you want to speed up time at any point, use the Speed Slider that is located at the bottom of the small, overhead map (top-left). Drag the slider with the mouse pointer or use [CTRL] and [T] to alternate between 0 percent and 100 percent time compression.

In short, click a unit to select it, then click again to indicate where you want it to go.

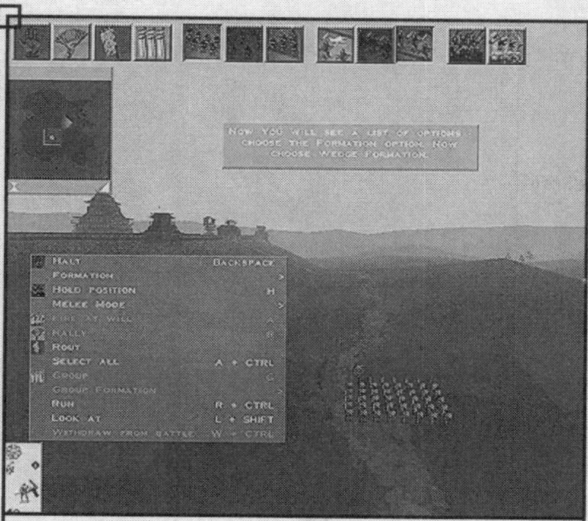

The second lesson deals with formations, their importance and their benefits.

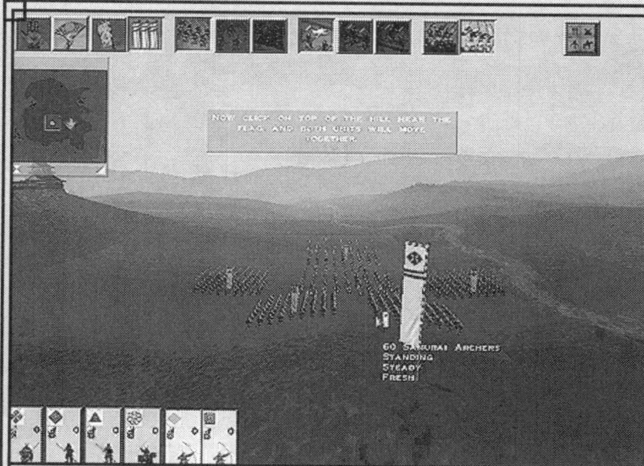

Learn to rearrange single units and whole armies made up of hundreds of soldiers.

COMBAT TRAINING—FORMATIONS

While the first training session is certainly simplistic, it nevertheless teaches the fundamentals of troop command and movement better than a manual ever could. After clicking on Continue to move to the Combat Training module, the patient Japanese general returns to instruct you on unit formations and groups. In short, the Combat Training section reveals the following important info:

- How to order individual units into formations.
- An introduction to the different types of units available.
- How to group units together.
- How to order grouped units into formations.

You should have no trouble passing and completing Combat Training as long as you are a good student and follow the spoken (and onscreen) instructions. Instead of right-clicking on the flag to access the Formations option, you can also use the shortcut on the icon menu bar that sits at the top of the screen. Details of what each box does are highlighted when you move the mouse pointer over them. An explanation of the Group command follows the basic Formations walkthrough. Again, instead of right-clicking on selected units here, simply click on the Group icon (displaying three white flags) on the menu bar. To select all of your troops, use the keyboard shortcut, [CTRL] and [A]. Lastly, predefined army formations can be accessed via the Control Panel Toggle on the far right-hand side of the menu bar.

You can organise your troops into smaller groups, creating useful sub-divisions within the main force.

THE TUTORIAL

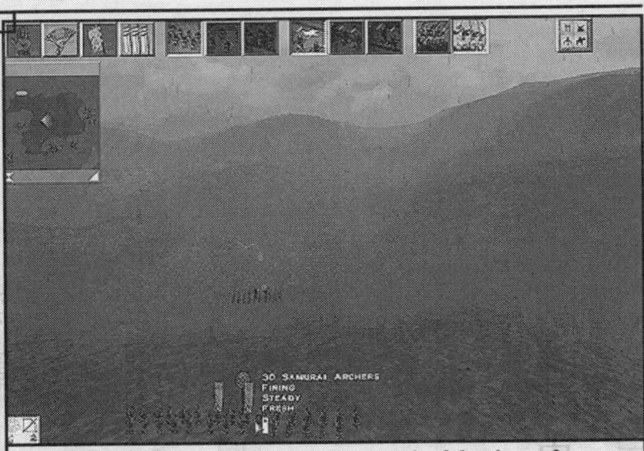

In this simple encounter, your squad of Archers faces a unit of Yari samurai.

Although the Yari samurai are stronger, the Archers have the advantage of height...

FIRST ENCOUNTER—THE ADVANTAGE OF HEIGHT

As its name suggests, First Encounter puts all the walking and formation drills behind you and tests you with a simple combat situation. But the important lesson that needs to be learned here is the value of a height advantage. It's a tactic that you will find useful throughout the game, whether you're fighting in an Historical Battle or defending a border outpost against an assault by samurai spearmen. In fact, the first part of the First Encounter module reveals:

- The importance of height advantage.
- How to fight hand-to-hand by left-clicking on the enemy.
- How to fire ranged weapons by left-clicking on the enemy.
- How to charge into battle by double-clicking on the enemy.

This is a short and sweet exercise which begins has a troop of 30 Archers defending a hilltop against 34 enemy Yari samurai approaching foolishly from below. If at any time you want longer to assess the situation, press [P] to pause the action (you can still move the mouse and the camera while the game is frozen). To attack the enemy, force with your ranged weaponry, click on the Archers and then left-click on the samurai steadily approaching your position. However, due to the poor weather conditions and the low skill of the Archers, you won't be able to kill all of the samurai with bow fire. Wait until they are about two-thirds of the way up the hill, then hold down [ALT] (which changes the cursor to a sword) and double left-click on the samurai. This causes your Archers to abandon their bows and charge into a hand-to-hand melee. As your Archers are still fighting with a height advantage, they should easily defeat the struggling samurai who will be tired and suffer a penalty for fighting uphill.

Fighting downhill, the Archers can even beat the samurai in hand-to-hand combat.

FIRST ENCOUNTER—THE ADVANTAGE OF COVER

Where the previous training scenario pit you against only one enemy and allowed you to attack from an advantageous position, the tables are turned in this next lesson. While you now have 40 Archers, 40 Yari samurai and 40 Heavy Cavalry at your disposal, enemy Arquebusiers stubbornly hold the hilltop in front of you. Yet, although it seems initially daunting, this situation exists to teach you the following:

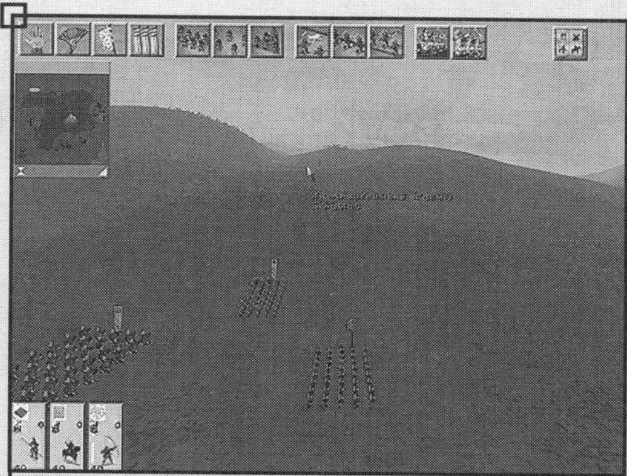

This training scenario is a little harder—here the enemy has the height advantage.

- It is possible to hide and set ambushes in the forest.
- A combination of ranged attack and close combat is the most effective strategy.
- Charging your men constantly will tire them, especially uphill or in snow.
- Units that fire projectiles are generally weaker at hand-to-hand combat.

Taking into account the four points above, the best strategy would seem to be an attack through the trees to hit the enemy's left side or right flank. Unlike the bow and arrow, the Arquebus gun can only fire in a straight line. Thus you can position your Archers directly in front of them, but hidden behind the lip of the hill—from here they can arc arrows into the ordered ranks of the enemy. Meanwhile, in a classic pincer movement, move the Yari samurai up to the top of the tree-covered hill and the Cavalry around to the right to the wood behind the enemy. As your samurai advance, you should spot that there is a third rank of Arquebusiers hidden in the woods. With the Archers still firing, order the samurai to charge into the Arquebusiers in the woods and the Heavy Cavalry to charge into the back of the Arquebusiers on the hill. Once forced to flee by this sudden attack, the Arquebusiers will be unable to use their weapons. Forced to rely on their hand-to-hand skills, they will be no match for your forces.

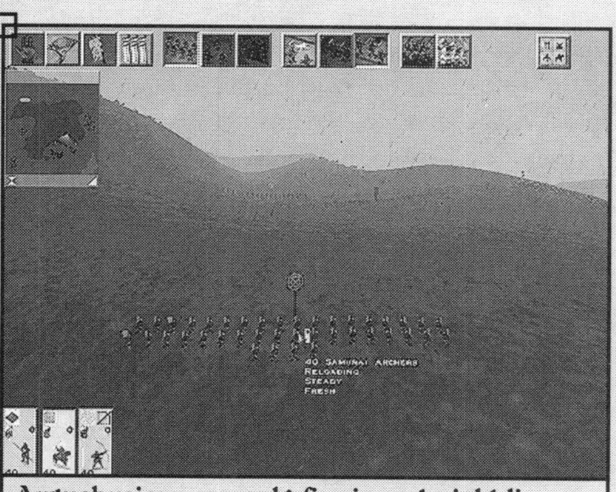

Arquebusiers can only fire in a straight line, but Archers can fire "over" the brow of a hill.

Send the infantry to attack from the left flank and the Cavalry to strike from the right.

It's the ultimate test—two equally matched forces. Remember the importance of "height".

1. At the start of the final scenario, press [P] to pause the game. This allows you to move the camera and survey the landscape. A good knowledge of where you are fighting is just as important as how you fight.

LEARN FROM THE PAST—THE FIRST ENCOUNTER

The final Tutorial segment draws together everything you have been shown so far and places you in command of an army of 320 men. You will be tested against a similarly equipped enemy force in a random scenario and success relies on what you have already learned, plus the last-minute pointers that this lesson gives on matching your units correctly against different types of enemy.

- Archers are effective against slow-moving Spearmen.
- Fast-moving Cavalry excel against Archers.
- Entrenched Spearmen will gain victory over Cavalry.

2. In this match-up, the enemy has the same units as you. In order to tip the balance in your favour, you need to use the terrain to your advantage. Remember: Most units are at their strongest when attacking downhill.

A good general will know how to use the accumulated knowledge to gain victory and honour in the field of battle. No matter which scenario you play, the key to beating the opposing army is to make full use of the forces you have and to position them in the most advantageous location. Thus, Archers should be placed on high ground where they can fire down onto the plains to cause maximum damage. The Yari samurai units can form a defensive wall against the attempts of the enemy Cavalry to break the lines of your bowmen, while your own Cavalry can be used in a mobile role to harass the enemy. The Yari Cavalry are expendable—but take care of the Heavy Cavalry as this is the unit that your general commands. If he dies, the rest of your troops will suffer a Morale penalty making them less effective.

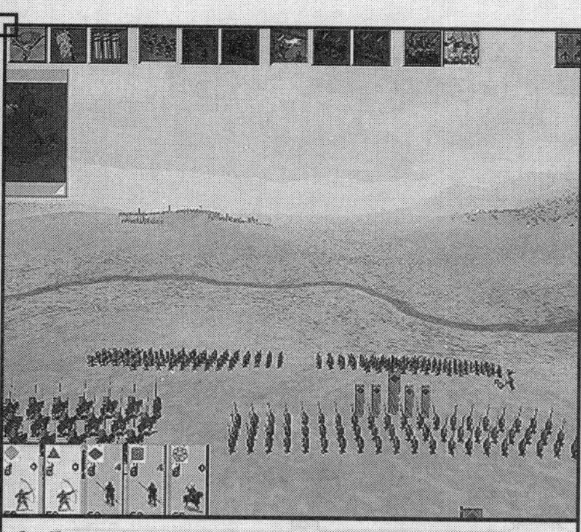

3. Scan the surrounding area. When you've located a suitably defensible hill, move your two Archer units to a vantage point atop it. From here they will not only be able to get a good view of the battlefield, but gain a much greater field of fire.

4. As for the Cavalry units, Heavy Cavalry is significantly more effective than Yari Cavalry, able to wreak havoc should it manage to break through the enemy samurai and onto the Archers beyond. When the battle starts, hold both these units back behind the Yari samurai and the Archers. Their increased mobility will allow them to plug holes in the defensive line should it be breached.

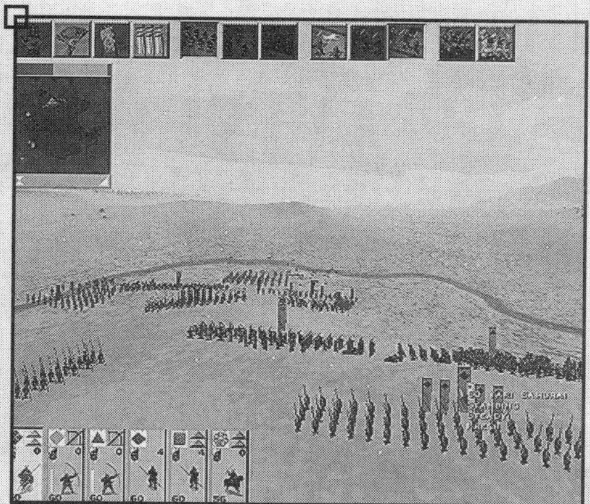

5. Similarly, your ground troops need to be arranged in readiness to cause maximum disruption and damage to the enemy lines. For starters, order the two Yari samurai units to take up a holding position in front of the samurai Archers. The enemy must now move upwards to engage your main force in battle. Give the order to charge when they are halfway through their climb.

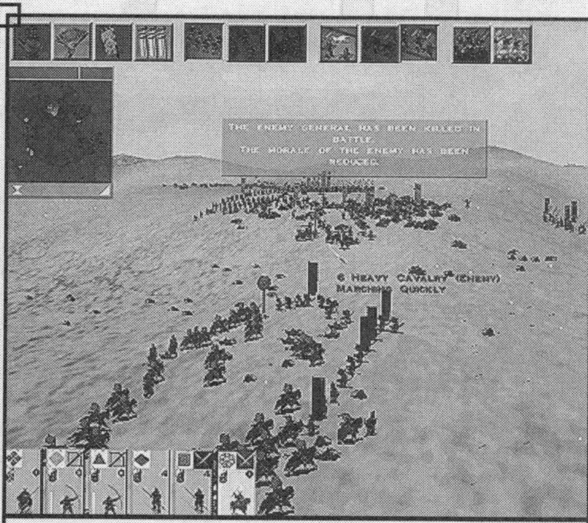

6. Finally, you may find that adopting a defensive posture forces the AI-controlled enemy into a rethink of its attack strategy—especially if you hold the high ground. The danger here is that you could be tempted to break formation in order to pursue. If you must change position to follow the enemy, recreate the same formation farther up the battlefield. Victory here will mark the end of the Tutorial section.

ANALYSIS

啓発

Know the other and know yourself,
One hundred challenges without danger.
Know not the other and yet know yourself,
One triumph for one defeat.
Know not the other and know not yourself,
Every challenge is certain peril.

Sun Tzu (translated by R.L. Wing in "The Art of Strategy")

KNOWLEDGE IS POWER

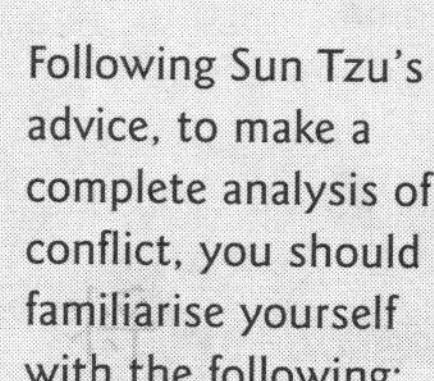

In the thirteen chapters that form the basis of *The Art of War*, Sun Tzu suggests that a wise strategist should undertake a full analysis of any situation before conflict is attempted. What the translated passage on the left implies is simply this: By knowing yourself, you can also know your enemy. This is especially true in *Shogun: Total War*. Because whether you are playing a Custom, Historical or Campaign battle, it's vitally important that you know the strengths and limitations of your troops and the effects that the environment will have on them. When you have analysed this knowledge, you will be in a strong position to know the strengths and limitations of your enemy's troops, and the effects that the environment will have on them.

This section of the guide, therefore, takes a look at the factors that determine whether your forces will charge to glorious victory on the battlefield or suffer a humiliating defeat at the hands of sixty peasant farmers. From the type of troops that you employ to the weather conditions that they fight in, *Shogun: Total War* takes into account a number of variables to resolve both ranged and hand-to-hand combat.

Learn the basic lessons: to know yourself is also to know your enemy.

Following Sun Tzu's advice, to make a complete analysis of conflict, you should familiarise yourself with the following:

Improve your efficiency by understanding the effects that the landscape has on your troops.

THE BASIC UNIT TYPES

With eleven different troop types available, to know the secrets of your own Archers is to know the secrets of your enemy's Archers.

TERRAIN

Use the high ground to your advantage, suggests Sun Tzu. But what if you have to engage an enemy on a flat, featureless plain?

WEATHER

Not all battles take place on bright, clear days with no wind. Snow, rain and even fog can play havoc with your tactical planning.

FATIGUE

Even little computer-generated samurai get tired running around a battlefield in heavy computer-generated armour.

MORALE

A good general should concentrate on persuading the enemy general that it is in his best interests to run away.

COMBAT

Why did your overwhelming force of 120 Yari samurai get massacred by only twenty-four Warrior Monks? Understand how combat works and you'll understand how to win.

THE BASIC UNIT TYPES

The key to success in *Shogun: Total War* is the correct use of the game's different unit types. By using, say, Archers in combination with Yari samurai, you can benefit from the strengths of each troop type while minimising the inherent weaknesses of the two units. For Custom, Historical and Campaign battles, generals have up to 11 different troop types at their disposal—Yari Ashigaru, Yari samurai, No-Dachi samurai, Warrior Monks, Naginata, samurai Archers, Arquebusiers, Musketeers, Yari Cavalry, Cavalry Archers and Heavy Cavalry. Each individual troop type is detailed here.

NOTE

The Attack and Defence factors quoted in the tables in this chapter refer to hand-to-hand combat only.

YARI ASHIGARU

Troop Type: Peasant Footsoldier (Ashigaru translates as "light feet")

Weapon: Long Spear

As expansionist samurai leaders needed an almost endless supply of soldiers to fight for them, peasants often signed up as Ashigaru—light-footed troops with low-grade armour and weaponry. There are a multitude of uses for this humble Yari Ashigaru unit (Yari = "spear"). While they may be poor in combat and lack the bravery displayed by rival units, their cheapness allows you have lots of them.

Because of this expendability, Ashigaru can either be used to absorb enemy arrow fire (therefore depleting enemy ammunition), or as an advance force designed to draw an enemy out of position. Their primary function is to add mass to an army, but the best way to use them is to keep them at the back of your formation so they don't affect the morale of the professional troops ahead of them. Towards the end of the battle when the enemy are tiring, the fresh Ashigaru units can be useful in turning the tide of combat. Armed with long spears, they are also reasonably effective against Cavalry Archers and Yari Cavalry.

YARI ASHIGARU	
Attack Factor	-1
Defence Factor	-1
Armour	2
Morale Bonus	-4
Walk Speed	7
Run Speed	12

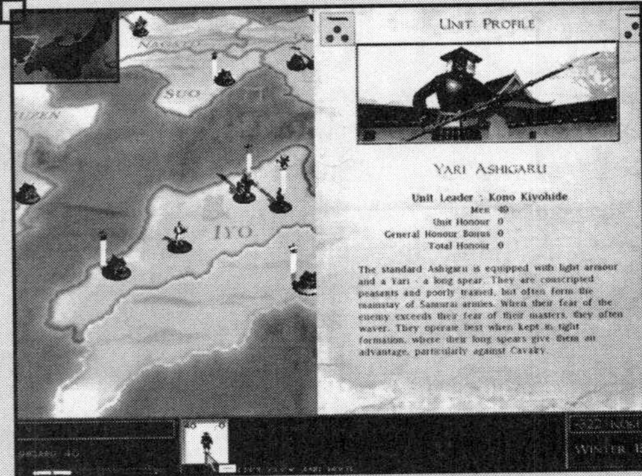

As peasants conscripted into the army, the Ashigaru are a poor substitute for trained samurai.

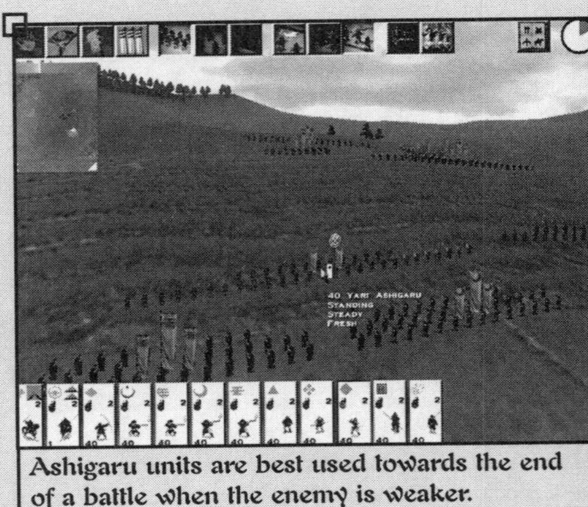

Ashigaru units are best used towards the end of a battle when the enemy is weaker.

YARI SAMURAI

Troop Type: Footsoldier
Weapon: Long Spear

Yari samurai, literally "samurai who carry spears", are the mainstay of the medieval Japanese army. Wielding what is essentially a sword blade attached to a long, wooden pole, these spearmen are quite tough in combat, well armoured, and highly effective against Cavalry units. While their flexibility allows them to be used effectively to attack enemy units, it is the Yari samurai's defensive properties that make them valuable to generals. Forming a strong, protective shield, ranged weapon units (such as Archers, Arquebusiers and Musketeers) can easily withdraw behind them for protection. Similarly, lightly armoured troops (i.e. Ashigaru, Warrior Monks) can shelter behind them while their ranks absorb enemy arrow-fire.

Yari samurai can be used very effectively when instructed to hold a defensible position (such as a hilltop) and can prove powerful with spears lowered charging into an enemy approaching from below. The Yari samurai unit provide generals with a good, all-round fighting force despite being one of the slower troops on the battlefield. Their only major weakness is that they can become vulnerable to Cavalry charges if caught while disordered or while their spears are pointing in the opposite direction.

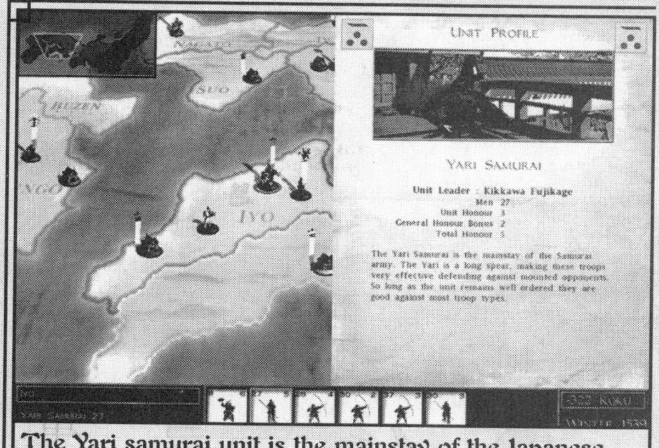

The Yari samurai unit is the mainstay of the Japanese army—a samurai armed with a spear.

YARI SAMURAI	
Attack Factor	0
Defence Factor	2
Armour	3
Morale Bonus	2
Walk Speed	6
Run Speed	10

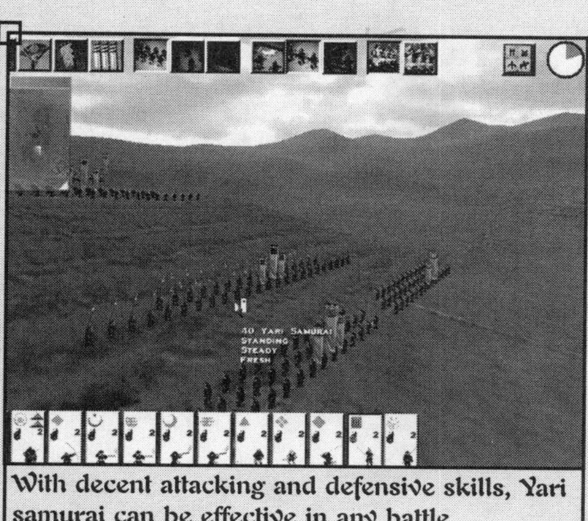

With decent attacking and defensive skills, Yari samurai can be effective in any battle.

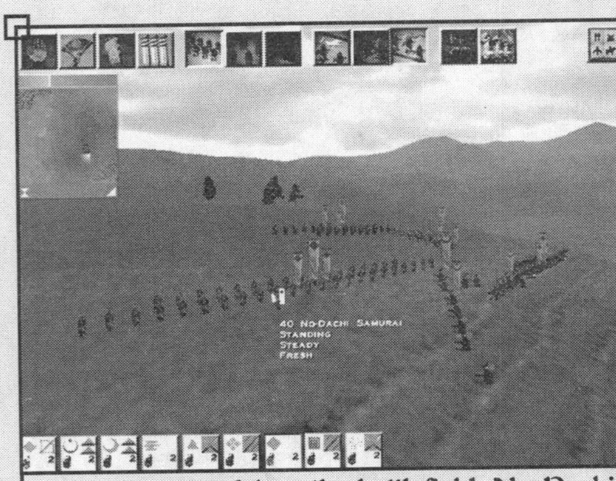

Although powerful on the battlefield, No-Dachi are extremely vulnerable to missile fire.

NO-DACHI SAMURAI

Troop Type: Footsoldier
Weapon: Long Sword

The No-Dachi sword was a long, heavy field weapon that often required two hands to wield it properly. As a result, No-Dachi samurai have a high Attack rating, but a poor Defence because they lack sufficient armour. No-Dachi samurai therefore kill fast and die fast, lethal in closely fought hand-to-hand combat, but vulnerable to arrow-fire. Consequently, No-Dachi samurai should be held back at the rear of an army until they are needed. Like a Cavalry unit, they are useful for breaking a hole in the enemy lines—although their low Defence rating ensures that few will live to receive a general's thanks afterwards. No-Dachi samurai can also be used to make opportunistic attacks against an enemy and, in some cases, to act as scouts for the main body of the army.

Since No-Dachi samurai possess a very high morale bonus, units can often operate independently of the general. For defensive situations, hide them in wooded areas (giving them some protection from arrow-fire) where they can then be used to terrorise and ambush an approaching enemy.

NO-DACHI SAMURAI	
Attack Factor	5
Defence Factor	-2
Armour	1
Morale Bonus	8
Walk Speed	7
Run Speed	12

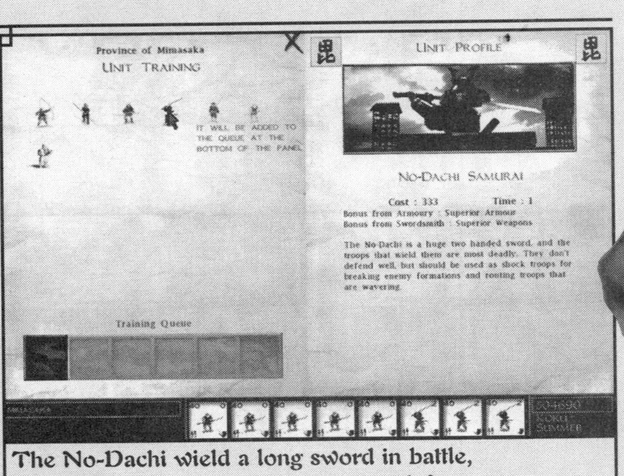

The No-Dachi wield a long sword in battle, combining a high attack with a poor defence.

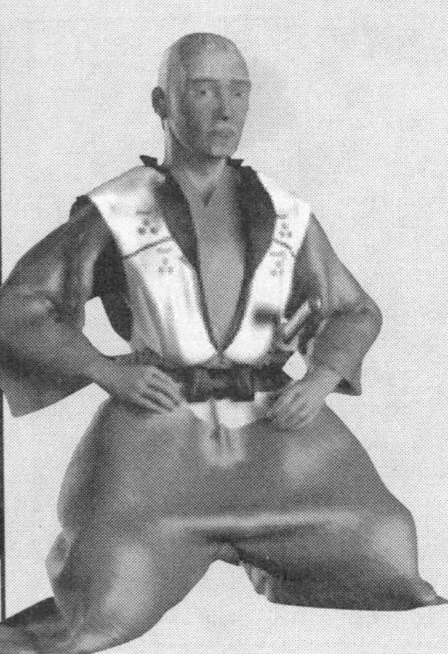

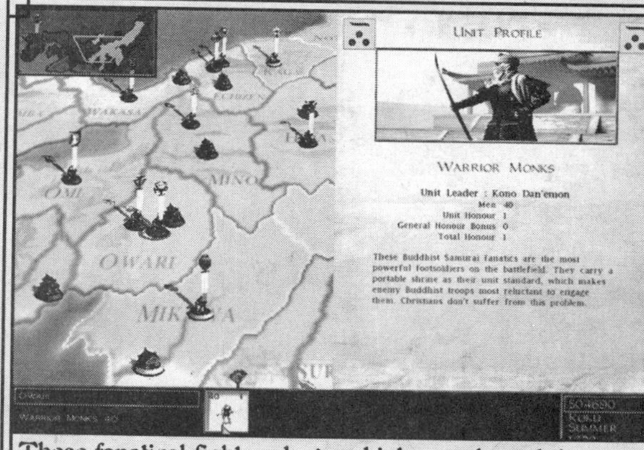
These fanatical fighters have a high morale and thus no fear of death.

WARRIOR MONKS

Troop Type: Footsoldier
Weapon: Naginata (sword)

The original Japanese word for the Warrior Monk is "sohei", meaning "priest-soldiers". A combination of fanatical ordained priests and warriors recruited by the Buddhist Temples, Warrior Monks are famed for their devotion to the military cause. Boasting a high Attack score, plus reasonable Defence and Speed ratings, the Warrior Monks are one of the most powerful units on the ancient battlefield. In hand-to-hand combat, they have the ability to defeat every other unit in the game and, thanks to their high morale bonus, they keep fighting bravely even if they are taking heavy losses. The Ikko-Ikki movement in 16th Century Japan believed that death in combat granted them a one-way ticket to paradise—They welcomed the challenge of battle and often approached bleak situations with undiminished fanaticism.

While in Campaign mode, Warrior Monk units are expensive to access and expensive to train, but the raw power they bring to an army is well worth the time and effort. It's worth noting, however, that like the powerful No-Dachi samurai, Warrior Monks are particularly vulnerable to ranged weapons fire. You should expect as much when you realise that the Warrior Monk's idea of protective armour is a tightly wrapped white sheet.

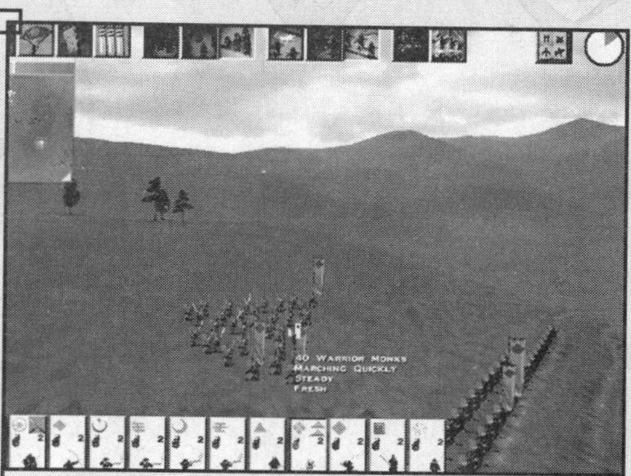
Very few units can stand up to an army that deploys many Warrior Monks in its ranks.

WARRIOR MONK	
Attack Factor	5
Defence Factor	2
Armour	1
Morale Bonus	8
Walk Speed	7
Run Speed	12

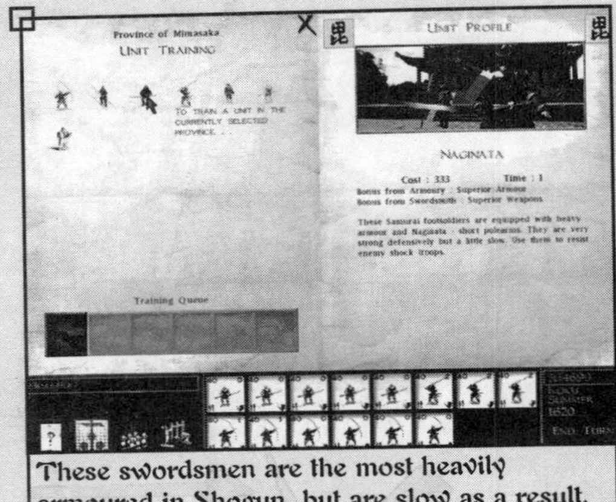

These swordsmen are the most heavily armoured in Shogun, but are slow as a result.

NAGINATA

Troop Type: Footsoldier
Weapon: Naginata (sword)

Armed with the curved Naginata sword, these samurai are amongst the strongest and best-protected in the game. Only Heavy Cavalry units can match their high Defence Factor, making Naginata the best defensive troops a general can lay his Yugake-covered hands on. Admittedly, the Naginata are slow and lack the skill and fervour to make an impact when thrown into surging attacks. But, thanks to their heavy armour and a high Defence Factor, these soldiers can withstand attacks for quite some time. They are particularly valuable for leading assaults across well defended bridges or into besieged Castles. Assign any other troop type to either of these roles and they will be cut to pieces by defensive missile fire before they reach their objective. Similarly, arranging a unit of Naginata in a loose formation in front of your army is a good way of absorbing initial enemy ranged weapons attacks.

When used intelligently, Naginata units can even hold their own against a Heavy Cavalry charge. Turn to them during a Campaign to defend strategically important provinces, or in a Custom Battle when you're either defending against an invading enemy or storming one of the game's well protected Castles.

Naginata move slowly, but their high Defence rating makes them strong against missile units.

NAGINATA	
Attack Factor	0
Defence Factor	6
Armour	1
Morale Bonus	0
Walk Speed	6
Run Speed	10

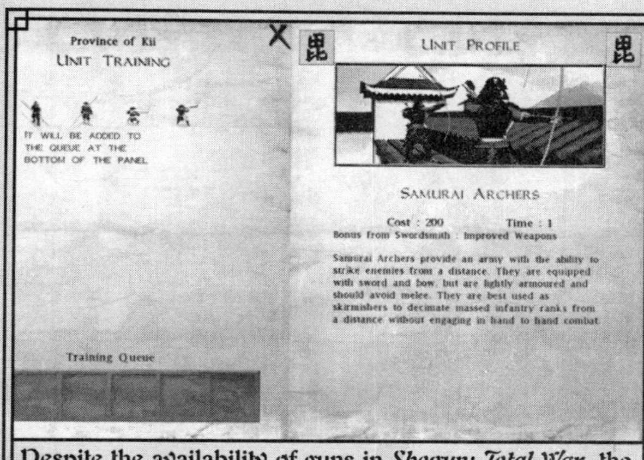

Despite the availability of guns in *Shogun: Total War*, the bow remains a formidable weapon.

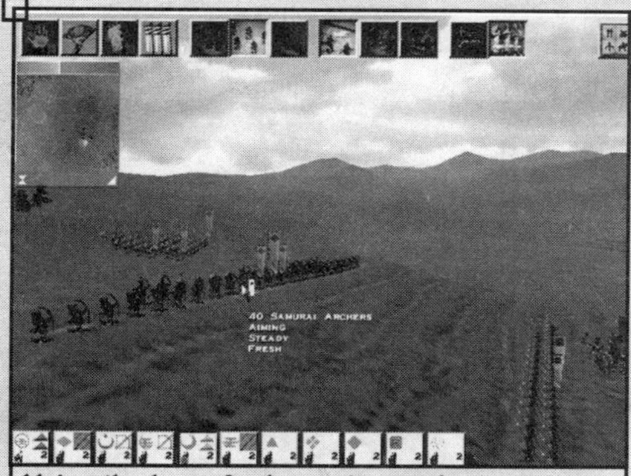

Using the bow, Archer units can be devastating, but they can also fight effectively hand-to-hand.

SAMURAI ARCHERS

Troop Type: Ranged Weapon
Weapon: Bow

Though not the most powerful troop type, samurai Archer units are arguably the most useful. Their primary use, is to provide ranged weapons fire for an invading or defending army. Unlike the gunpowder weapons described later in this guide, the bow and arrow doesn't need a direct line of sight to be effective.

Samurai Archer units are at their most deadly when they have a height advantage over an enemy. Firing from a hilltop not only gives the samurai Archer a wider field of fire, but also increases the damage caused by the arrows loosed. Used in large numbers, these "artillery" units can often seriously damage an opposing force before it reaches hand-to-hand combat range. Admittedly, samurai Archers are particularly vulnerable to Cavalry charges—although by positioning a unit of Yari samurai directly behind an Archer unit you can protect them from this threat. But it's worth remembering that when their ammunition is exhausted, samurai Archers are also quite proficient in close combat. They should easily beat Yari Ashigaru in a straight fight, and can also stand up to Yari samurai if they have a small advantage (i.e. less fatigue, or if they are attacking downhill).

SAMURAI ARCHERS	
Attack Factor	0
Defence Factor	0
Armour	1
Morale Bonus	0
Walk Speed	6
Run Speed	10

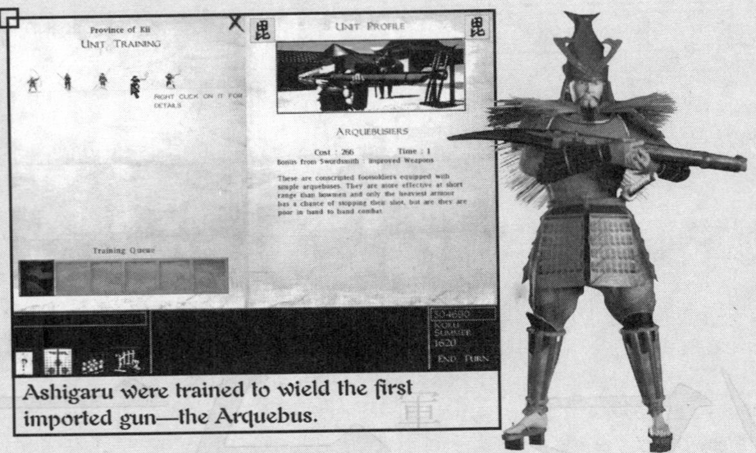

Ashigaru were trained to wield the first imported gun—the Arquebus.

ARQUEBUSIERS

Troop Type: Ranged Weapon
Weapon: Arquebus

Although Japanese samurai had faced catapult-launched gunpowder bombs during the Mongol invasion in 1274, not to mention Chinese fire lances (ancient flamethrowers), it was the Portuguese who introduced the gun into the east. *Shogun: Total War* designers, Creative Assembly, have acknowledged that some players may be disappointed with the effectiveness of the Arquebusiers in the game, expecting them to outshoot the Archer units.

The truth is that they can't outshoot Archer units because the early Portuguese weapons were very crude, and inferior to a bow in the hands of a skilled archer. Nevertheless, guns like the Arquebus proved immensely popular because any peasant could be taught to fire a gun in a short space of time. It took years of training to produce a skilled archer.

The key to using guns is to have lots of them. Due to its low accuracy, the Arquebus causes little damage at long range. But fired at close range, especially by multiple units, a volley of Arquebus gunfire can be both physically and mentally destructive. Guns such as the Arquebus and the improved Musket should be employed with patience. Over time they *will* wear the enemy down—samurai armour is much less effective against bullets than it is against arrows. A word of caution, however: the Arquebus has a slow reload time and often doesn't work in the rain!

ARQUEBUSIERS	
Attack Factor	-6
Defence Factor	-3
Armour	2
Morale Bonus	-4
Walk Speed	7
Run Speed	12

Arquebusiers prove their worth on the battlefield when deployed in massed ranks.

MUSKETEERS

Troop Type: Ranged Weapon
Weapon: Musket

As an improved version of the Arquebus, the Musket is blessed by the former's strengths but afflicted by its weaknesses. Again, due its poor accuracy, Muskets don't cause much damage at long range. But at very close range their volleys can be devastating. In fact, the effect of huge casualties, together with the morale penalty for being shot at by gunpowder weapons, may often cause enemy units to rout.

To maximise their effectiveness, if you deploy Musketeers in three or more ranks, they will use a classic revolving firing system (i.e. the front rank fires, then retires to the rear to reload while the next rank fires). This means that their rate of fire is effectively three times what it would be if the whole unit fired at once. If Musketeers (or Arquebusiers) are deployed in one or two ranks, the whole unit will fire impressively at once, but will then take a long time to reload for the next volley.

Without their guns, Musketeers and Arquebusiers fight very poorly in hand-to-hand combat situations. It's usually safer to employ gunners in the default Skirmish mode, allowing them to retreat if enemy troops get too close. If, however, you do command them to hold their position, they will pause until the enemy are very close to maximise the destructive potential of their attack. Remember: Like the Arquebus, the Musket's awesome battlefield power can be dampened by poor weather.

MUSKETEER	
Attack Factor	-6
Defence Factor	-3
Armour	2
Morale Bonus	-4
Walk Speed	7
Run Speed	12

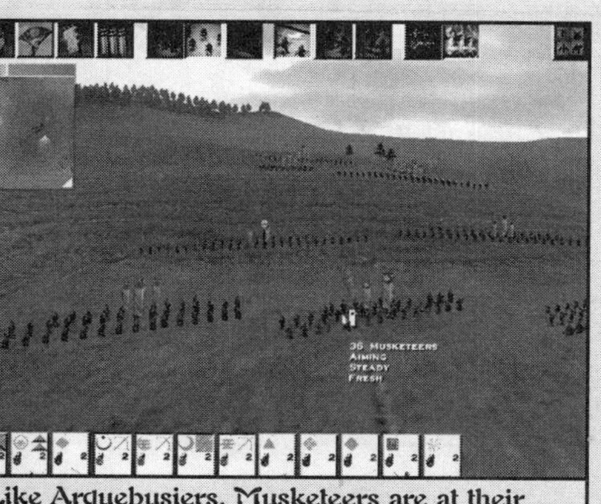

Like Arquebusiers, Musketeers are at their most effective when used in large numbers.

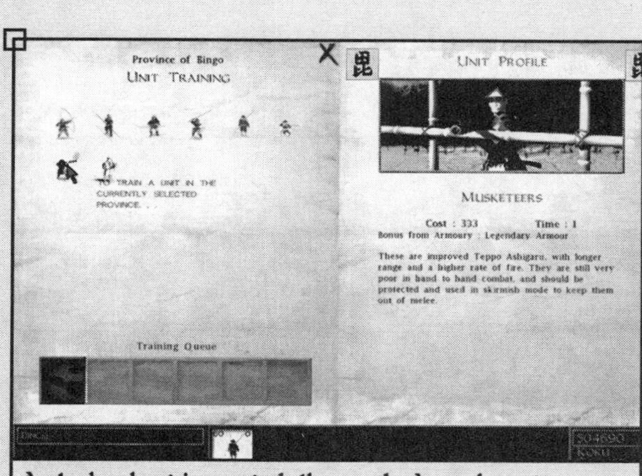

As technology improved, the crude Arquebus was replaced by the more efficient Musket.

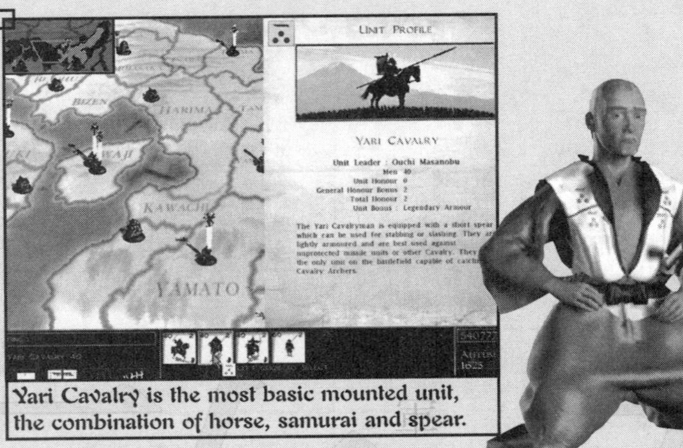

Yari Cavalry is the most basic mounted unit, the combination of horse, samurai and spear.

YARI CAVALRY

Troop Type: Horse Cavalry
Weapon: Spear

As this unit is the mainstay of the Cavalry forces, it should come as no surprise that Yari Cavalry is jack-of-all-16th-Century-Japanese-trades, master of none. As the game designers at Creative Assembly point out, the Yari Cavalry fight well against other Cavalry types and have the speed to run down Cavalry Archers. Not only that, but they are also particularly effective against the lighter infantry types. However, generals expecting to sweep away peasant armies with a thunderous, do-or-die horse charge may be disappointed by the results. Not only will Yari Cavalry "do", but they will also "die" in the process.

While Yari Cavalry units enjoy limited success, they are somewhat vulnerable to the various forms of medieval missile fire (arrows and bullets to be precise). The Yari Cavalry too can suffer if they come against a well-drilled battalion of Yari samurai or Yari Ashigaru. Just as the Daimyos of ancient Japan discovered, when you pit Yari against horse the clash often results in a win for the guy with the spear. Similarly, while Yari Cavalry units can run down samurai Archers, Arquebusiers and Musketeers in a dramatic frontal charge, they will suffer heavy casualties as they attack. A much better and safer way of utilising these troops, is to use their speed to outflank your opponent so that you can charge into enemy units from the side or rear.

Although weak against missile troops, a Yari Cavalry charge can annihilate an infantry line.

YARI CAVALRY	
Attack Factor	2
Defence Factor	3
Armour	3
Morale Bonus	2
Walk Speed	10
Run Speed	24

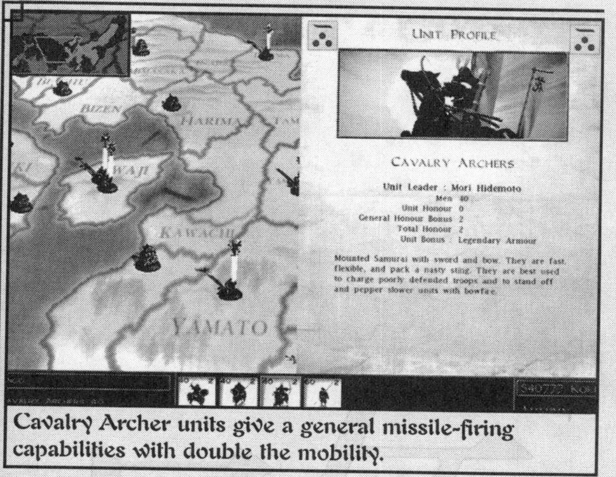

Cavalry Archer units give a general missile-firing capabilities with double the mobility.

CAVALRY ARCHERS

Troop Type: Horse Cavalry/Ranged Weapon
Weapon: Bow

This seems like the ideal solution—the artillery power of samurai Archers combined with the speed and mobility of Yari Cavalry. But the outwardly impressive Cavalry Archer unit isn't quite as powerful as its name might suggest.

The good news is that Cavalry Archers can terrorise infantry units to great effect, especially if the opposing force lacks support from missilemen of its own. Although Cavalry Archers don't possess the same sort of accuracy as their mud-trudging equivalents, their excellent mobility goes some way to making up for any wayward shooting. Thus an eager unit of Cavalry Archers can harass an opposing army and get away quickly before it incurs too many casualties.

In the default skirmish mode, for example, Cavalry Archers will perform this manoeuvre automatically, but it's best to keep an eye on them just in case. Should your fragile Cavalry Archers get sucked into a messy melee with infantry, they stand more than a good chance of being hacked to pieces. Horses are very easy targets to hit. But while Cavalry Archers will suffer badly at the hands of sword- and spear-wielding grunts, they can easily defeat infantry missile troops.

CAVALRY ARCHERS	
Attack Factor	1
Defence Factor	2
Armour	3
Morale Bonus	0
Walk Speed	8
Run Speed	20

These mounted bowmen are at their most effective when they aggressively harry an approaching enemy.

UNIT TYPES

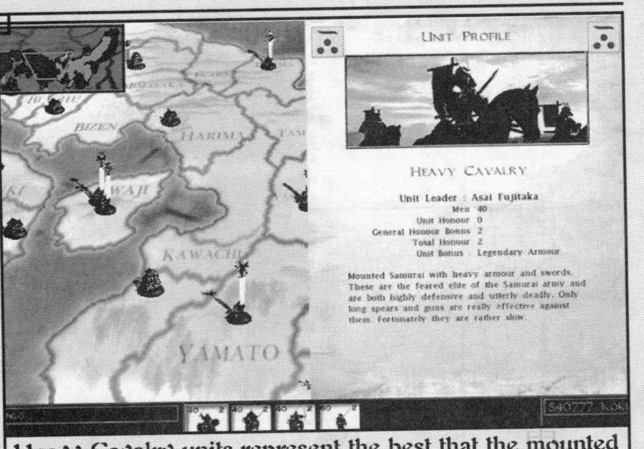

Heavy Cavalry units represent the best that the mounted soldier has to offer—they're almost unbeatable.

HEAVY CAVALRY

Troop Type: Horse Cavalry
Weapon: Sword

Heavy by name, heavy by nature, this Cavalry type is by far the most powerful mounted unit in *Shogun: Total War*. The Heavy Cavalry is an elite unit, expensive both to recruit (in Custom Battles) and to access (in the Campaign mode). But, if you can add Heavy Cavalry elements to your forces, you'll discover that these armoured horsemen stand up well to any troop type thrown against them.

While Heavy Cavalry are still vulnerable, they are only threatened by missile fire (less so than other cavalry units) and by those rare occasions when a squad of Yari samurai or Warrior Monks take them by surprise. As long as you use them wisely and on flat ground rather than a hillside, as few as 40 Heavy Cavalry can pack a dramatic and tide-turning punch. The only real rule you need to follow with Heavy Cavalry, and this is relevant for all cavalry units, is this: keep them out of the woods. Most units find fighting amongst trees difficult, but this is doubly true for mounted units who have much less space to move through. Sending a Cavalry unit into the woods is a disastrous strategy that will cause the troops to break formation and become disorganised. They are then easy pickings for any infantry units that happen to be skulking nearby (see Terrain).

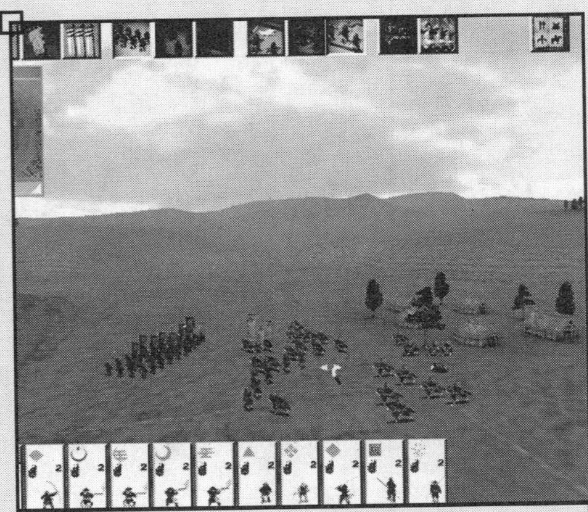

Thanks to heavier armour, these cavalry units can break through any enemy formation.

HEAVY CAVALRY	
Attack Factor	2
Defence Factor	6
Armour	5
Morale Bonus	4
Walk Speed	8
Run Speed	20

TERRAIN

As has been mentioned before in this guide, where you fight is almost as important as how you fight. Knowing the different types of terrain that you will encounter is yet another part of the complete pre-conflict analysis favoured by Sun Tzu. Be aware that there are several features of the environment that can affect the fighting efficiency of your troops.

LOWLANDS

Since most of the good advice in this Terrain section involves fighting on high ground, it follows that most of the bad advice involves fighting on low-lying land. Without the Attack and Defence bonuses accumulated by gaining a height advantage, fighting on lowland areas is a straightforward test of manpower and tactics. Whereas a beleaguered force of 120 Yari samurai and 40 Archers on a hilltop could hold its own against a much larger force, the same units will struggle to defeat an opponent if heavily outnumbered on lower ground. Fighting this way requires a great deal more skill and strategic thought, but typically the general with the largest army will win the day.

In short, never commit to an attacking strategy without the benefit of some height advantage. Unless, of course, you happen to be leading 1,000 highly motivated Warrior Monks into battle against 100 fearful Ashigaru. Remember that, just like many other real-time strategy games, victory can be achieved through sheer weight of numbers.

Beware of overconfidence, however. History often records the victories of much smaller forces when faced by a seemingly superior and stronger enemy. A well organised and cleverly lead army using troops, terrain and tactics to best effect can still triumph when the odds are stacked against it. The battle of Mikata Ga Hara in *Shogun's* Historical Battle section (see page 66) is a prime example of defeat on paper, victory in practice.

HIGHLANDS

There's a whole section devoted to the importance of height in the Tutorial section (see page 16), so it's no surprise that the most important terrain type is the hill. "When the hill is high, never face up," said Sun Tzu in *The Art of War*, followed by another pearl of wisdom: "When the hill slopes behind, never back down."

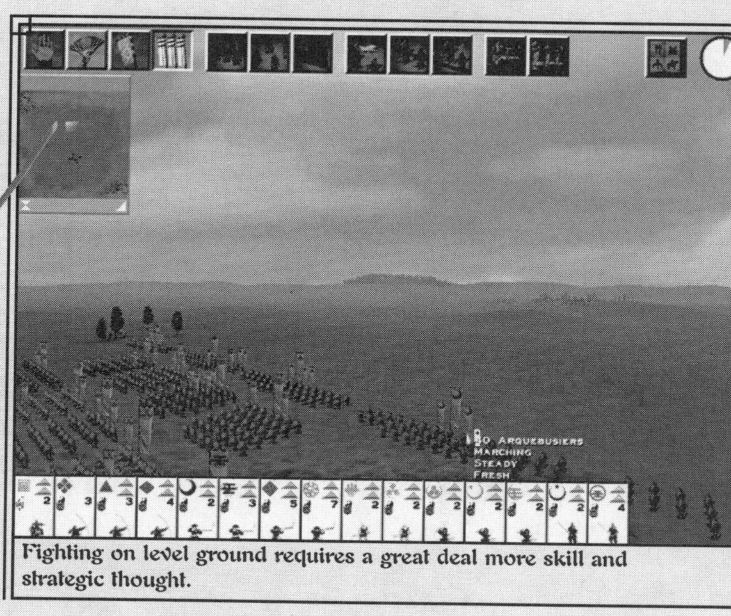

Fighting on level ground requires a great deal more skill and strategic thought.

When defending a province or an area of the battlefield, basing your strategy around hills and steep mountainsides gives you numerous tactical advantages. The specific effects that height has on both defending and attacking troops are examined later in this guide, but there's more to camping out on a hilltop than just getting a hefty Attack bonus. For starters, an army defending a hill has an unparalleled, almost panoramic view of the battlefield as the opposing force approaches.

If you have Archer units, placing them on high ground not only increases the effective range of their missile fire but also augments the damage that they cause to enemy units. As far as infantry and cavalry troops are concerned, friendly units receive a bonus for attacking downhill, while hostile units suffer a penalty because they have to exert more effort to fight uphill. Obviously, the higher and steeper the hill, the greater the advantage your soldiers gain from it. Even weak hand-to-hand units like Ashigaru and Archers can prove surprisingly effective in a hillside battle.

Sun Tzu connected victory in battle with an understanding of the importance of height.

A classic defensive posture is to place Archer units at the highest point of your chosen hill, with infantry (such as Yari samurai) arranged in front of them. The Archers should be able to pepper any approaching enemies with bow-fire, while the samurai can charge into units that stray too close.

Attacking an enemy that holds the high ground is another matter entirely. The computer AI in *Shogun: Total War* is clever, and armies will often choose to dig in on a hillside (usually with some tree cover) if you are playing the invading force. Unless you have vastly superior troop numbers and can afford to suffer high casualties, it is advisable *never* to attack uphill. Not only will your troops start to tire as they climb towards the enemy positions, but should hostile units charge into your ranks while you are ascending a slope, you will suffer terrible Defence and Attack penalties.

How then do you engage an enemy camped smugly on a hillside? Few of the provinces and battlefields have hills that can't be approached

Always keep the hill at your back. Fight down, but never fight up.

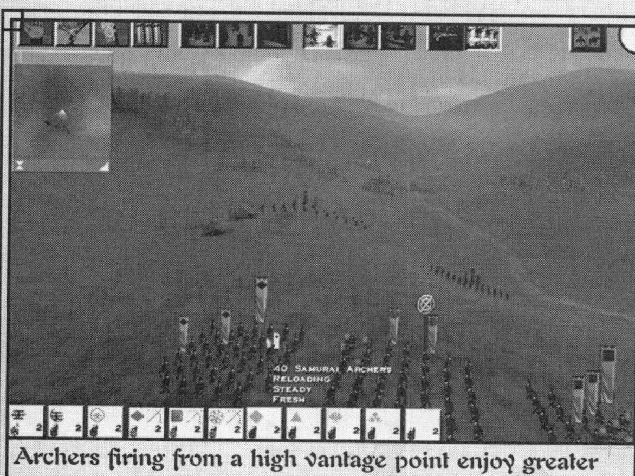

Archers firing from a high vantage point enjoy greater range and inflict more damage.

from more than one angle. The trick is to outflank the enemy force, marching your soldiers onto high ground to lessen the height advantage. By moving your forces around to the side of an enemy's position, one of three things may happen. (1) The opposing army shifts position to protect its vulnerable flanks—troops receive an Attack bonus for attacking from the side; (2) the opposing army moves to attack you *before* you can manoeuvre your troops into an advantageous position; or (3) the enemy general will realise that his strategy has been compromised and will move his force to another part of the battlefield.

If you can't gain a height advantage, attempt to engage an enemy on the same level. Finally, make sure that you have the correct troop types for the battle. Cavalry units don't operate efficiently on highland battlefields, while the Naginata's strong defensive properties are best used to defend your lands against attack, rather than to invade new territories. Analyse your situation from every angle to gain the all-round knowledge to fight anybody, anywhere, any time.

CASTLES

In the later stages of the Campaign mode, and during some Custom and Historical Battles, you must attack or defend a Daimyo's Castle.

When defending a province, always pick the highest point and dig in for a long fight.

Attacking or defending Castles requires well trained troops—a lot of them.

Because such fortifications are always built atop strategically important hills, defenders should follow the rules laid out in the Highlands section to mount their defence. Well-trained Footsoldiers and an abundance of missile troops form a strong basis for a Castle defence, while heavily armoured Naginata and and Archers have a fighting chance if you must attack Castle walls rather than defend them.

In short, for the defender, missile troops should be arranged against the walls within the castle compound. To win the day, the enemy must successfully storm the castle gate, so this should be protected with your strongest troops—No-Dachi, Warrior Monks or the heavily-armoured Naginata. For the attacker, a successful assault requires well armoured troops such as Naginata and Heavy Cavalry. Use these unites to draw enemy Monks and Samurai. Again, the seeds of victory must be planted in preparation. A strong defence requires a strong blow to break it.

River crossings can prove to be both difficult to attack and tricky to defend.

BRIDGES

River crossings can prove to be both difficult to attack and tricky to defend. For the attacker, the challenge is to move troops quickly across a bridge that will undoubtedly suffer under a hail of arrows from defending Archer units. Minimising casualties is the first and only priority when attacking provinces that have a river. Using a large army may be enough to scare enemy forces away before you even cross the bridge, while any army that faces you without missile troops of their own is staring defeat in the face. You can also tempt enemy infantry to attack one of your units by marching it across the bridge and then marching it straight back again—if this incursion draws in a hostile unit, you can use your Archers to whittle away their numbers.

For defending a bridge, use Archers, Archers and more Archers. Plus the odd Yari samurai unit to mop up any stubborn enemy resistance. Cavalry Archers, with their excellent mobility and ranged weapon capability are also particularly useful here.

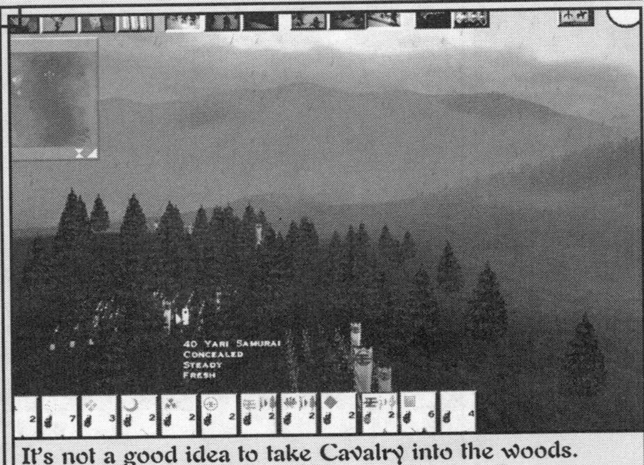

It's not a good idea to take Cavalry into the woods.

WOODS

Woods are another important feature of the *Shogun: Total War* landscape. Not only do they offer concealment and protection from missile fire, but note that Cavalry units fight particularly poorly in woods. This is because the riders are distracted by the hazards of low branches and because horses are much more cumbersome than men on foot when manoeuvring amongst trees. Woods also break up formations, allowing men on foot to get amongst the Cavalry to attack individual soldiers.

WEATHER

In addition to the type of terrain you fight *on*, the sort of weather you fight *in* also has an effect on how your troops perform during a battle. As the designers of the game point out, the weather in *Shogun: Total War* not only enhances the atmosphere of the battlefield. The pixel snow and rain also have an impact on the morale, fatigue and attitude of your soldiers. Napoleon's invasion of Russia in 1812, which saw an army of 422,000 soldiers reduced to 10,000 in harsh winter conditions, shows that even the greatest generals should not underestimate the weather.

While you can never control the weather, you *can* predict it to some extent, especially when playing a Campaign or Custom Battle. In these modes, conflicts take place during spring, summer, autumn or winter and thus certain weather types can be expected to feature in each. This section of the guide features the main weather types—wind, rain, snow, fog—and how these types may affect the fighting efficiency of Footsoldiers and Cavalry on the ancient Japanese battlefield.

The weather in *Shogun: Total War* not only enhances the atmosphere, it affects how troops perform on the battlefield.

WIND

While light or heavy wind on the battlefield doesn't really affect the efficiency of Footsoldiers, it can play havoc with ranged weapons troops. For Archers, any wind on the battlefield can drastically affect the accuracy of the arrows that they fire, reducing the damage that they inflict on an enemy. The higher the wind, the worse the effects—Archers with a low honour rating are rendered almost useless. Light wind is less of a problem for Arquebusiers and Musketeers, although their aim may be affected should the wind be stronger.

High winds can have a dramatic effect on the accuracy of ranged weapons units.

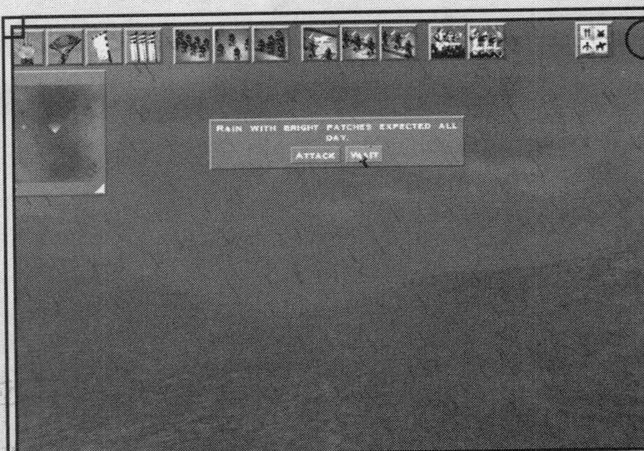

Rainstorms on the battlefield restrict visibility and render gunpowder weapons useless.

RAIN

The effects of rain on an army are much more pronounced, so much so that they can sometimes change the entire context of a confrontation. Not only does rain hit the efficiency of ranged weapons units, it can also have a dramatic impact on sword- and spear-wielding skirmishers.

Most significantly, rain stops Arquebusiers and Musketeers from firing their weapons — it dampens the gunpowder and the fuses used in both guns, and puts out the primitive matches that were used to light them. Similarly, while a downpour makes the Arquebus and the Musket almost useless, it also reduces the accuracy of an army's Archers—their efficiency is affected by damp bowstrings. Rain also has an effect on heavily armoured troops. Due to the conditions, rain soaks into armour making it heavier. Combined with the fact that wet weather also makes soldiers cold and miserable, the *Shogun: Total War* battle model increases the rate at which sodden soldiers become fatigued to compensate.

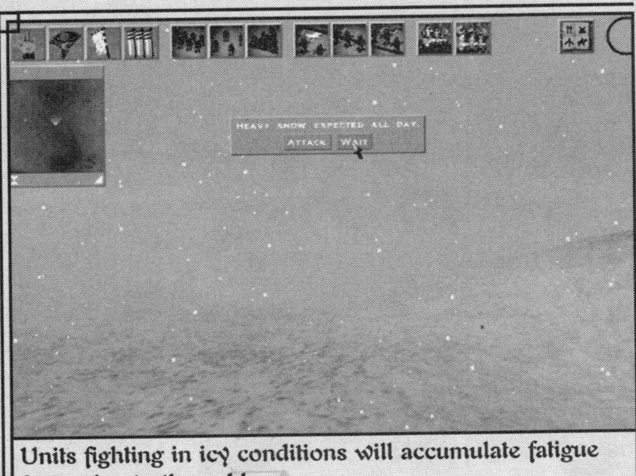

Units fighting in icy conditions will accumulate fatigue faster due to the cold.

SNOW

Snow is very similar to rain in that it has a marked effect on the effectiveness and accuracy of ranged weaponry. Fortunately, a severe snowstorm has much less effect on Archers, Arquebusiers and Musketeers than a rainstorm. However, extreme cold weather affects troops in heavy armour, who accumulate fatigue much faster than other units in such a situation. Thus, the heavily armoured Naginata will suffer on snowbound battlescapes, as will Heavy Cavalry units. Both rain and snow can also affect visibility during conflicts.

FOG

In addition to rain, snow and wind, fog is the last weather type that can either aid or ruin a confrontation. Unlike the previous trio of inclement conditions, fog on the battlefield is constant—i.e. it doesn't miraculously clear in the way that rain sometimes stops. Thankfully, fog has no real effect on actual game mechanics. Consequently, it doesn't render the Arquebus and the Musket useless, nor does it increase the rate at which your virtual samurai gain virtual fatigue. Fog on the battlefield simply affects visibility. And this is true for both player and computer AI alike.

On the one hand, fog can seriously damage a general's ability to: (a) see the enemy soldiers, and (b) manoeuvre his own troops into an advantageous position from which the enemy can be effectively attacked. If it affects you in this way, it also affects the AI that has been programmed to have as much difficulty peering through the gloom as the player does. On the other hand, battlefield fog can contribute to victory rather than hinder it. In battles where "Heavy Fog" is encountered, you can use the poor visibility to outflank unwitting opponents before circling around them to attack from the rear. This sort of approach will only work under the cover of Heavy Fog. Light Fog may seem to offer a similar opportunity, but the enemy has a greater chance of spotting you before you can sneak into missile firing or melee range.

Fog on the battlefield reduces visibility allowing you to sneak up to units without being spotted.

FATIGUE AND MORALE

(See Confrontation, page 40.)

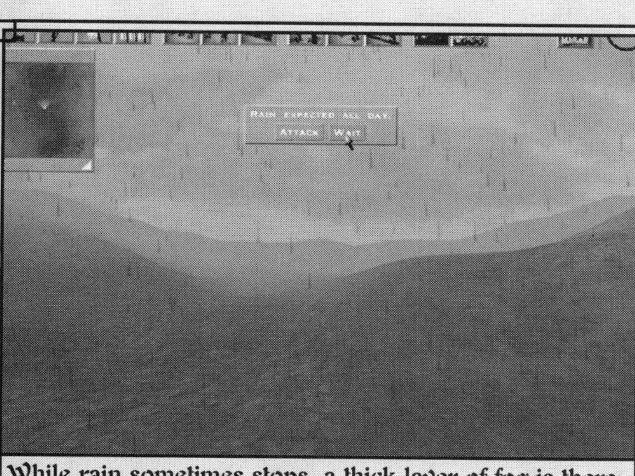

While rain sometimes stops, a thick layer of fog is there for the duration of the battle.

WEATHER

CONFRONTATION

戦争

Generally, those who occupy the place of
conflict early,
Can face their opponent in comfort.
Those who occupy the place of conflict late,
Must hasten into conflict troubled.

Thus, those who are skilled in conflict,
Take the initiative over others
So that others do not take the initiative.

Sun Tzu (translated by R.L. Wing in "The Art of Strategy")

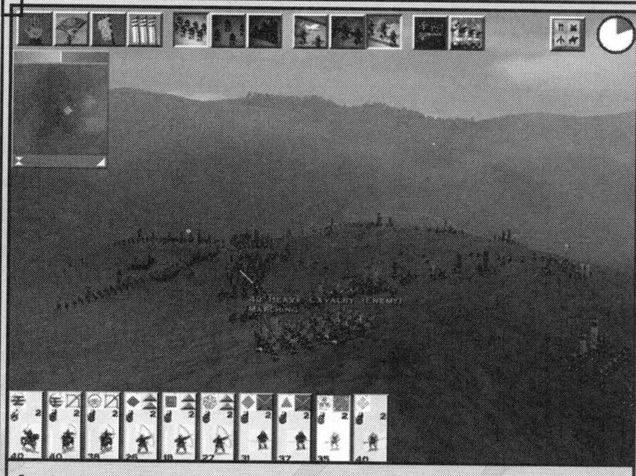
A strategy should offer a strong chance of success even before the battle commences.

To enter into combat is to have first analysed the situation, estimated the costs, prepared your forces and planned the attack. Sun Tzu teaches that a strategy should offer a strong chance of success even before the battle commences. It must be obvious that victory is attainable before an Arquebus is loaded and a sword unsheathed. When your own army is ten times greater of number, he suggested, surround the enemy. When five times greater, attack the enemy. When two times greater, scatter the enemy. The most important lesson you can learn from any confrontation is when to challenge and when not to challenge. To secure yourself against attack, believed Sun Tzu, was the foundation of a good challenge.

In this section of the guide, we'll take a look at what factors affect a conflict, how battles are calculated, and what you can do to stack the odds in your favour. First of all, this means taking a look at the effects of both Fatigue and Morale on the fighting performance of an army's soldiers. This is followed by an explanation of the various Attack and Defence penalties that are applied during a battle, and the formations that you can use to plan for an attack or prepare a defence. Lastly, this section of the guide discusses how best to command your troops in battle. What's the best way to attack a bridge? Which troop types are the most effective? Just how much influence does an army's general have on the Ashigaru and Samurai units around him? The answers appear on the following pages, along with in-depth game information and battle strategies.

In order to win, you must know what factors affect the gaining of victory.

THE BATTLE SCREEN

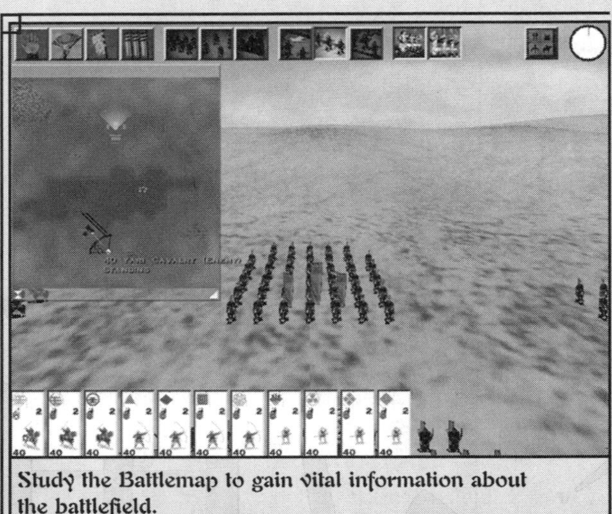

Study the Battlemap to gain vital information about the battlefield.

When entering a battle in *Shogun: Total War*, be it a Campaign, Historical or Custom Battle, you'll encounter the same familiar Battle screen. This screen consists of four main elements: the Icon Bar at the top, the Battlemap below the Icon Bar, the 3D Window, and the Troop Display that runs along the bottom. Combined with the point-and-click functions of the mouse (i.e. select army, move army, etc.), *Shogun* generals can control armies as small as a single man or as large as 1,920 men.

THE ICON BAR

Running across the top of the screen, the Icon Bar allows instant onscreen access to some of the game's more important commands. From left to right, these commands are: Halt, Rally, Rout, Group, Close Formation, Loose Formation, Wedge Formation, Skirmish, Hold Formation, Engage At Will, Hold Position, Fire At Will. The far-right icon is the Control Panel Toggle that is used to access the nine different Group Formations also available.

THE BATTLEMAP

Moveable and resizable, the Battlemap shows a zoomed-out view of the current battlefield, complete with contours and other terrain information (bridges, rivers, trees, buildings). The Battlemap also contains the Speed Slider (used to advance the game speed from between 0 percent and 100 percent of normal speed), plus the Kill Ratio bar that displays the casualties suffered by both combatants.

TROOP DISPLAY

At the bottom of the screen is the Troop Display, showing the types of unit currently available in the army, the number of soldiers in the unit and their overall morale. Units can be selected by clicking on them in the 3D Window or by clicking on their icons in the Troop Display. Units can also be selected by clicking on them via the Battlemap.

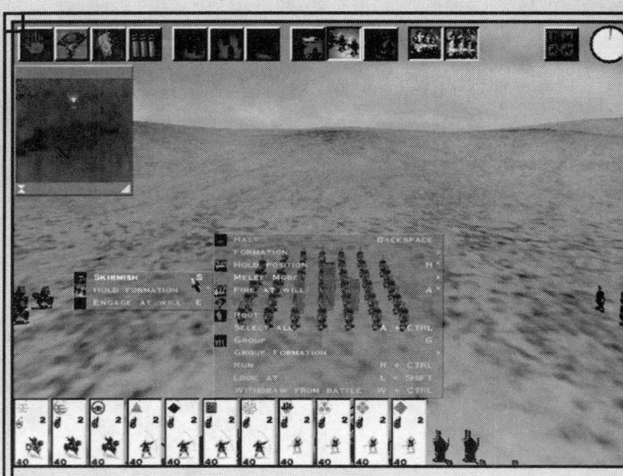

The number and status of your soldiers is illustrated by the Troop Display at the bottom of the screen.

FORMATIONS

When controlling units or groups of units during a battle, the Icon Bar allows Shogun generals access to a range of troop commands and orders. By knowing when to use these instructions, you can increase the efficiency of your soldiers and overall army performance.

SINGLE UNIT FORMATIONS AND ORDERS

Close Formation

The default troop formation—soldiers attack as a strong, coherent unit making them much more effective in battle.

Loose Formation

The attacking potency of a unit is lessened in a Loose formation, but by keeping the soldiers apart, they are slightly less vulnerable to ranged weapons fire.

Wedge Formation

The Wedge Formation is typically used for attacking and breaking through enemy lines, where its arrowhead shape makes it particularly effective. Casualties, however, are often higher.

Skirmish

Missile troops such as Arquebusiers, Musketeers and Archers are placed in Skirmish mode by default; should the enemy get too close, the missile troops will fall back to a new position and try to attack again.

Hold Formation

Units given this command will attempt to keep their lines intact as they fight. The formation is a defensive one and reduces the damage they suffer as well as inflict. This command is particularly effective when used with Yari samurai and Yari Ashigaru.

In the Close formation, samurai fight side-by-side as a formidable fighting unit.

Engage at Will

If spearmen fight better in closely arranged lines, then Warrior Monks, No-Dachi and Naginata units excel when left to their own devices.

Hold Position

A unit instructed to "Hold Position" will attempt to defend its current location until routed or destroyed. If a unit is forced out of position, it will attempt to move back to the lost position until ordered to do otherwise.

Fire at Will

Missile units will automatically attack any enemy unit in range. They will continue attacking until forced to retreat or until they run out of ammunition (if Limited Ammo option is used).

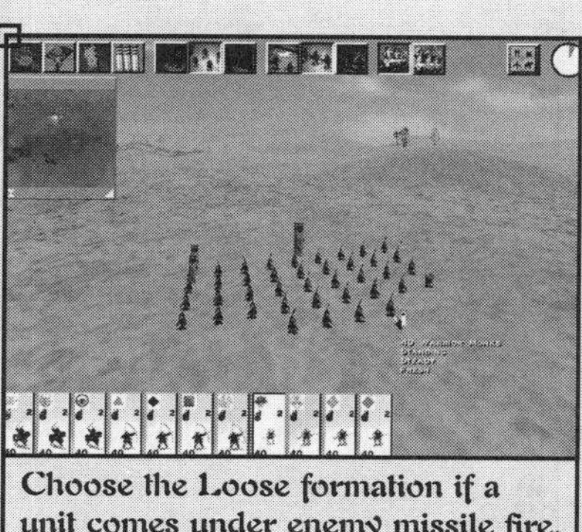

Choose the Loose formation if a unit comes under enemy missile fire.

The Wedge formation is particularly effective at penetrating enemy lines.

The Centre Offensive formation benefits from having the general leading from the front.

GROUP FORMATIONS AND ORDERS

In addition to the Single Unit Formations on page 43, groups of units (or an entire army) can be ordered to take up one of nine different Group Formations.

Single Line

Cavalry, Spear and Missile units form a straight line across the battlefield with the general (and horse guard) in the centre.

Defensive

Spear units form the leading edge of this formation, protecting the Missile and Cavalry units that are positioned behind them. The general sits safely at the back. A good basic formation for all battlefield situations, particularly useful when marching.

Square Formation

The classic defensive Square requires enough Spear units to surround and protect the centre of the formation that contains the Missile Units, Cavalry and general.

Skirmish Left

Missile and Spear troops are arranged on the left-flank with the mobile Cavalry units in a free role on the right. The employment of this formation will depend on the types of units faced and the terrain encountered.

Skirmish Centre

A front-line of Missile troops leads Spear and Cavalry units into battle. The Missile troops attack until forced to retreat, whereupon the Spear units enter into hand-to-hand combat. The often-vulnerable Cavalry units are kept to the rear.

Skirmish Right

Missile and Spear troops are arranged on the right-flank with the mobile Cavalry units in a free role on the left. Again, the employment of this formation will depend on the types of units faced and the terrain encountered.

Left-hand Offensive

Reversing the Skirmish Left formation, Spear troops lead Missile units into battle, supported by Cavalry (led by the general) on the left flank.

In addition to the unit formations, a general has access to several army formations like the Line.

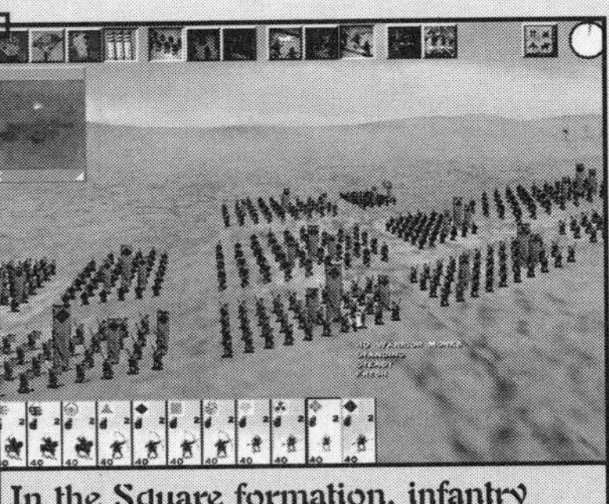

In the Square formation, infantry form a fence around weaker units.

Centre Offensive

The general leads the Spear units into battle supported by the Missile Units and the Cavalry which gain some protection at the rear of the formation.

Right-hand Offensive

Reversing the Skirmish Right formation, Spear troops lead Missile units into battle, supported by Cavalry (led by the general) on the right flank.

BATTLEFIELD CALCULATIONS

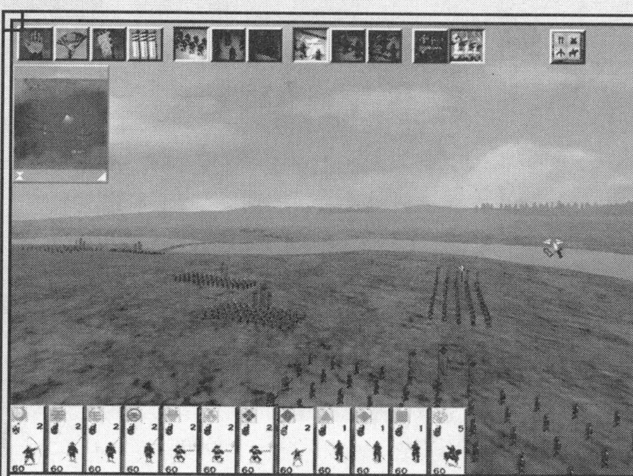
Shogun: Total War features a complex battle model for enhanced realism and historical accuracy.

The battlefield simulation model in *Shogun: Total War* is a complex system of ancient strategies (from Sun Tzu's *The Art of War*) and common sense. As such, the model aims to combine realism and the psychology of massed troop bodies, within the context of a game that is easy to control and easy to play. Thus, the authenticity of the battlefield simulation largely frees you from having to learn the rules of the game, since the rules of the game are largely a matter of common sense.

For example, if someone asked you to wear heavy Japanese armour and to march up a steep hill, you would probably move slowly and be tired when you finally got to the top. So this is exactly what happens to the soldiers in the game. Similarly, if somebody asked you to stand in a field all day in the pouring rain, you would no doubt become cold, miserable and tired. Again, this is how the soldiers in the game are affected during a rain-lashed battle. And what if you were ordered into a situation where the most likely outcome appeared to be decapitation by an enemy samurai? You may choose a heroic warrior's death, but it's more likely that you will flee from the situation as quickly as possible. It should come as no surprise then, that when your *Shogun: Total War* soldiers are faced with the same dilemma, they'll run for the hills as fast as they possibly can.

By understanding how the game works, you gain an understanding of how best to play it.

CLOSE COMBAT

All hand-to-hand combat in *Shogun: Total War* is calculated on a man-to-man basis. Each man makes one attack each animation cycle, but may be attacked many times during the same time. The chance of a man making a kill during his attack depends on his Attack factor (see Basic Unit Types on page 22), the opponent's Defence factor, the honour and fatigue of both parties, and on other factors such as morale, whether the attacker is charging, or whether the attacker is striking the defender's side or rear.

Virtual life and death takes into account factors such as a soldier's morale and fatigue level.

The basic method of calculating close combat results is to take the Attack factor for the attacking man's type, subtract the defender's Defence factor, and then add or subtract any situational factors (see below). This gives a final factor that is then used to determine if the attacker kills or pushes back the defender. Each factor increase in this final value gives a 20 percent increase to the chance of killing the defender. Refer back to the numbers in the Unit Types section (pages 22-32).

Combat Situation Factors

- \+ (attacker's personal honour + attacker's unit honour) /2
- \- (defender's personal honour + defender's unit honour) /2
- \+ (attacker's general's rank - defender's general's rank) / 2
- \+ Charge Bonus if charging (depends on type)
- \- Defender's extra armour (from Armoury—Campaign mode only)

Charging into an enemy from the flank or rear is more effective than a frontal assault.

By using height to your advantage, your samurai gain valuable bonuses in battle.

- -4 If cavalry facing Yari armed infantry
- +4 If Yari armed troops (infantry or cavalry) attacking cavalry

- +5 Attacking flank
- +7 Attacking rear
- +12 Charging into flank or rear
- +4 If defender is running away
- +6 If the attacker pushed back the defender in a recent attack

- +/- Height advantage or disadvantage
- -2 Cavalry attacking Infantry in woods
- +2 Infantry attacking Cavalry in woods
- +5 Defender has no space to fight properly (e.g. on a bridge)

- +3 Attacker is in wedge formation
- +3 Defender is in wedge formation
- -2 Attacker is in Hold Formation mode
- -2 Defender is in Hold Formation mode

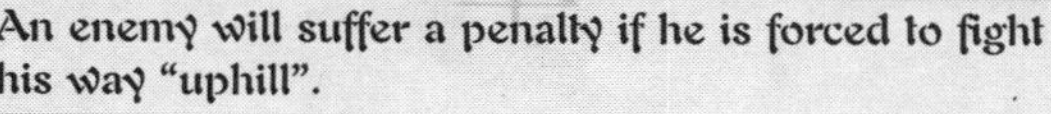
An enemy will suffer a penalty if he is forced to fight his way "uphill".

THE IMPORTANCE OF FATIGUE

Troops get progressively more tired as a battle goes on. Just how tired they get depends on what they are doing on the battlefield. Walking on level ground, for example, is fairly undemanding, whereas marching up a hillside is extremely tiring. Similarly, troops that run or charge also get tired quickly, while constant combat drains the energy out of samurai at an even higher rate. Ultimately, the more fatigued a unit is, the higher the penalties it suffers to its Attack, Defence and morale factors. The fatigue modifiers for both attackers and defenders are listed below:

Adjustment for Attacker's Fatigue

-2 Quite Tired
-3 Very Tired
-4 Exhausted
-6 Totally Exhausted

Adjustments for Defender's Fatigue

+1 Very Tired
+2 Exhausted
+3 Totally Exhausted

Troops that are described as "Fresh" or "Quite Fresh" suffer no penalties for fatigue at all. In contrast, troops who are "Quite Tired", "Very Tired", "Exhausted" and "Totally Exhausted" suffer progressively higher penalties. Totally Exhausted units cannot run or skirmish. Tired men are also reluctant to fire their weapons or seek out new opponents in combat.

March your soldiers too hard and they'll be too tired to fight when they engage the enemy.

Fatigue and low morale contribute to poor performances on the battlefield.

THE IMPORTANCE OF MORALE

Morale and its effects are also extremely important in *Shogun: Total War*. According to the game's designers at Creative Assembly, units can have one of several morale levels that can affect the soldiers that belong to them in different ways.

"Steady" is the default morale level of all troops. It's an indication of their willingness to do battle, loyalty to their general and above average bravery. Of the other levels featured in the game, only Rout has any major effect. But each one, indicated whenever you hold the mouse pointer over the unit or its icon, gives a commander an idea of how soldiers are faring in battle. If units are tagged as "Impetuous", it means they are overconfident, likely to pursue routed enemy units rather than obey orders to hold their position. Samurai in units described as "Uncertain" will hesitate before seeking new opponents but their loyalty is still unquestionable. When troops are described as "Wavering", however, it means that while their units have not fled the battlefield yet, they are considering it. As commander, the Troop Display will alert you to any "Wavering" units—unit icons will flash with the Rout icon (a white flag) to indicate a faltering unit. If the Rout icon disappears, the unit has regained its confidence. If it becomes a permanent fixture, the unit has turned tail and retreated.

The morale level of any unit is dependent upon that unit's type, its honour level, and by a large number of situational factors. The main morale-moulding factors are the level of casualties sustained, how the unit is doing in melee, the rate at which new casualties are occurring, their fatigue and the presence of threatening enemy units. Historically, soldiers were very unhappy when an enemy could attack them in the flank or rear. Accordingly, sending a unit behind the enemy army can reduce the morale of many units.

By killing the opposing general, you rob the enemy of his leadership and morale bonus.

Protect your commander, you'll notice he carries a Golden standard.

RANGED COMBAT

Like the melee system, the shooting model in *Shogun: Total War* is straightforward and fairly realistic. In essence, each soldier automatically picks an enemy soldier to shoot at. The computer then calculates the exact angles required for the soldier to hit his chosen target. After this, the game adjusts these angles by a random percentage based on the skill of the shooter, the accuracy of his weapon and the weather conditions. Finally, the computer tracks the arrow or bullet until it hits something. Consequently, missile troops are more likely to hit targets at close range.

One of the questions that regularly comes up during most chaotic battles is this: Can you hit your own troops with missile fire? In reality, the answer is yes, so in *Shogun: Total War* the answer is also yes. Note, however, that units ordered to "Fire At Will" will *not* fire into melees and will stop firing at an enemy if they are hitting their own men as well. But, units that have been *specifically* ordered to fire at a particular enemy, will carry on until you tell them to stop regardless of friendly casualties. Thus, it's perfectly legitimate to send an Ashigaru unit up against a unit of Heavy Cavalry with the sole purpose of keeping it stationary while Archers pound them with arrows. This is especially useful in the Campaign mode, where Ashigaru units are cheap to recruit and quick to train.

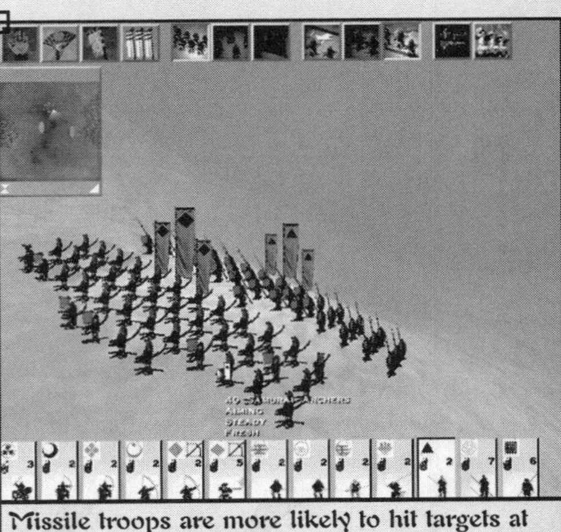

Missile troops are more likely to hit targets at close range.

As mentioned earlier in this guide, woods provide some cover against arrows and gunfire. There are no special rules for shooting into or out of wooded areas, but obviously many of your arrows will hit the trees if you conceal a unit of Archers deep within such natural cover. While they will be relatively well protected from enemy arrow-fire, they will only be able to fire accurately themselves if they move out into the open to give them an unobstructed field of fire.

Arquebusiers need a clear field of fire. Archers can fire "over" soldiers who are standing in front of them.

Not only does the type of terrain affect firing accuracy, it also affects how well a firing soldier can see the target. In game terms, soldiers who stand in the first two ranks of a unit (the first three ranks in a Loose Formation) are deemed to have a good view of their target. Those that stand behind these front ranks cannot see the target as clearly and therefore fire with reduced accuracy. Of course, if the view of the men in the front ranks is obscured by intervening units or terrain, they will also suffer the reduced accuracy penalty and those behind will be further penalised.

Consequently, Archers are at their most effective when deployed in shallow formations with a high and unobstructed view of the battleground. If you are defending on flat or gently sloping ground, for example, your missile units will do most damage if they are deployed in front of your other troops, where they have a clear view of the advancing enemy. On the other hand, if you are defending your position with the advantage of a steep slope, your missile troops can be deployed behind ranks of Arquebusiers or Yari samurai and still have a clear view of the enemy ahead.

Lastly, to defend against missile troops (especially samurai Archer units), veteran generals suggest employing a Loose Formation over a Close or Wedge arrangement. Under fire, the advantages are obvious. In Close Formation, if an arrow misses its intended target, it's more likely to hit somebody else. In a Loose Formation, which is most effective at defending against hopeful, long-range missile fire, the defending soldiers stand a chance of avoiding the arrows and gain a tiny armour bonus as a result.

Gunners are best deployed in two or three ranks, allowing them to fire continually.

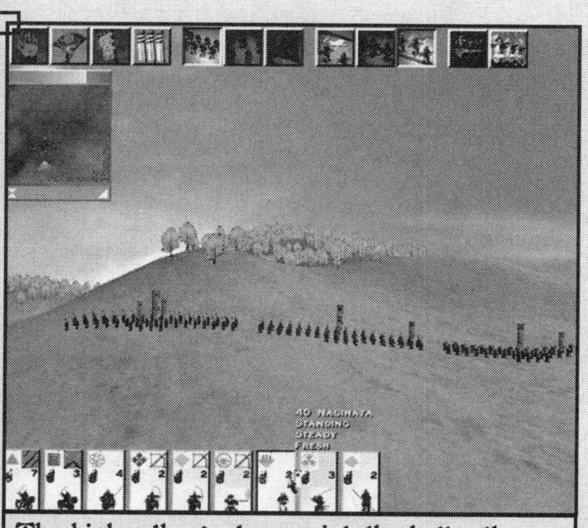

The higher the vantage point, the better the view a unit has of the battlefield.

BATTLE STRATEGIES

BATTLEFIELD STRATEGIES

Sun Tzu teaches that a great general takes into account a large number of factors before entering into battle. These will range from the type of terrain that he faces and the weather conditions, to how best to position his army in the most advantageous location from which to engage the enemy. The following pages contain some of the core tactics and strategies that you need to adopt to become a successful leader to your men.

The key to successful strategizing is to make use of different types of forces.

STUDY YOUR SURROUNDINGS

A good general examines the landscape he will fight on in minute detail. A great general not only knows the position of every tree, hill and river crossing, but he can see the tactical possibilities generated by them. Before every battle in *Shogun: Total War*, you will have the opportunity to rove freely around the battlefield before combat begins. Once you're happy that you know the location of the major features, you can enter into combat. However, when the enemy army has been placed on the battlefield (it is invisible to you during the pre-fight battlefield tour), press [P] to pause the action and then enlarge the Battlemap to study the situation further. Even though the camera is restricted to a view around your own forces, you can move the mouse pointer over enemy troops on the Battlemap to determine their type and strength.

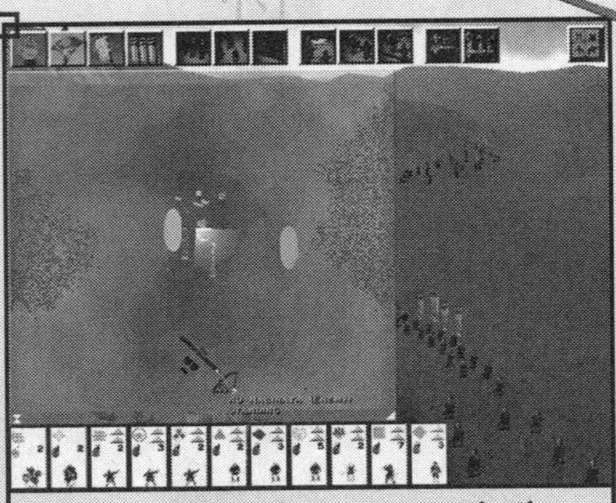

Enlarge the Battlemap to study the composition of the enemy force.

MY LORD, I HAVE A CUNNING PLAN...

With the game still paused, you can not only discover the enemy's strength and numbers, but you can start to devise a plan to counter them. At its most basic level, *Shogun: Total War* operates a scissors, paper, stone combat system—fast-moving Cavalry excel against Archers, Archers are effective against slow-moving Spearmen who will gain victory over Cavalry. As ever, the key to successful strategizing here is to make use of different types of forces, using them in combination to achieve your aims.

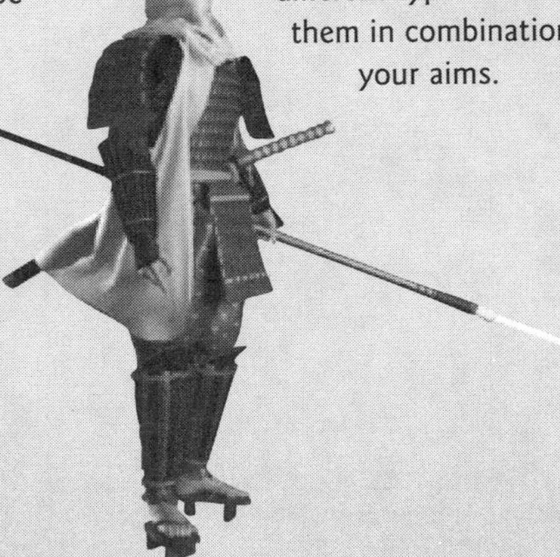

USE THE WEATHER

Some battles in the game (notably those in the Campaign mode) provide the opportunity to time your attack and take advantage of weather conditions. In a Campaign or Custom Battle, conflicts can be fought in spring, summer, autumn or winter in certain climate conditions. Clear days are more likely during the summer months, rain showers will plague operations in the spring, while snow should be expected on higher ground in the winter. In addition to these basic conditions, the Campaign mode also gives generals the chance to wait for the weather to change. Heavy rain, for example, may give way to a clear day and vice versa. You can use the terrain to your tactical advantage, so why not use the weather in the same way? A battle waged during the winter against an enemy who favours mounted units will inevitably swing in your favour as horses suffer in such conditions.

Use the weather to your advantage—gunpowder weapons, for example, are useless in the rain.

DIRECTING AND POSITIONING

Sun Tzu believed that the ideal strategy was to move or "direct" an opponent until they were perfectly positioned to their disadvantage. This has wider implications during a Campaign game but by moving your forces unexpectedly on the battlefield, you can often make an opponent re-evaluate its own position and shift to accommodate your new strategy. Thus, if an enemy is dug in to expect a frontal attack, simply start to march around him, taking advantage of the confusion as its units are reordered and repositioned. Similarly, use trees to launch ambushes and mass troops in one area of the battlefield before attacking another. By carefully manipulating the situation, you can position yourself for triumph even before a sword is drawn or an arrow is fired.

By outflanking a stubbornly placed enemy, you can force them to shift position.

HEIGHT: USE IT OR LOSE IT

The advantage of height in a conflict cannot be stressed enough. If used properly and skilfully, height advantage over an enemy can help a small army win victory over a much larger opponent seemingly against the odds. If you follow the advice on page 52 and study your surroundings *before* moving your troops, you can often locate a suitable patch of raised ground from which to launch an attack or mount a defence. Archers firing from such a location not only gain a better view of the battlefield, but inflict slightly more damage as a result. Similarly, as Sun Tzu points out, it is always better to fight downhill than uphill. "When the hill is high," wrote the master strategist, "never face up; when the hill slopes behind, never back down."

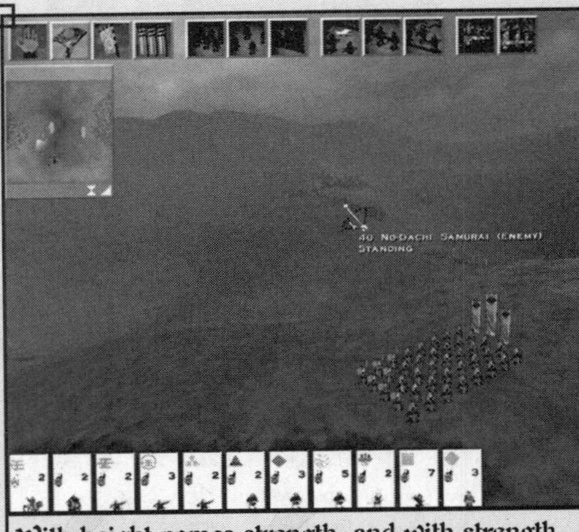

With height comes strength, and with strength, power. It's the most important tactic of all.

THE ADVANTAGE OF MISSILE TROOPS

If you haven't realised by now, the samurai Archer is by far the most useful unit on the battlefield, capable of devastating ranged weapon attacks and, in some cases, half-decent hand-to-hand combat support. If a good mix of troop types is essential to a successful battle, then no army (however small) should be without a complement of Archers. Even when the Portuguese and the Dutch introduce the Arquebus and the Musket to Japan in the Campaign mode, the Archer still has an important role to play. Arguably, while volleys of gunfire can inflict heavy casualties on an enemy line, Arquebusiers and Musketeers have a slow reload time and are next to useless in close combat situations. If you're playing with limited ammunition, gunners rarely run out of bullets due to their slow rate of fire. Archers, however, use up their arrows quickly so beware you don't commit them against units that should be attacked by Footsoldiers and Cavalry.

Missile troops can be used to reduce an army's forces before the hand-to-hand carnage begins.

THE ROLE OF THE GENERAL

As mentioned earlier, morale is very important on the battlefield and one of the better ways to reduce the morale level of an opponent is to kill the enemy general. Easy to identify (he carries a Golden standard), the death of a general will have an adverse effect on all units in the army. If units are under pressure, the news that their general is dead, is likely to make them rout, which may lead to mass panic in the ranks. It's therefore advisable to be very careful with your general's unit. Leaving him safely at the back is one option, but by having him close to the fighting troops boosts the morale of adjacent units. If the general routs, then the units close to him no longer gain a bonus from his presence, but there is no further penalty.

Guard against panic and low morale in the ranks by keeping one or two good units well back out of the battle, so that even if the rest rout, you have not lost the battle. Their presence will also help the other troops to rally and allow time for reinforcements to arrive if you have them. Note that samurai units are much less worried by the sight of fleeing Ashigaru, than by fleeing samurai. Ashigaru make no such distinction. Players can boost the morale of their troops by keeping units close together. Units that have other units protecting their flanks, or in support behind, receive a morale bonus. In addition, units in Close or Wedge formations tend to have higher morale than units in a Loose formation.

If units are under pressure, the news that their general is dead will likely cause them to rout.

AVOIDING FATIGUE

The two main causes of fatigue are fighting (which is unavoidable) and running long distances. Consequently, it is better to walk your troops until you close with the enemy. Save running for real emergencies or for seizing fleeting opportunities. Attacking, on the other hand, should always be done via a charge, as this gives a bonus on impact. Fresh troops kept in reserve can have a big impact on tired enemy units and can defeat opponents that they normally could not. Yari Ashigaru brought along to bolster the numbers, for example, can be very useful in the later stages of a game.

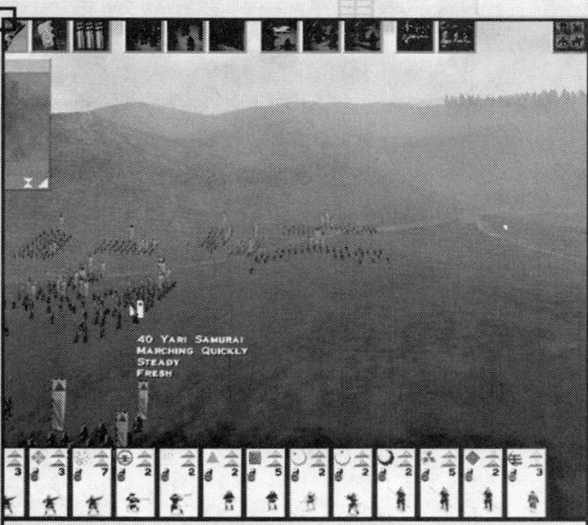

Attacking should always be done via a charge because this gives a bonus on impact.

KNOWLEDGE

知恵

Winning strategists are certain of triumph
Before seeking a challenge.
Losing Strategists are certain to challenge
Before seeking a triumph.

Sun Tzu (translated by R.L. Wing in "The Art of Strategy")

LEARN FROM THE PAST

To prepare for the future, you must learn from the past. To this end, alongside its Custom Battle and Campaign options, *Shogun: Total War* features six Historical Battles—the perfect way to practise your battle tactics and to familiarise yourself with advanced troop types. Not only do these six confrontations dare you to recreate ancient history, they introduce units that are not instantly available in the Campaign mode. Units such as Warrior Monks, No-Dachi samurai and Musketeers are waiting to be commanded, in a variety of military challenges ranging from large-scale clashes to foolhardy river crossings.

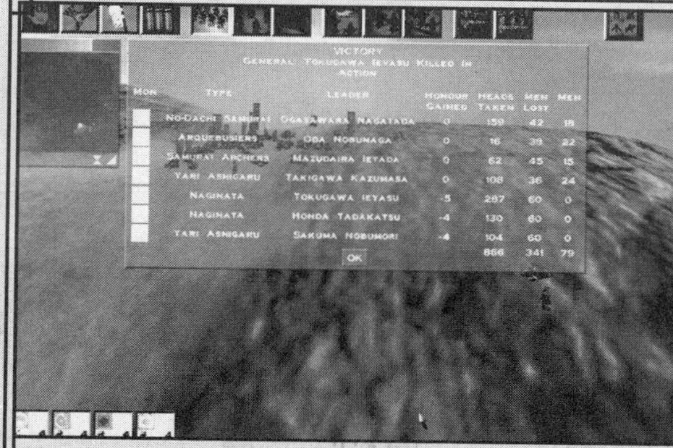

The battle at Mikata Ga Hara seems impossible to win. But there is a simple solution.

By far the best way to prepare yourself for the trials of the Campaign mode, is to first tackle Tutorial mode, then to test your embryonic command skills in some of Japan's most celebrated battles. Each of the six battles in the Historical Battles section is rated with one of three difficulty levels—Easy, Moderate and Hard. At Anegwa you are expected to marshal 840 troops against an opposing army of 900. At Nagakute, the numbers are fewer but the challenge is equally as great, while Mikata Ga Hara flings you into a snow-covered battlescape with forces that are outnumbered by 2:1. Nagashima tests your quick-thinking and patience by giving you an army of Musketeers rendered useless by heavy rain, Yamazaki is yet another case of two armies divided by a river that only one of them is forced to cross. Lastly, and most significantly, the fourth battle of Kawanakajima is a fight for a heavily defended fortress. When you've beaten all of these scenarios, you'll be more than prepared for the Campaign mode that stretches your strategic thinking on several different levels.

You can learn valuable lessons for the future, by playing battles set in the past.

ANEGAWA

In 1568, Oda Nobunaga marched on Kyoto and established Ashikaga Yoshiaki as a "puppet" Shogun under his control. However, the powerful Asakura clan still defied the Oda to the north. Nobunaga mobilised his army to teach them a lesson, and following several victories, he was marching on the Asakura capital when he heard that the Asakura had allied with the Asai clan. Nobunaga withdrew to Kyoto and regrouped to tackle this combined threat. When he set out again, the Asai-Asakura force met his army on the banks of the Anegawa River.

Battle: Anegawa (1568)
Difficulty: Easy
Objective: Controlling the Nobunaga forces, drive the Asai from the battlefield.
Weather conditions: Clear

Forces:	**Nobunaga (Player)**	**Asai (Computer)**
	180 Yari Samurai	240 Yari Samurai
	180 Yari Ashigaru	240 Yari Ashigaru
	180 Samurai Archers	120 Samurai Archers
	120 Arquebusiers	120 Arquebusiers
	60 Cavalry Archers	60 No-Dachi Samurai
	120 Heavy Cavalry	120 Heavy Cavalry
Total:	840	900

The battle at Anegawa pitches Oda Nobunaga against the Asai. Fighting takes place across the river.

HISTORICAL PERSPECTIVE

History records that the Oda armies fought the combined Asai/Asakura forces in a huge hand-to-hand battle in the middle of the river Anegawa. The battle took place in the shadow of the Asai Castle of Odani, with Nobunaga relying on assistance from the Tokugawa family. Rather than one battle, the Anegawa conflict was practically two—the Tokugawa clashing with the Asakura and the Oda in fierce fighting with the Asai. When the Tokugawa repulsed the Asakura attack, they were then free to lend support to the Oda forces. The Tokugawa altered the flow of battle by hitting the Asai's right flank, whereupon the Asai collapsed under the pressure and the Oda forces won the day.

Originally the battle at Anegawa took place in the shallow river. Here you fight around it.

BATTLE NOTES

The battle of Anegawa took place on a clear day, so weather is not a factor in this particular battle. The landscape around the Anegawa River is low, flat and altogether featureless, cut in two by the waterway that is bridged in three separate places. The majority of the conflict will take place on this middle ground and you can expect the Asai forces to counterattack as soon as you set foot on one of the bridges. At the beginning of the battle, only the centre bridge is actively defended by the enemy. Look closer, however, and you can see that the Asai have units in the distance covering both the left- and right-hand bridges. If there's a key to success here it is in good organisation—you have 840 troops split into six different troop types. If you allow the enemy to advance they will cut off all access to all three bridges. But attack too quickly, without thinking and your units will be trapped on the wrong side of the river against an overwhelming force.

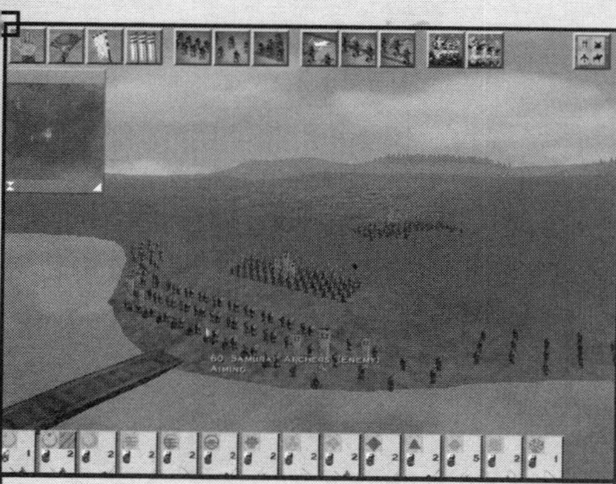

The Anegawa battlefield is cut in two by a river, which is bridged in three places.

The Asai have slightly more soldiers and hold a very strong defensive position.

ENEMY TROOP MOVEMENT

The Asai have 60 Yari samurai, 60 Arquebusiers and 60 samurai Archers guarding the central bridge. But as this only adds up to 180 men, it means that they have 720 in reserve. This 720-strong reserve is split into two elements; each one in a position to reinforce the remaining bridges before you can even get one Ashigaru unit across. Enlarge the Battlemap and you'll be able to see that 240 Asai stand back from the right-hand bridge—60 Heavy Cavalry, 60 samurai Archers and 120 Yari Ashigaru. The larger of the two elements, comprising 480 men lurks in range of the left-hand bridge. Here, 120 Yari Ashigaru, 120 Yari samurai, 60 No-Dachi, 60 Heavy Cavalry, 60 Arquebusiers and 60 samurai Archers prepare to make life for the Oda very difficult.

PLAYER TROOP MOVEMENT

As the battle starts, the majority of Nobunaga's troops are positioned towards the central bridge, with only four units in reserve (located opposite the left-hand bridge). The forces here are strong, but they are poorly placed. As you look, 180 Yari samurai, 60 Yari Ashigaru, 120 Heavy Cavalry, 120 samurai Archers, 60 Arquebusiers and 60 Cavalry Archers are arranged haphazardly on this side of the river. Of their number, the front three units (60 Ashigaru, 60 Yari samurai and 60 Heavy Cavalry) are in immediate danger of facing a volley of gunfire from the Asai Arquebusiers across the river. What you need to do is re-arrange the main body of this army, lock it into a formation and combine it with elements from the reserve. These four units consist of 120 Yari Ashigaru, 60 Arquebusiers and 60 samurai Archers (plus the general).

As the battle begins, the Oda have a total of 840 men at their disposal.

Use your missile troops to wear down the enemy prior to a direct assault.

FIGHTING AT ANEGAWA

Unlike Custom Battles or Campaign clashes, you can't alter the positions of your troops prior to the start of the battle. But you can use the calm before the storm to arrange your units into groups, i.e. Archers, Cavalry, etc. Once you've clicked the mouse to start the battle, press the [P] key to pause the action and issue the first round of orders to your troops.

First things first, withdraw the threatened Ashigaru, samurai and Heavy Cavalry units so that they can't be torn apart by the enemy Arquebusiers. Consolidation is the next task, so regroup the Oda forces bringing the left-most units into play towards the main force and move the mounted units (120 Heavy Cavalry, 60 Cavalry Archers) to a position on the left. This battle is a war of attrition—line up the ranged weapon troops on the banks of the river near the right-hand and central bridges, then send across Ashigaru units to tempt the enemy into committing his forces. The Ashigaru or samurai are needed here to keep the enemy busy as you attack them with Arquebus (set in three ranks for maximum effect) and Archer fire from across the river. Action here, will draw the main body of the Asai force towards this right-hand bridge. As the enemy's units become depleted, march the cavalry units across the left-hand bridge where they can attack the crumbling enemy from the rear. Make sure that you keep back a samurai unit (plus the Archers commanded by the general) to cope with the final "mopping up" procedure.

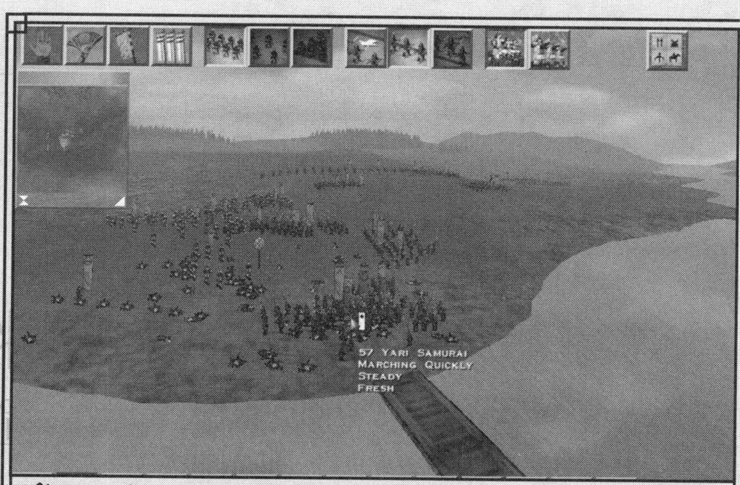

When weakened, drive your soldiers across the bridge to push the Asai back.

NAGAKUTE

By 1584, there was a stalemate between the great rivals Tokugawa Ieyasu and Toyotomi Hideyoshi as they each built a series of fortifications and field defences around their domains. To break the deadlock, Hideyoshi's ally Ikeda Nobuteru suggested a raid on Mikawa province and managed to take the Castle of Iwasaki. But Tokugawa was prepared for this strategy and he launched his army at Hideyoshi's forces, meeting them near the village of Nagakute.

Battle: Nagakute (1584)
Difficulty: Moderate
Objective: Deplete the Ikeda forces to a more manageable level.
Weather conditions: Clear

Forces:	**Tokugawa (Player)**	**Ikeda (Computer)**
	120 Yari Samurai	120 Yari Samurai
	60 Yari Ashigaru	60 Yari Ashigaru
	60 Samurai Archers	120 Arquebusiers
	120 Arquebusiers	60 Yari Cavalry
	60 Cavalry Archers	
	60 Yari Cavalry	
Total:	480	360

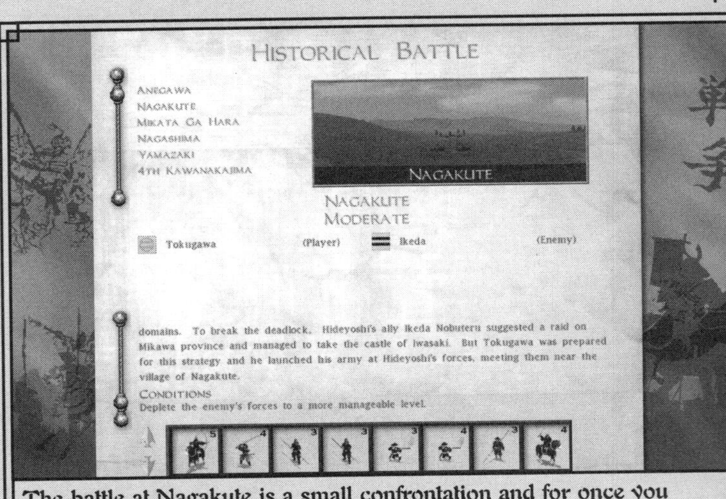

The battle at Nagakute is a small confrontation and for once you outnumber the enemy.

The battle takes place in a wide, shallow valley surrounded by hills.

HISTORICAL PERSPECTIVE

The battle of Nagakute gets its name from the small village that this famous confrontation was fought around. While you only have 480 troops to command in this *Shogun: Total War* recreation, the Tokugawa army actually numbered closer to 9,000 men before the battle started. As usual, it began with a long range exchange of gunfire, as both sides possessed Ashigaru gunners carrying the Arquebus. History records that the weather was clear and fine on this day in 1584, and that the battle did not actually last very long. Expecting a prolonged fight, the Ikeda forces suffered a blow to their morale when one of their leading figures, Mori Nagayoshi, was shot from his horse. As the battle raged on, the Ikeda finally retreated after samurai warriors attacked and killed Ikeda Nobuteru, the Ikeda's commander.

BATTLE NOTES

The battle of Nagakute takes place in a wide valley with gently sloping sides and, like the real battle, the weather is fine and doesn't affect troop performance. As in many of these Historical Battles, the enemy here expects you to come to him and after an initial advance, takes up defensive positions on the low hills beyond the huts that represent the village of Nagakute itself. The Tokugawa forces begin the day split into three groups, each one a fairly decent defensive position. However, it's perhaps advisable to reorder the troops to combat the twin elements of the Ikeda army—one camped on hills to the southeast, the other slowly approaching from the southwest.

Nagakute gets its name from the small village of Nagakute near where the battle was fought.

NAGAKUTE

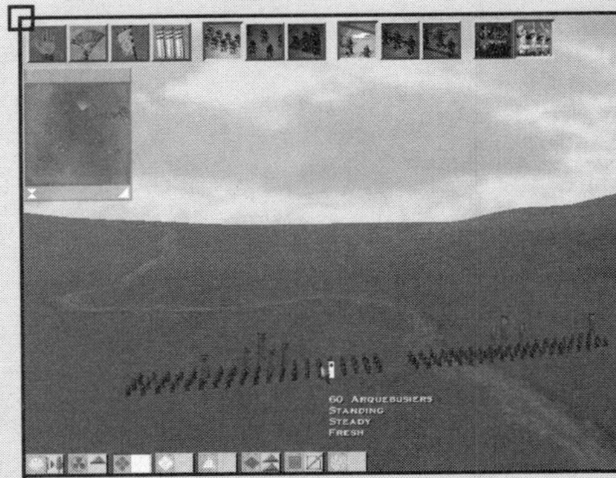

Gunpowder weapons are most effective when deployed in ranks of two or three.

ENEMY TROOP MOVEMENT

As mentioned in the Battle Notes section on the previous page, the Ikeda forces here are split neatly into two smaller forces. After advancing only a short distance, both will take up defensive positions on the low hills. In the southwest corner (as you look at the scenario's Battlemap), 60 Arquebusiers hold a fragile front line with 60 Yari samurai and 60 Yari Cavalry sheltering behind them. On the opposite side, in the southeast corner, 60 Arquebusiers stand in front of two more units—60 Yari samurai and 60 Yari Ashigaru. If you split your own forces to attack both of these groups at the same time, you ultimately lack the ranged weapons advantage that the Tokugawa's 120 Arquebusiers have, thanks to the support of the Archer and Cavalry Archer units. The enemy won't budge as you take the time to order your forces for the battle ahead.

PLAYER TROOP MOVEMENT

As mentioned earlier, commanding the Tokugawa forces, you'll start this scenario with your forces split into three separate groups. In the west (as you look at the Battlemap), 60 Yar Cavalry, 60 samurai Archers and 60 Yari Ashigaru hide silently in the trees. In the centre, 60 Yari samurai and 60 Arquebusiers skulk behind the last hillock in the valley. And finally, hidden in the trees to the east, 60 Cavalry Archers, 60 Arquebusiers and 60 Yari samurai await your orders. Again, as you are the attacking force, the enemy will advance to the centre of the battlefiel and take up defensive positions. Take the time to reorder your forces—creat a main force of 120 Arquebusiers, supported by samurai Archers and a unit of Yari samurai. Meanwhile, prepare to instruct the Yari Cavalry an the Yari Ashigaru in the west to outflank the Ikeda forces on the left-hand side.

As soon as the enemy reaches the valley, it will head for valuable high ground.

By positioning your troops on the hills, you can sweep the enemy Ikeda away.

FIGHTING AT NAGAKUTE

Just as the history books afford a glimpse into the real tactics employed (i.e. the battle began with an exchange of Arquebus fire), you can recreate a similar situation here. As the battle begins, let the enemy advance to its two defensive positions. Concentrate on constructing a main force of Arquebusiers (two units, laid out to a depth of three ranks), Archers (in a line behind them) and samurai (also in a line), but be prepared to hold position and formation in the event of a counterattack.

As you wait and watch, the Ikeda forces will advance to what they hope are defensible positions, employing classic formations on the hillside with their Arquebus units at the front. In the west, the Ikeda forces have taken up a position very close to the two Tokugawa units (60 Cavalry Archers, 60 Yari Ashigaru) that remain there. Send the Cavalry Archers to harass the western Ikeda faction, while moving your Yari Cavalry and Ashigaru into a position where they can charge down the hillside, hitting the Arquebusiers, Yari samurai and Yari Cavalry in the flank. Just as the Cavalry Archers get the attention of the Ikeda Yari Cavalry unit, attack the unprotected Yari samurai unit with a Yari Cavalry charge of your own. At the same time, advance the Arquebusiers and Archers to meet the enemy Arquebusiers. You'll find that the Yari Cavalry has already done the damage. Hold back your other ground troops and repeat the attacking thrust with the second group of Ikeda forces.

Yari Cavalry is particularly effective in this battle. Outflank the Ikeda and charge!

MIKATA GA HARA

The battle of Mikata Ga Hara came about during the drive south by Takeda Shingen against the Tokugawa fortress of Hamamatsu. At this time the Takeda were the most powerful clan in Japan and Tokugawa was heavily outnumbered. Not only did Takeda Shingen have the advantage of numbers, but also the formidable might of the Takeda cavalry. Despite the odds and against the advice of his generals, Tokugawa attacked.

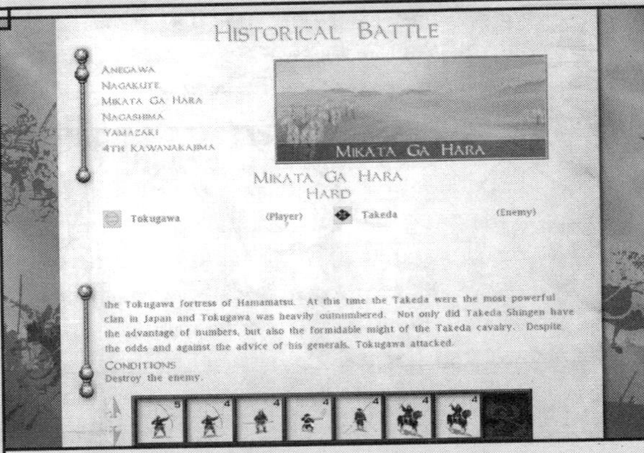

The battle of Mikata Ga Hara takes place on a harsh, frozen landscape.

Battle: Mikata Ga Hara (1572)
Difficulty: Hard
Objective: Commanding Tokugawa's forces, destroy the enemy.
Weather conditions: Snow (clear)

Forces:	Tokugawa (Player)	Takeda (Computer)
	120 Yari Ashigaru	180 Yari Ashigaru
	60 Samurai Archers	180 Samurai Archers
	60 Arquebusiers	60 Arquebusiers
	60 No-Dachi Samurai	180 Heavy Cavalry
	120 Naginata	120 Naginata
		120 Yari Samurai
		60 Cavalry Archers
Total:	420	900

HISTORICAL PERSPECTIVE

History records that Tokugawa Ieyasu was outnumbered by a factor of 3:1 and that the battle of Mikata Ga Hara was less of an actual "battle" and more of a desperate retreat. Even with an army of 11,000 men, Tokugawa Ieyasu faced the overwhelming strength of the Takeda who relied on their highly skilled cavalry units for dominance on the battlefield. Bravely, the Tokugawa forces withstood the initial cavalry charges, opening fire on the Takeda samurai with their Arquebus troops. Quickly, the Tokugawa lines began to crumble, divisions were overrun, and it became apparent to Shingden as it grew dark that the Tokugawa army was in retreat. Thanks to the loyalty of his men, Tokugawa Ieyasu was able to withdraw from the battlefield and return to the fortress of Hamamatsu with what remained of his shattered army.

History records Mikata Ga Hara as a retreat, so a dramatic change of tactics is required. Start moving your troops to the mountain as soon as the battle begins.

BATTLE NOTES

Mikata Ga Hara is a featureless snow-covered battlescape, not flat but not hilly enough to offer much of an advantage to the defending player. The only real high ground is located in the south of the battleground (if you look at the Battlemap). But this area has about 900 heavily armed and armoured Takeda soldiers marching confidently down it. Outnumbered by a factor of 2:1, it's practically impossible to meet the Takeda forces in a straight fight and hope to win. The key to success here is to do something unexpected, something that the marching Takeda aren't prepared for and ultimately can't cope with. It's certainly true that the Takeda forces are strong, but perhaps they rely too much on their Heavy Cavalry units. This is a weakness that you can exploit.

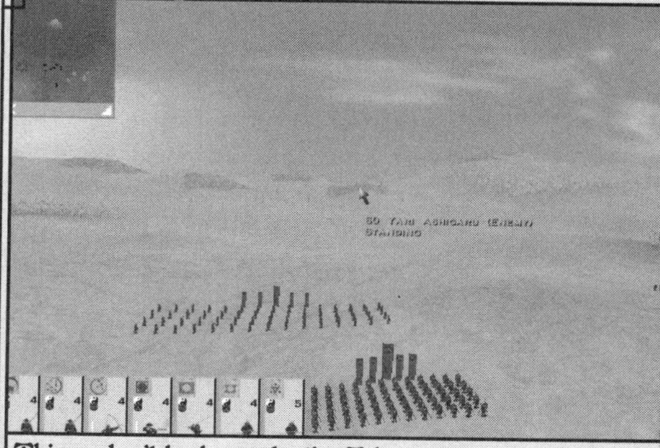

Things don't look good—the Tokugawa are outnumbered by 2:1.

ENEMY TROOP MOVEMENT

The Takeda forces, mighty though they are, have a long march ahead of them before they are close to engaging their enemy. To start with, they assume a familiar formation: missile troops (60 samurai Archers, 60 Arquebusiers) at the front supported by Footsoldiers (Yari samurai) and Heavy Cavalry. Behind this vanguard, march the weaker Ashigaru units, and further back the remaining cavalry and missile units (120 samurai Archers, 60 Cavalry Archers) begin the long trudge south. At the back, the Takeda's own Naginata units (numbering 120 men) provide a hefty, and heavily armoured reserve force. Unless the opposing Tokugawa force dramatically shift position, the Takeda will continue to march downhill until battle is joined.

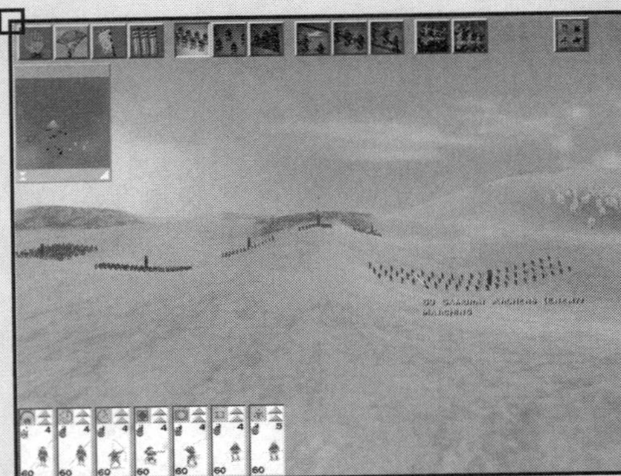

The opposing Takeda begin the battle with the advantage of height and numbers.

PLAYER TROOP MOVEMENT

Although the Tokugawa are heavily outnumbered, and perhaps outclassed, note that two Naginata units and a No-Dachi squad make up 180 of the army's 420 man total. As the battle begins, the Takeda forces start high on the southern edge of the map and will take some time to march from their high starting point to the low plain where the Tokugawa forces are cowering. Here, 60 Arquebus Ashigaru and 60 samurai Archers hope to slow down the approaching hordes, protecting the ground troops behind them. Of these, 120 are experienced Ashigaru units, while 120 Naginata and 60 No-Dachi samurai make up the rest. Don't worry too much about changing the basic formation here —if you choose to stay here, any tactical shape you employ won't stop the Takeda from rolling over the Tokugawa army and grinding it into the snow.

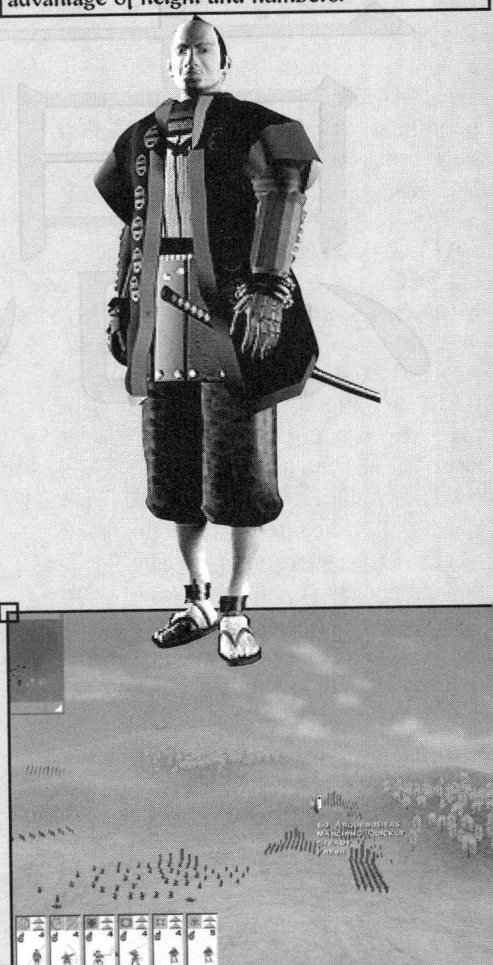

Start moving your troops to the mountain as soon as the battle begins.

FIGHTING AT MIKATA GA HARA

Admittedly, the prospects for the Tokugawa forces look bleak, especially when history also records that Tokugawa Ieyasu returned to Hamamatsu with only five men of the 11,000 who faced the Takeda. But, as Sun Tzu is proud to point out, by surprising the enemy, by doing the "unexpected", there is a chance for victory. The key to success at Mikata Ga Hara is to use the situation to your advantage, fighting on your own terms rather than those defined by the Takeda.

What this requires is a dramatic shift in tactics. Instead of waiting for the Takeda to sweep down the mountain to attack your forces with the advantage of numbers, height and charging speed, select your entire army (use [CTRL] and [A]) and march them up the high peak that dominates the landscape to the southwest. Using the trees as cover for your repositioning, stay as far away from the approaching Takeda as possible—losing some samurai to Takeda missile fire at this point is unavoidable. Keep moving until your forces have occupied the top of the mountain, an enviable position with an unparalleled view of the battlefield. By now the Takeda will have turned to pursue, but to get to you they either have to climb the steep hillside or attack through the snow-covered woods. Cavalry are rendered almost powerless amongst the trees and by sending in the two Naginata units, you can decimate the Takeda's mounted support.

In addition, co-ordinate your defence from the mountain-top, using the Archers to fire at the troops below and the remaining ground forces (No-Dachi, Ashigaru) to attack the rest of the Takeda forces. Victory is suddenly within your grasp.

Draw the Takeda Cavalry into the trees where it can be defeated easily.

Claim the mountain-top and make the Takeda fight uphill to reach you.

MIKATA GA HARA

NAGASHIMA

Some of the most formidable tests Oda Nobunaga faced were in fighting against the Ikko-Ikki Warrior Monks and it took a decade of campaigning before he finally broke their power. The Ikko-Ikki were utterly fearless in battle and devoted to honing their skills as warriors through relentless training. Following a disaster in 1571 where Nobunaga's army was severely defeated in an attack on the monastery fortress of Nagashima, he took personal control of the operation and launched a second attack in 1573.

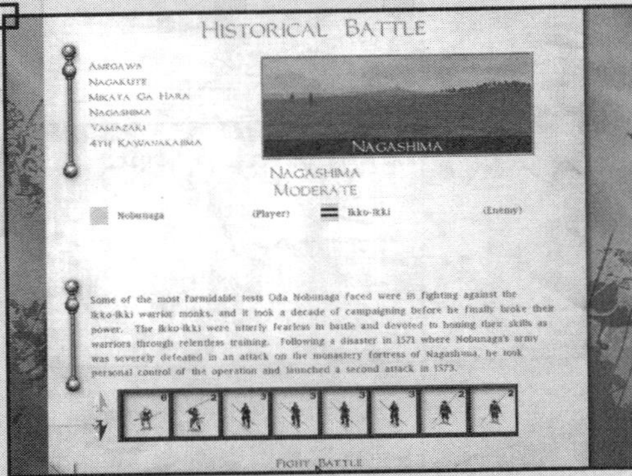

At Mikata Ga Hara you fought Cavalry in the snow, here you face Warrior Monks in the rain.

Battle: Nagashima (1573)
Difficulty: Moderate
Objective: Commanding Nobunaga's forces, kill all enemy troops.
Weather conditions: Rain showers

Forces:	Nobunaga (Player)	Ikko-Ikki (Computer)
	240 Yari Samurai	180 Yari Ashigaru
	120 Samurai Archers	180 Samurai Archers
	240 Musketeers	240 Warrior Monks
	60 Cavalry Archers	120 No-Dachi
	60 Heavy Cavalry	
Total:	720	720

Yes, you have 240 Musketeers. But in the rain, they have 240 muskets that won't work.

BATTLE NOTES

Just as history recounts a battleplan ruined by the elements, you'll discover that this recreation in *Shogun: Total War* stays horribly true to the facts. Of the 720 men under your command in this scenario, half are missile troops. Due to the torrential rain, the Musketeers cannot fire and the Archers have their accuracy reduced because the water affects the bowstrings. Consequently, you have 240 Yari samurai and 120 mounted Cavalry with which to repel the enemy charge. It's a tall order, especially as the Ikko Ikki ranks consist of the feared Warrior Monk units which, though lightly armoured, fight with sky-high morale and so very little fear of death. To succeed at Nagashima where Oda Nobunaga failed, you will need to protect your missile troops until the rain stops and the gunpowder weapons can be used to maximum effect. Know this: the break in the weather *will* come.

HISTORICAL PERSPECTIVE

Oda Nobunaga reopened his offensive against the Ikko-Ikki in July 1573, taking personal charge of the operations in an attempt to ensure victory. Having recruited heavily, Nobunaga was able to command a sizeable army, a large part of it consisting of Arquebus-wielding Ashigaru. Unfortunately, just as the battle was about to begin, the heavens opened and it began to rain. The downpour played havoc with Nobunaga's plans, rendering the majority of the guns that he was relying on absolutely useless. As water soaked the matches that were needed to fire the Arquebus weapons, Nobunaga was forced to defend with his older weapons as the Ikko Ikki seized the chance to launch a fierce counterattack. As the Ikko Ikki advanced, pushing Nobunaga back, the rain stopped allowing both sides to use their guns. But the break in the weather was too little too late for Nobunaga who was ultimately forced to retreat for the second time in two years.

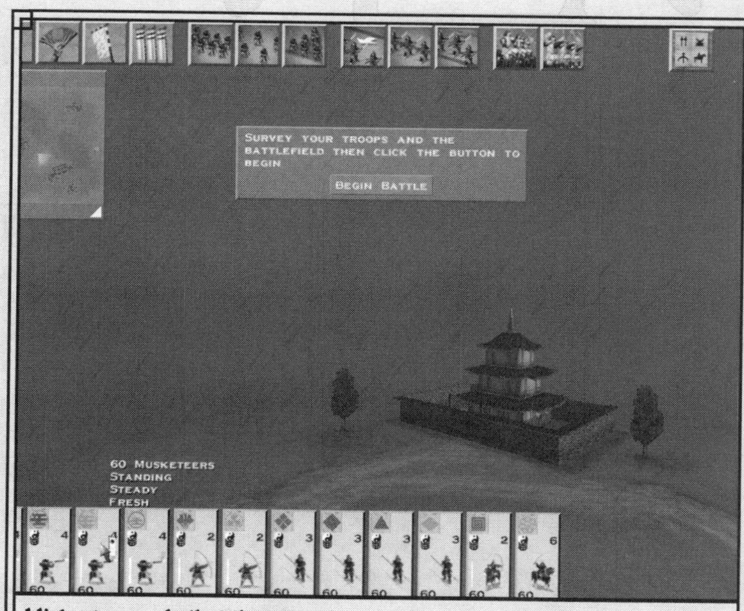

History records that the rain played havoc with Oda Nobunaga's plans for conquest of the Ikko-Ikki.

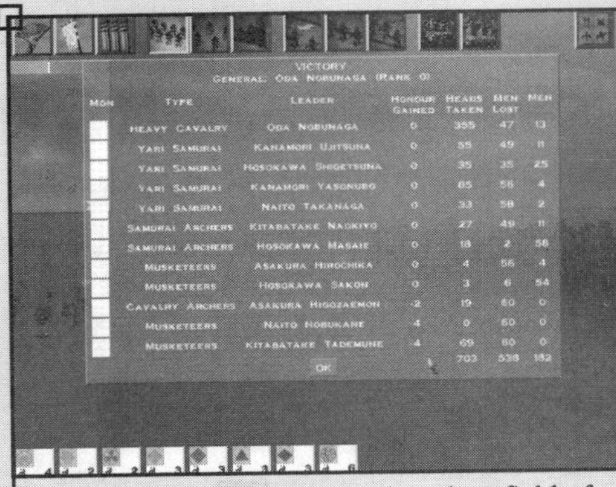

Deploy your Musketeers with a clear field of fire and use the Archers to inflict early damage.

ENEMY TROOP MOVEMENT

When this historical battle begins, it's difficult to tell exactly where the enemy are and where they will come from. Visibility is poor thanks to the driving rain, and the Battlemap is helpfully blank. Suffice it to say, however, that the Ikko-Ikki are advancing in the gloom beyond the small Castle to the immediate left of the Oda forces. Deploying a basic attacking formation, their lines are lead by three units of samurai Archers, flanked on each side by 60 No-Dachi samurai. Behind them, 180 Ashigaru provide support for the main body of the army—four units (240 men) of Warrior Monks, one of the most fearsome and effective units on the *Shogun: Total War* battlefield. Almost unbeatable in hand-to-hand combat, these fanatical fighters are best attacked from a distance with ranged weapons. Not only is it impossible to see where the enemy is likely to attack from, but your forces are initially laid out in a Skirmish Centre formation.

PLAYER TROOP MOVEMENT

The missile weapons (in this case, the Musketeers) are positioned at the front, followed by the Yari samurai, the Archer units and the cavalry bringing up the rear. While the 240 Musketeers would form a strong front-line on a clear day, in the rain they are poorly equipped to meet the expected enemy charge. The four units of Yari samurai behind them, however, can operate in any weather and this makes a case for them replacing the Musketeers at the front of the Nobunaga lines. Another option is the 120 men that make up the two samurai Archer units who, while the rain affects their accuracy, can still provide ranged weapons support. Finally, safe in the rear sit 60 Cavalry Archers and 60 Heavy Cavalry. If you haven't already realised by now, these two units will be instrumental in causing the majority of the damage to the enemy's Warrior Monks.

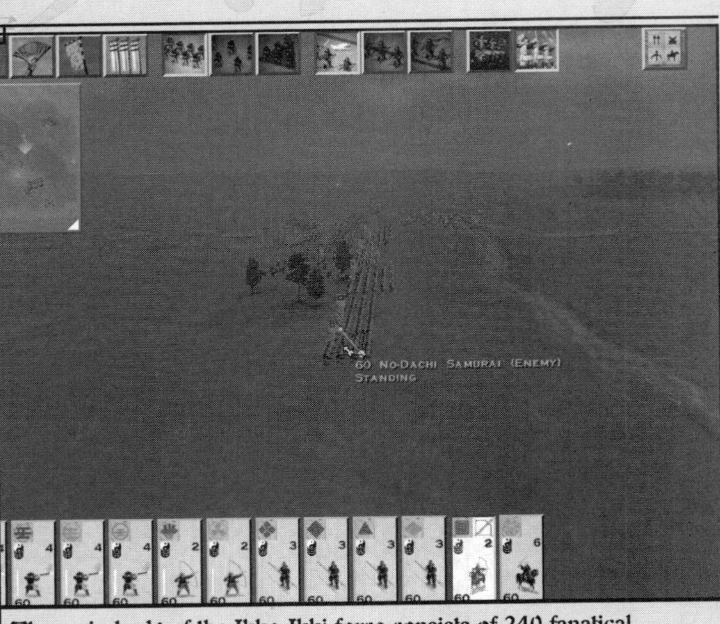

The main body of the Ikko-Ikki force consists of 240 fanatical Warrior Monks, supported by No-Dachi samurai.

FIGHTING AT NAGASHIMA

The biggest headache for any general is to have 240 men that they can't use and this is precisely what you are faced with at Nagashima. Due to the heavy rain, the four units of Musketeers that make up a third of Nobunaga's forces are rendered useless. This leaves the Archers, Yari samurai and mounted units to take most of the strain. Your task is simple: delay the Ikko-Ikki advance until the weather clears, so the guns can be briefly used to redress the imbalance.

You begin the scenario holding a reasonable defensible hill. The surrounding landscape doesn't offer a better alternative, so dig in here in preparation for the attack by the Ikko-Ikki forces. While the Musketeers can't be used in the rain, they still need to form the front line, ready to open fire as soon as the weather changes. Unfortunately, the forecast for the battle is for showers and no sooner do you get your Muskets firing at the enemy than the rain begins again. As always, the Archer units can be used to provide covering fire and their number is bolstered by the presence of the Cavalry Archers. The most important unit on the battlefield, however, is the Heavy Cavalry. Used wisely (i.e. hitting the flanks or rear of the enemy), they are more than a match for the Warrior Monk units. Be careful not to waste them against the Ashigaru or the No-Dachi. There are 240 white-robed monks to get rid of and without these troops, the Ikko-Ikki forces are significantly less of a threat.

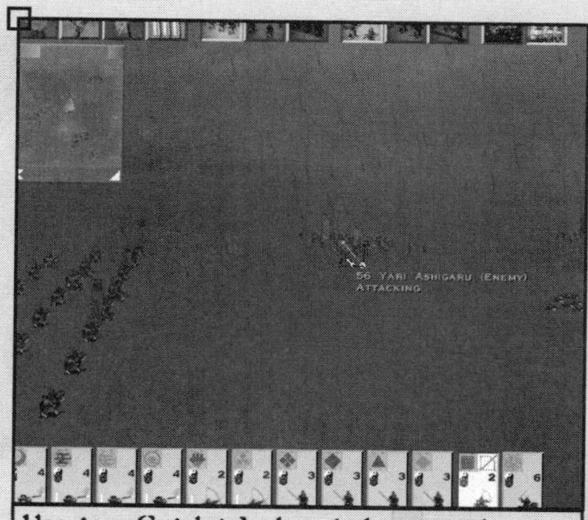

Use your Cavalry Archers to harass and confuse the advancing enemy.

Make use of the intermittent clear weather to attack with the Musketeers.

NAGASHIMA

YAMAZAKI

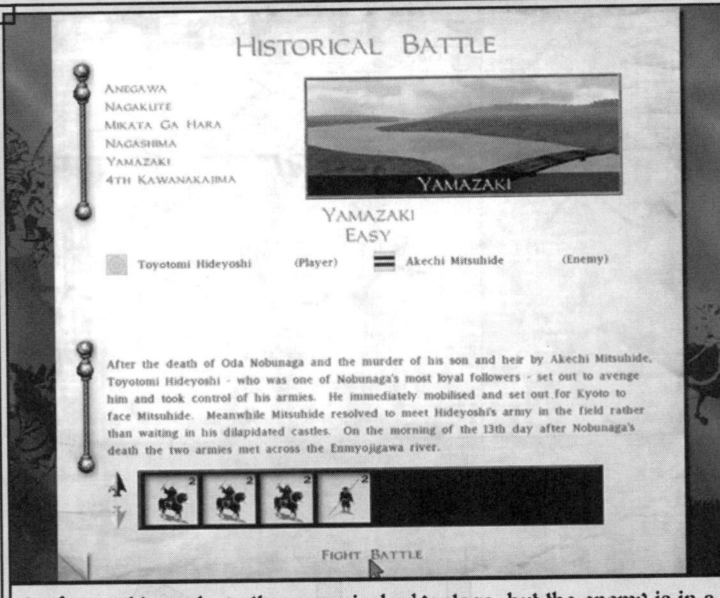

At Yamazaki you have the numerical advantage, but the enemy is in a strong defensive position.

After the death of Oda Nobunaga and the murder of his son and heir by Akechi Mitsuhide, Toyotomi Hideyoshi—one of Nobunaga's most loyal followers—set out to avenge him and took control of his armies. He immediately mobilised to Kyoto to face Mitsuhide. Meanwhile, Mitsuhide resolved to meet Hideyoshi's army in the field rather than waiting in his dilapidated Castles. On the morning of the thirteenth day after Nobunaga's death, the two armies met across the Enmyojigawa river.

Battle: Yamazaki (1582)
Difficulty: Easy
Objective: Commanding Oda Nobunaga's forces, annihilate the enemy.
Weather conditions: Clear

Forces:	Toyotomi Hideyoshi (Player)	Akechi Mitsuhide (Computer)
	180 Yari Samurai	120 Yari Samurai
	180 Yari Ashigaru	60 Yari Ashigaru
	120 Samurai Archers	180 Samurai Archers
	180 Arquebusiers	60 Arquebusiers
	60 Heavy Cavalry	60 Heavy Cavalry
Total:	720	480

Yamazaki is a river battle much like Anegawa, but here there are two bridges instead of three.

BATTLE NOTES

Like most river-based scenarios in *Shogun: Total War*, the Yamazaki landscape is wide and flat, edged by slightly higher ground to both the north and south. The tactic of gaining a height advantage is useless here, however, most of the actual fighting takes place close to the river Enmyojigawa and that splits the battleground in two. With the aim of destroying the Mitsuhide forces, the first objective is to make it across the river with as few casualties as possible. There are two bridges across the river, both guarded by elements of the enemy army. Due to the fact that the terrain is flat and featureless, tactics should be based around ranged weapons troops and the mobility of Cavalry units. Archers and Arquebusiers have the power to strike at the enemy across the river, while the Heavy Cavalry can be used to harry the enemy when his lines are finally broken.

HISTORICAL PERSPECTIVE

Toyotomi Hideyoshi and Akechi Mitsuhide met in a river battle close to a small village called Yamazaki. History records that Hideyoshi was able to field 36,000 troops against Mitsuhide's 16,000, dominating not only in terms of sheer numbers but due to careful positioning on the battlefield. Although Akechi Mitsuhide had a good defensive stance on his side of the Enmyojigawa river, the sheer weight of the Hideyoshi advance was enough to crush him. After Shinobi from Hideyoshi's army had caused midnight confusion in the enemy camps, Hideyoshi swept across the river crossings, encircling and massacring his under-strength opponent. Mitsuhide managed to flee during the carnage, escaping as far as the village of Ogurusu where he was killed by bandits. Thus, barely thirteen days after Mitsuhide had murdered his way to the title of Shogun, he was dead.

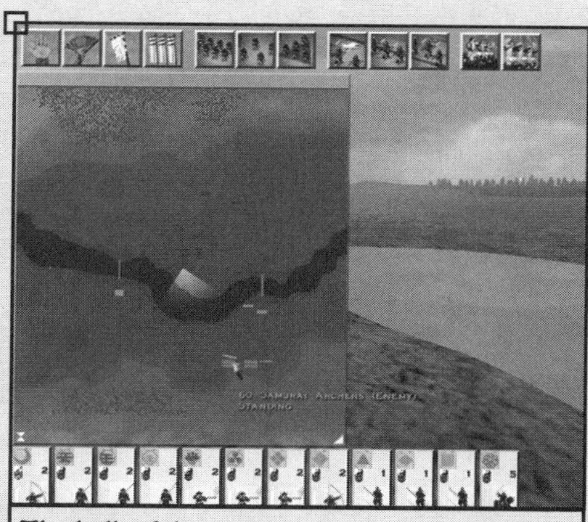

The bulk of the enemy force is massed around the eastern bridge.

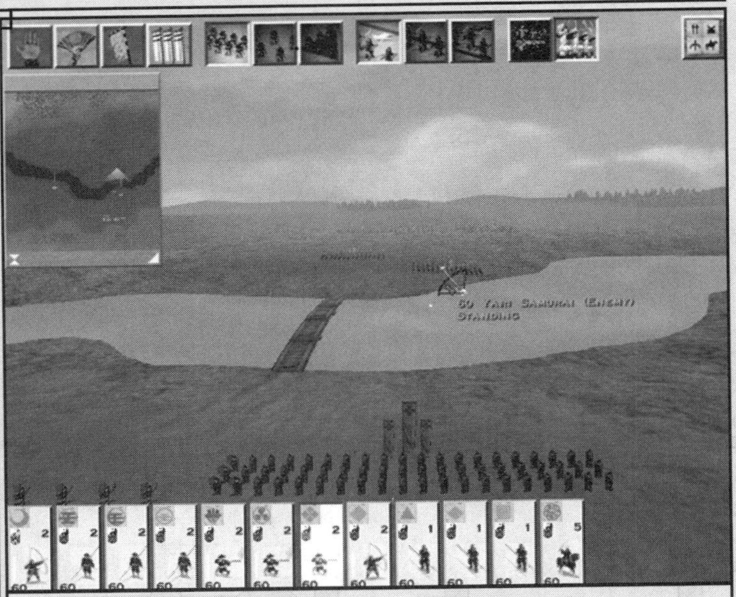

Akechi Mitsuhide will snipe at invaders from distance, supporting them with Yari Troops.

PLAYER TROOP MOVEMENT

There's little initial order in the ranks of Hideyoshi's army at the start of the scenario, but as Mitsuhide is content to defend rather than attack, you have plenty of time to reorder and redistribute your units. Take a look at the Battlemap and you can see that 60 samurai Archers and 60 Arquebusiers face the 420 enemy troops across the eastern bridge. The bulk of the Hideyoshi army stands steady between the two river crossings. 120 Arquebusiers and 60 samurai Archers provide the ranged weapons option, while 120 Yari Ashigaru wait ready to be sacrificed in a series of costly sorties across the bridges. Hanging back, three Yari samurai units and an extra squad of 60 Ashigaru make up the reserves. While the enemy will continually shift the positions of its troops to the east, it will not yet dispatch any units to reinforce the Heavy Cavalry unit to the west.

ENEMY TROOP MOVEMENT

With fewer men at his disposal and two bridge crossings to defend, Mitsuhide's forces will initially set up in a familiar bridge-defence formation. Thus, on the eastern flank, the bridge here will be defended by the massed ranks of 120 Yari samurai, 60 Yari Ashigaru, 60 Arquebusiers and 180 samurai Archers. This strategy leaves the western bridge guarded only by 60 Heavy Cavalry. It's a good tactical choice, as the mounted unit can sit beyond arrow and bullet range, but is able to quickly charge in to defend against incursions across the bridge. Once set in these defensive positions, Mitsuhide's forces will not budge unless their enemy make a dramatic tactical change to their positions and formation. The Battlemap gives you an excellent overall view of the Mitsuhide defensive strategy.

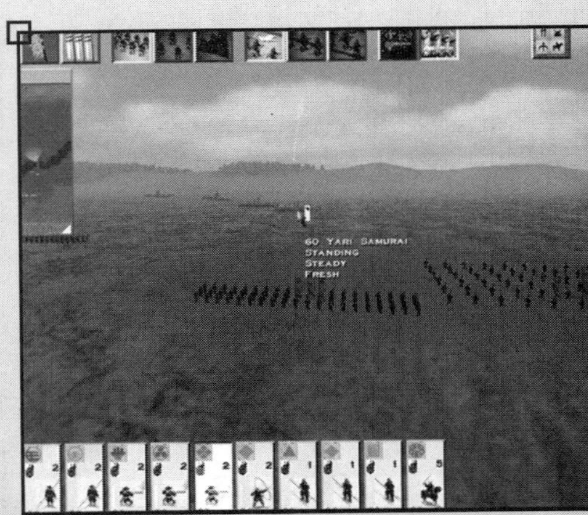

With the enemy set out to defend, you have plenty of time to organise your forces.

FIGHTING AT YAMAZAKI

Like any bridge action in *Shogun: Total War*, ranged weapons units are all important. Using Archers you are able to strike across the river while only risking one ground unit at a time. Similarly, the Mitsuhide army is at its most vulnerable on the western bridge. While it is guarded by the considerable might of enemy Heavy Cavalry, there are no missile troops to cut down an advance party as it charges into battle across the bridge. The key to unlock the Mitsuhide defence (which is much stronger than it looks), is to fight fire with fire. Or in this case, Heavy Cavalry with Heavy Cavalry. Your own Heavy Cavalry unit is your most potent weapon and, once you can get rid of the enemy's own mounted troops, you can effectively control the battlefield.

To gain a foothold on the opposite side of the river, use the "entrapment" bridge tactics detailed earlier in this manual. Line up both Archer units near the western bridge and march a unit of expendable Ashigaru across to tempt the enemy Cavalry into an attack. As they start to charge, order the Ashigaru to retreat so that they are not caught in the arrow-fire with the charging horses. Repeat this process until the enemy Cavalry is at about half of its normal strength, then launch a concerted attack with your own Cavalry to defeat it. This will no doubt draw some reinforcements from the bridge to the east, but by using units one-at-a-time, you can whittle away at the Mitsuhide defences before mounting a final invasion with every unit you have left in your army. Mitsuhide can't stand up against this superior force.

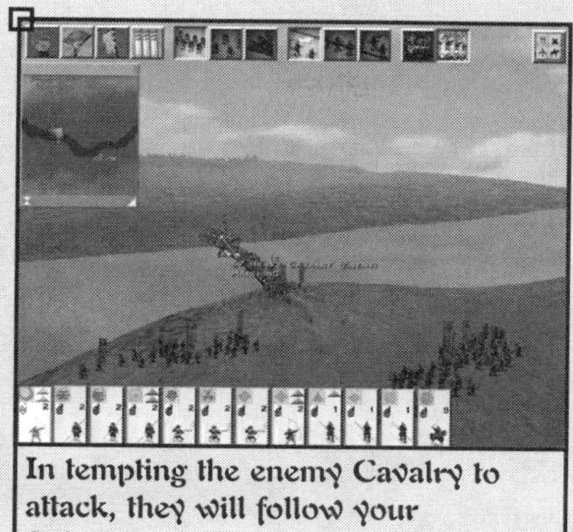

In tempting the enemy Cavalry to attack, they will follow your Ashigaru onto the bridge and become trapped.

An advantage of attacking the Cavalry first is that the enemy general is commanding them.

4TH KAWANAKAJIMA

The Kawanakajima plain is an area of flatland where the territories of the Uesugi and the Takeda clans met. Five battles were fought on this plain between the two clans, and the fourth was one of the bloodiest and most spectacular battles in Japanese history. Uesugi's army had taken position atop Mount Saijo. Takeda split his army in two and intended to take Uesugi by surprise with the first section of his army, while the second section waited to cut them down as they were routed. However, Uesugi mobilised before the Takeda strike force could arrive and descended on the Takeda position on the plain. The Takeda army was expecting to face a disorganised and routing enemy, but now were faced by the full strength of the Uesugi army advancing upon them.

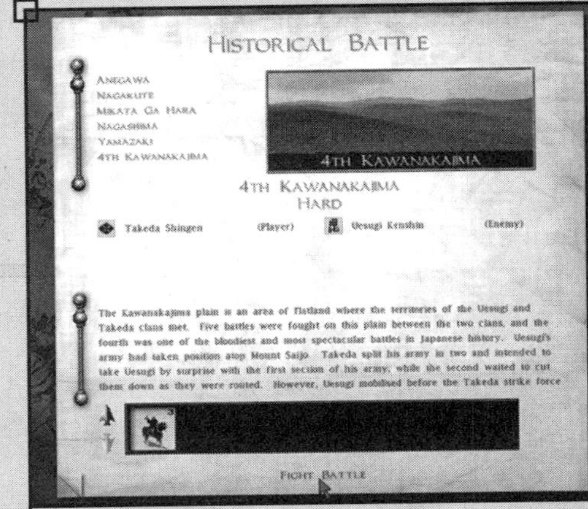

Can you fight an enemy you can't see until it's right on top of you? Kawanakajima provides the answer.

Battle: 4th Kawanakajima (1561)
Difficulty: Hard
Objective: Commanding the Takeda forces, destroy the enemy.
Weather Conditions: Fog

Forces:	**Takeda Shingden (Player)**	**Uesugi Kenshin (Computer)**
	120 Yari Samurai	240 Yari Samurai
	120 Yari Ashigaru	120 Yari Ashigaru
	120 Samurai Archers	180 Samurai Archers
	60 No-Dachi Samurai	60 Arquebusiers
	60 Cavalry Archers	60 No-Dachi
	60 Heavy Cavalry	60 Heavy Cavalry
		120 Yari Cavalry
		60 Cavalry Archers
Total:	540	900

HISTORICAL PERSPECTIVE

The Kawanakajima conflict simulated here is the fourth meeting between the forces of Takeda Shingen and clan Uesugi. In their first meeting on the plain in 1553, the two armies were involved in little more than skirmishes before Takeda withdrew. Two years later, and Takeda Shingen advanced again onto the Kawanakajima plain, where he met Kenshin Uesugi in battle at a castle known as Asahiyama. Kenshin abandoned his attempts to take the castle from Takeda Shingen, and retreated to the river where he arranged his armies to wait for him to make a countermove. Shingen, however, did not attack and eventually both forces withdrew to deal with weightier matters. The third time Takeda Shingen invaded was in 1557, where he managed to penetrate deeper into Uesugi territory than ever before. Again, Kenshin led an army to face him and rather than fight, Takeda Shingen withdrew. there was also a fifth battle, but this also resulted in skirmishing and little else.

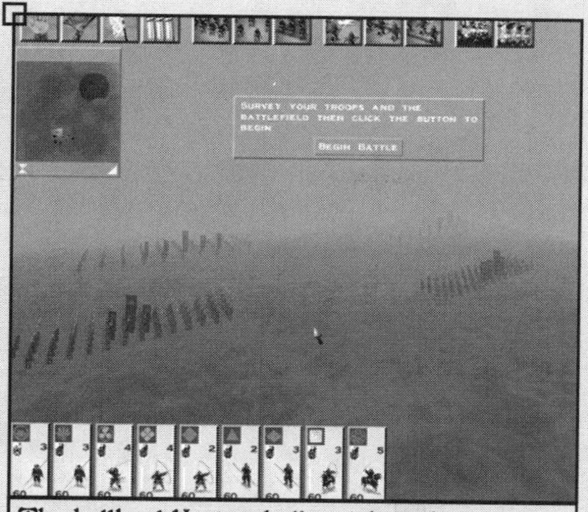

The battle at Kawanakajima takes place in foggy conditions causing reduced visibility.

BATTLE NOTES

As the 4th Kawanakajima battlescape is covered with fog when the battle begins, it's difficult to know where to set up a defence and where the enemy will be coming from. Thus, before you tackle the 4th Kawanakajima battle, do a little sneaky research. Load up the Custom Battles section of the game and generate a random confrontation between two armies using the 4th Kawanakajima landscape. Choose to fight the battle in spring or summer to ensure good weather, allowing you to survey the battlefield without the fog. What you'll discover is that the Kawanakajima plain is a featureless stretch of undulating terrain, its low hills divided by shallow, rocky hollows. Your starting point is almost in the centre of the battlemap—point the camera south to take a look at what is basically a large chunk of raised ground at the edge of the map.

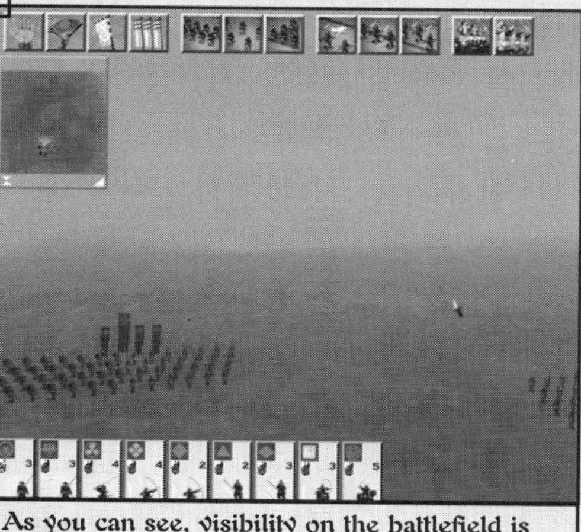

As you can see, visibility on the battlefield is about 100 yards, no more.

ENEMY TROOP MOVEMENT

You won't be able to see them, but the massed ranks of the Uesugi army lie hidden in the mist to the northeast of where you start the battle. They are stretched across the plain here, using a wide formation that allows them to see a large area of the terrain in the fog. Sixty Cavalry Archers will have galloped ahead in a scouting role, followed by the main body of the force. In order, this consists of 60 front-line Yari samurai with 60 samurai Archers behind them. This advance force is supported by Yari samurai and Yari Ashigaru units, while two units of samurai Archers follow closely. Another 120 Yari samurai support the missile troops, and provide a buffer zone between themselves and the six units bringing up the rear. Here, No-Dachi samurai and Yari Ashigaru are kept in reserve, trotting alongside 60 Arquebusiers, 120 Yari Cavalry soldiers and 60 Heavy Cavalry.

Only by sending your Cavalry Archers to scout will you beable to detect the approach of enemy mounted units.

PLAYER TROOP MOVEMENT

By far the best way to see where the enemy is attacking from is to employ your Cavalry Archers as scouts, much like the Uesugi army is doing somewhere in the fog. Like the Uesugi, Takeda Shingden's forces (your forces) are arranged in a loose formation, hoping to cover as much ground as possible and thereby gain a greater view of the gloomy battlefield. As a defensive posture, however, it won't stand up to a concerted Uesugi attack without some alteration. As the battle begins, you'll see that the 120 Yari Samurai and 120 Samurai Archers are in a half-decent position on this raised area. On their flanks, however, the two units of Ashigaru are poorly placed, while the No-Dachi, Cavalry Archers and Heavy Cavalry stand in one of the hollows that cover the battlefield. Take our advice: don't leave your army here.

Your troops are vulnerable from all sides in this loose group formation.

FIGHTING AT 4TH KAWANAKAJIMA

Remember that in foggy conditions, the computer AI can't see other units any better than you can. This offers tremendous scope for moving around the advancing enemy to hit it from behind; this would be a good tactic if you had a surplus manpower. But, being outnumbered by almost 2 to 1 requires a stalwart defensive action.

For starters, reposition your army as far back against the edge of the map as you can—the mouse pointer will turn red if the part of the battlefield you're pointing at can't be used. Arrange the 120 Archers on the highest ground you can find, but leave some space to station the two Yari samurai units behind them. Now create a defensive front-line with the 120 Ashigaru under your command, positioning them slightly on the rising ground if possible. Finally, place your No-Dachi and Heavy Cavalry units on the flanks, and dispatch your Cavalry Archers to scout ahead for signs of enemy activity. The Uesugi army will approach from the northeast as you look at the battlemap. Preceded by their Cavalry units they will try to hit your lines in an attempt to break them. Hold your lines and respond with Archer fire and by committing the No-Dachi and Heavy Cavalry elements if necessary. When the Ashigaru eventually break (and they will), reinforce their positions with the stronger Yari samurai.

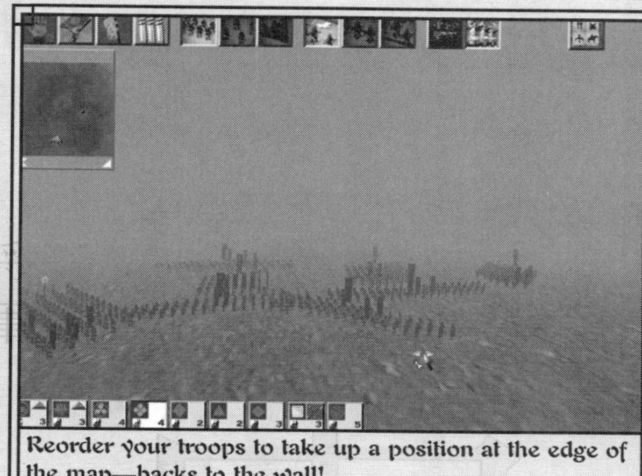

Reorder your troops to take up a position at the edge of the map—backs to the wall!

What unfolds from now on is a messy melee, but by actively controlling the No-Dachi and the Heavy Cavalry, you can halt the Uesugi advance and push them back into the mist.

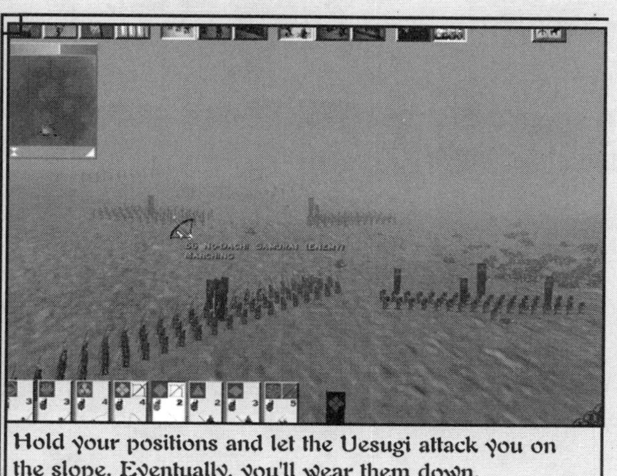

Hold your positions and let the Uesugi attack you on the slope. Eventually, you'll wear them down.

INTELLIGENCE

将軍

将軍

将軍

知能

将軍

将軍

将軍

将軍

Intelligence cannot be employed without
enlightenment and intuition.
Intelligence cannot be used without humanity
and generosity.
The work of Intelligence cannot succeed
without subtlety and ingeniousness.

Subtly, very subtly,
Nowhere neglect the use of Intelligence.

Sun Tzu (translated by R.L. Wing in "The Art of Strategy")

THE FIVE STRATEGIC ARTS

Ancient strategist Sun Tzu isolated what he called the "Five Strategic Arts", the five elements in the establishment of an overall situation that cannot be defeated. The first of these five arts is "Measurements", a knowledge of the type of opposing force that a leader faces. The second Strategic Art is that of "Estimates", an awareness of the resources that a general needs to counter the opposing force. The third art is the "Analysis" of the Estimates, the formulation of a plan that takes into account what threat the opposing force poses and looks at how to defeat it. The fourth of the Five Strategic Arts is "Balancing", the creation of a force that is strong and powerful enough to confront and defeat the opposing force. The last art is "Triumph", the successful culmination of the Measurements, Estimates, Analysis and Balance.

Nowhere are these Five Strategic Arts more important than in *Shogun: Total War's* Campaign mode. Starting a new Campaign game, players can choose to command one of seven colour-coded Japanese clans. Each clan has its own individual strengths and weaknesses, but their aim is the same—the domination of Japan and the defeat of their rivals. Combining real-time strategy battlescapes with *RISK*-style empire-building, the Campaign mode represents the ultimate test of leadership in the game. By knowing yourself, and the abilities of your opponents, you give yourself a solid foundation for the task ahead. The following pages detail the clans, building types, special units, provinces and tactics—vital information if you desire complete tactical knowledge.

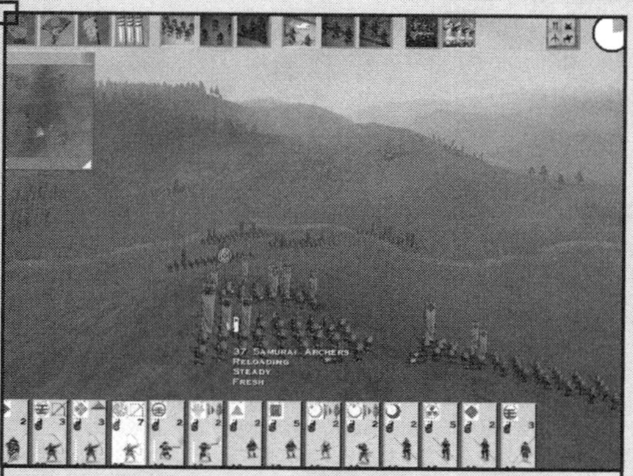

The Campaign mode combines 3D battles with a RISK-style game of conquest.

You can command Naginata in the Historical Battles, but you must develop them in the Campaign.

THE SEVEN CLANS

CLAN MORI (RED)

The Mori are famed for the skill of their Warrior Monks.

Resources: 8 provinces yielding an average of 1163 Koku per year.

Suo	139 Koku
Iwami	120 Koku
Hoki	103 Koku
Mimaska	123 Koku
Inaba	125 Koku
Bizen	190 Koku
Harima	220 Koku
Izumo	143 Koku

INTELLIGENCE

General Information: The Mori Clan have a great respect for tradition and religion, which makes warrior monks eager to fight for their cause. With religious fervour to support the spirit of their armies, they are eager to impose their power throughout Japan.

Daimyo Information: This Daimyo believes in a careful balance between quality and quantity of forces and aggressive campaigning against his enemies. He is untrustworthy as an ally, and his warring nature makes him an unpopular neighbour.

Military Strength: Initial standing army of 851 men.

Yari Ashigaru:	240
Yari Samurai:	300
Samurai Archers:	300
Daimyo and Guard:	11

Strategic Advantages: The Mori clan can recruit and maintain Warrior Monks for a lower cost.

Special units: 1x Emissary.
Buildings: Spear Dojo, Archery Dojo, Tranquil Garden.

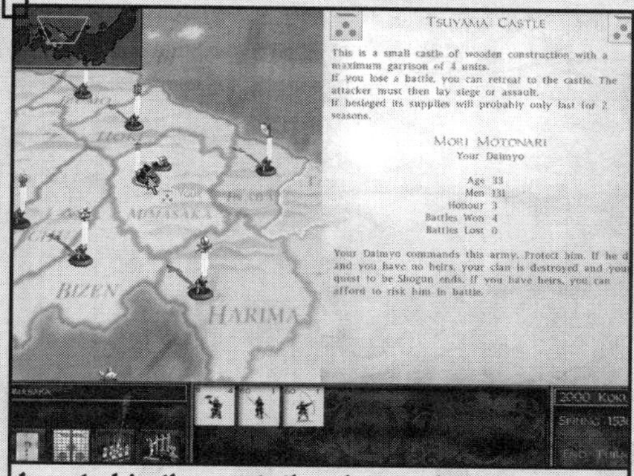

Located in the west, they have a large empire, but precious few resources.

To control the peninsula, the Mori must wipe out the Black Takeda forces.

ANALYSIS

Playing the Mori Clan not only places you in command of a versatile clan with a great deal of potential, but it also means that you don't have to face the untrustworthy Red faction in battle. Unlike some of its rival clans, the Mori's empire is situated in one defensible chunk of the Japanese mainland, bordered by the Green Shimazu to the west and the Gold Clan Oda to the east. Several unpredictable Rebel provinces nearby (Tajima, Awaji) also need to be watched closely, but the Mori's greatest problem is the three Takeda-controlled provinces that stubbornly cling to a foothold in the heart of the Red empire.

With a disappointing level of income (1163 Koku), the Mori's expansionist dreams are initially limited by the geography of their homelands. As the Mori's eight provinces are mostly highland areas, the subsequent lack of good farmland translates to a low annual yield. Thus, when the clan's starting capital has been spent, the Mori need to expand quickly to fund a growing army. As such, the three Takeda-held lands to the south are weak enough to be invaded within the first year. However, while Aki possesses the raw resources for a Mine, claiming it in addition to Bitchu and Bingo, add little to the Mori's family fortune. A better bet is a push to the south toward the fertile and therefore high-yield lands on the isle of Shikoku (Iyo, Tosa, Sanuki and Awa). Or, more dangerously, a brave advance west in order to conquer the rich outpost of the Imagawa.

Nevertheless, despite its initial weaknesses, the Mori clan has the strong advantage of being able to recruit and maintain Warrior Monks at a lower rate. These fanatical Buddhists are one of the best units in the game, and would-be Mori Daimyos should aim to access them as soon as possible. To do this, however, requires a hefty investment in a Large Castle and a Buddhist Temple. Unless the Mori can expand its empire early in the game, they will lack the resources they need to keep up with some of their richer Japanese neighbours.

Difficulty Level: Medium

CLAN SHIMAZU (GREEN)

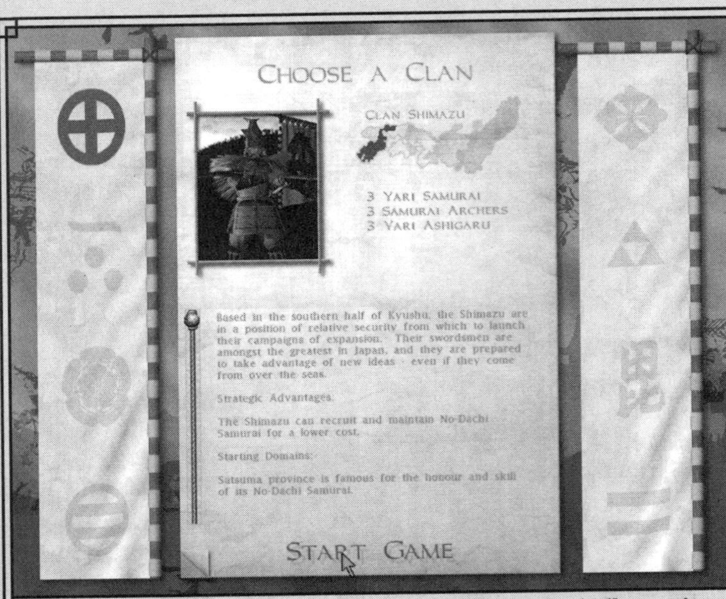

The Shimazu are renowned for their legendary No-Dachi Samurai.

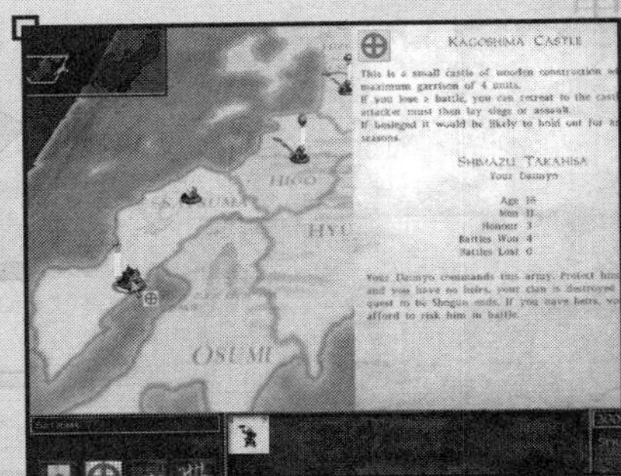

Located on the isle of Kyushu, the Shimazu have the easiest start of all the clans.

INTELLIGENCE

General Information: Based in the southern half of Kyushu, the Shimazu are in a position of relative security from which to launch their campaigns of expansion. Their swordsmen are amongst the greatest in Japan, and they are prepared to take advantage of new ideas—even if they come from overseas.

Daimyo Information: This Daimyo is largely content with what he has, preferring to isolate himself from warring factions and reap the prosperity of peace. This doesn't make him weak, but it does make him less likely to assault your borders than most. Once engaged in conflict he can be dangerous.

Resources: 7 provinces yielding an average of 1194 Koku per year.

Satsuma	180 Koku
Higo	178 Koku
Hyuga	174 Koku
Osumi	175 Koku
Bungo	120 Koku
Buzen	228 Koku
Nagato	139 Koku

Military Strength: Initial standing army of 491 men.

Yari Ashigaru:	120
Yari Samurai:	180
Samurai Archers:	180
Daimyo and Guard:	11

Strategic Advantages: The Shimazu can recruit and maintain No-Dachi for a lower cost.

Special Units: 1x Emissary.

Buildings: Spear Dojo, Archery Dojo, Tranquil Garden.

ANALYSIS

Like the Mori clan to the east, the Green Shimazu family control a large number of provinces that produce a disappointing level of income. If this faction is controlled by the computer AI, the Shimazu pursue an isolationist strategy, content to consolidate what they have, rather than embark on a quick and risky campaign of aggression. As a result, for players controlling either the Imagawa or the Mori nearby, any alliance forged with the Shimazu will last until the size of their forces puts such a strain on their resources that expansion is the only option. For players who choose to command the Shimazu clan, the big advantage of being Green is the defensible location that this family controls on the large Kyushu island.

The Shimazu also need more resources and greedily eye the Imagawa lands to the north.

Bordered by the Imagawa to the north, plus the Mori and several Rebel enclaves to the east, the Shimazu lands are rarely threatened at the start of a Campaign game. Even if a rival clan *does* decide to attack, the clan's troop-producing facilities sit safe in the Satsuma province at the bottom of the island. Despite its strong geographical location, an initial annual harvest of 1194 Koku doesn't give the Shimazu a good foundation for growth. With no bonuses to boost its turnover, the Shimazu need to invade new lands to contribute funds to their coffers. The most inviting target is surely the Imagawa outpost to the north. By attacking Chikugo, Hizen and Chikuzen, the Green forces can not only wipe out opposition on Kyushu, but gain an extra 320, 408 and 304 Koku respectively. By quickly capturing Hizen, the Shimazu can effectively cut the Imagawa lands off from their homeland in the east.

The Shimazu also have an advantage in that they can build No-Dachi samurai for 25 percent less than the other clans. However, these sword-wielding troops are difficult and expensive to access and are slightly less useful in battle than the Warrior Monks and Naginata. Unless the Shimazu decide to pick a fight with the Imagawa clan to the north, they can reap the benefits of peace and build up their forces in relative safety. Beware the Mori, however, who may covet Nagato on the mainland.

Difficulty Level: Easy

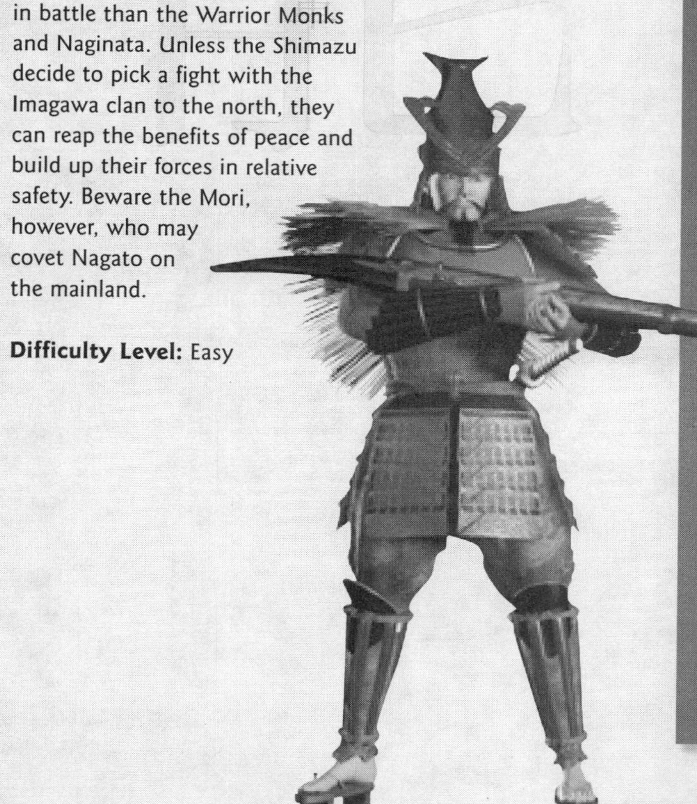

CLAN IMAGAWA (CYAN)

INTELLIGENCE

General Information: The Imagawa clan command an enviable position in the centre of Japan from which they can expand. However, to ensure that they do not become surrounded by enemies it is necessary to balance a careful web of alliances and to make use of the men of the shadows.

Daimyo Information: This Daimyo prefers that an enemy should die by the assassin's hand rather than face him in battle. He is blamed for many untimely deaths, but often rightly so. His armies are also strong, and adept at exploiting the confusion that arises when an enemy general falls to a Ninja's blade.

Resources: 6 provinces yielding an average of 1947 Koku per year.

Chikugo	320 Koku
Hizen	408 Koku
Chikuzen	304 Koku
Mikawa	260 Koku
Totomi	155 Koku
Suruga	100 Koku

Military Strength: Initial standing army of 731 men.

Yari Samurai:	360
Samurai Archers:	360
Daimyo and Guard:	11

Strategic Advantages: The Imagawa clan can recruit Ninja and Shinobi for a lower cost.

Special Units: 1x Emissary, 2x Ninja.

Buildings: Spear Dojo, Archery Dojo, Tranquil Garden, Ninja House, 2x Port.

The Imagawa value stealth and are famous for their Ninja and Shinobi.

ANALYSIS

The Imagawa's fledgling empire is split between Chikuzen, Hizen and Chikugo in the west and the provinces of Mikawa, Totomi and Suruga on the Japanese mainland. Thus, anybody who attempts to guide this Cyan clan's destiny, must be able to cope with two very different geo-political situations. In the centre of Japan, Imagawa holdings are bordered by the troublesome Oda clan to the east, the Uesugi to the north and the Takeda family to the west. Arguably, the lands here, Mikawa, Totomi and Suruga are *not* strategically important for the Imagawa's neighbours—they lack temptingly high farm yields and contain no Iron deposits for an Armoury, nor precious metals for a Mine. Totomi, however, is famed for the skill of its Archers.

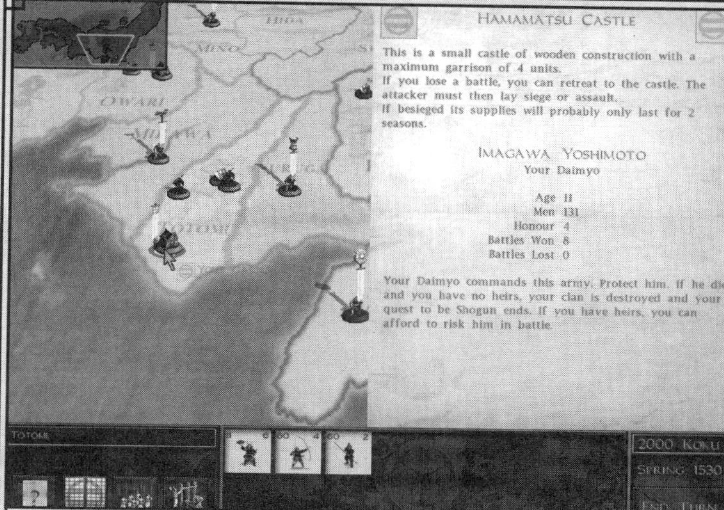

The Imagawa's kingdom is split into two areas that are linked together by a Port.

The situation is very different for the other three provinces on Kyushu. Chikuzen, Hizen and Chikugo represent a fragile foothold for the Imagawa clan in an area dominated by the Shimazu and threatened by the Mori. Yet, it is this Cyan-coloured beachhead on the island of Kyushu that offers the Imagawa a chance to flourish. Faced by three stronger enemies in the centre of Japan, the Imagawa's opportunities for expansion are limited. The majority of the Imagawa's income comes from the three Kyushu lands in the west, plus the 400 Koku generated by the two Ports. As a result, the leaders of these Cyan peoples can probably afford to sacrifice Suruga and Mikawa to keep the western provinces well defended.

While it may be tempting to abandon the central provinces in favour of pursuing a defensible empire on Kyushu, Totomi is the base for the Imagawa Castle, its basic troop-producing facilities, plus a Ninja House. As a result, while there are good reasons to pour resources into attacking the Shimazu on Kyushu, the Imagawa clan can't forsake any of their lands.

Difficulty Level: Medium

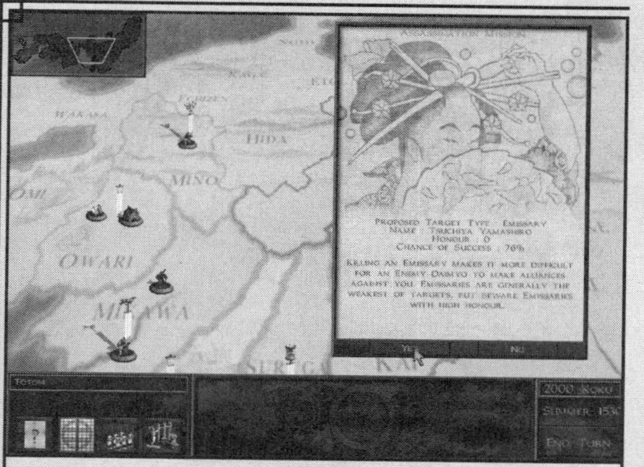

Use Ninja to assassinate key generals and annoying foreign Emissaries.

CLAN ODA (GOLD)

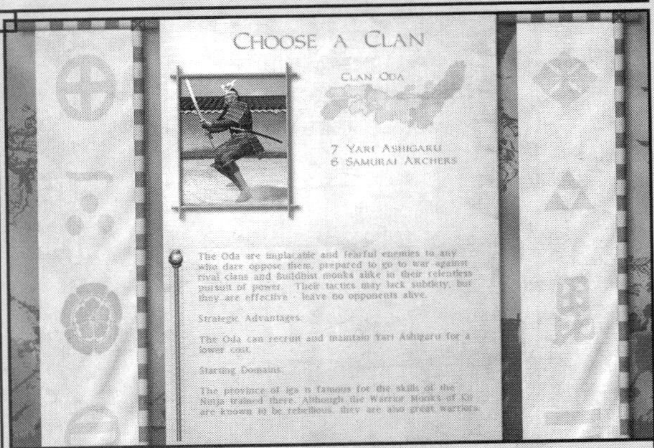

The Oda are renowned for their skill in recruiting Yari Ashigaru.

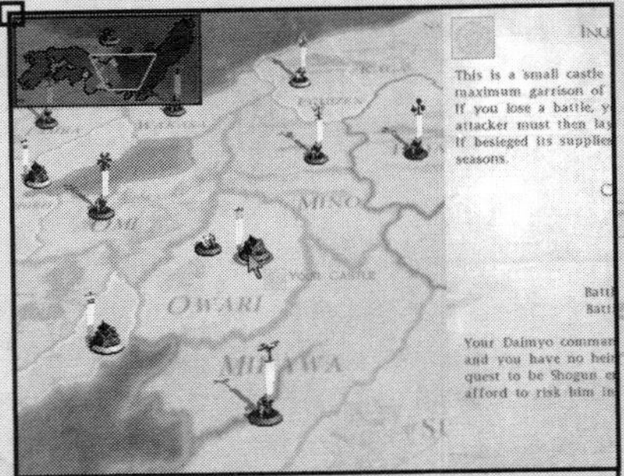

The golden empire is a sprawling realm located in the middle of Japan.

INTELLIGENCE

General Information: The Oda are implacable and fearful enemies to any who oppose them, prepared to go to war against rival clans and Buddhist Monks alike in their relentless pursuit of power. Their tactics may lack subtlety, but they are effective—leave no opponents alive.

Daimyo Information: This Daimyo is patient, persistent and relentless. He is not fond of diplomacy, preferring to slowly and systematically crush all opposition. If you win against him, he will fall back, regenerate and attack again. He prefers to use lightly armoured Ashigaru troops in great numbers. A most dangerous foe.

Resources: 9 provinces yielding an average of 2020 Koku per year.

Tamba	220 Koku
Wakasa	103 Koku
Omi	235 Koku
Kawachi	220 Koku
Owari	650 Koku
Iga	120 Koku
Yamato	202 Koku
Kii	270 Koku
Mino	260 Koku

Military Strength: Initial standing army of 971 men.

Yari Ashigaru:	600
Samurai Archers:	360
Daimyo and Guard:	11

Strategic Advantages: The Oda can recruit and maintain Ashigaru for a lower cost.

Special Units: 1x Emissary.

Buildings: Spear Dojo, Archery Dojo, Tranquil Garden.

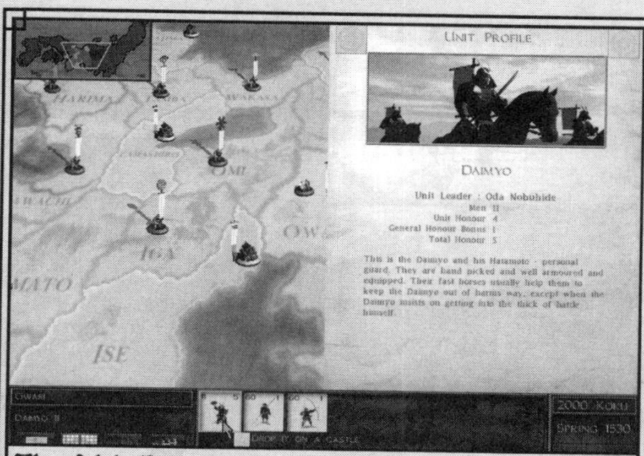

The Oda's Daimyo has a Hatamoto—a personal mounted guard of ten hand-picked Samurai.

ANALYSIS

While the Oda clan has the largest standing army in Japan, it needs it to defend the Campaign mode's largest empire. With nine provinces to defend, the Oda face the untrustworthy Mori hordes to the west, as well as the Imagawa and the Uesugi to the east. Worse still, the sprawling Oda territories are plagued by various Rebel-held provinces. So not only must an Oda lord deal with three rival Daimyos, but armies that march under the Golden banner also need to keep an eye on rogue states: Awaji, Tajima, Yamashiro, Ise and Echizen. As a new Campaign game begins, the Oda will need to concentrate on consolidation rather than instant expansion.

Happily, providing that the harvest is a good one, the Oda annually benefit from a hefty resource boost. Even with an average harvest, its lands produce 2020 Koku, a great slice of which is from the strategically vital Owari province. Owari, which can contribute an average of 650 Koku on its own, is also home to the main Oda Castle. This province is also famed for its Ashigaru, which the Oda can recruit and maintain for 25 percent less than the other six clans. This presents an interesting dilemma—while Ashigaru are cheap and can be trained without draining clan resources, they are weak compared to Yari samurai. An Oda commander must be careful not to employ too many Ashigaru in the ranks. Keep in mind that the Oda also control lands that can produce skilled Ninja (Iga) and Warrior Monks (Kii).

Large and vulnerable, players that take on the Oda challenge must make sure that they limit their conflicts to one front rather than trying to fight on three. While initially peaceful, the Rebel-held states pose a significant threat as the years pass. It may be tempting to try and conquer them early on, but Ashigaru Vs Warrior Monks is a confrontation that should be avoided.

Difficulty Level: Hard

CLAN TAKEDA (BLACK)

INTELLIGENCE

General Information: The Takeda are masters in the traditional arts of war and are ruthless in their quest to overcome their enemies by any means necessary. Facing a charge from Takeda Cavalry will test the will of even the bravest warrior.

Daimyo Information: This Daimyo specialises in the use of highly mobile and heavily armed forces to sweep foes from the battlefield. This strategy involves large Cavalry formations, Heavy Armour and high-quality weaponry. It can lead to unbalanced armies and this is an inherent weakness. He is expansionist and not particularly trustworthy.

Resources: 6 provinces yielding an average of 1527 Koku per year.

Aki	153 Koku
Bingo	130 Koku
Bitchu	114 Koku
Kai	200 Koku
Sagami	460 Koku
Izu	70 Koku

Military Strength: Initial standing army of 671 men.

Yari Samurai:	240
Samurai Archers:	60
Yari Cavalry:	180
Cavalry Archers:	180
Daimyo and Guard:	11

Strategic Advantages: The Takeda can recruit and maintain Cavalry for a lower cost.

Special Units: 1x Emissary.

Buildings: Spear Dojo, Archery Dojo, Tranquil Garden, Horse Dojo, 2x Port.

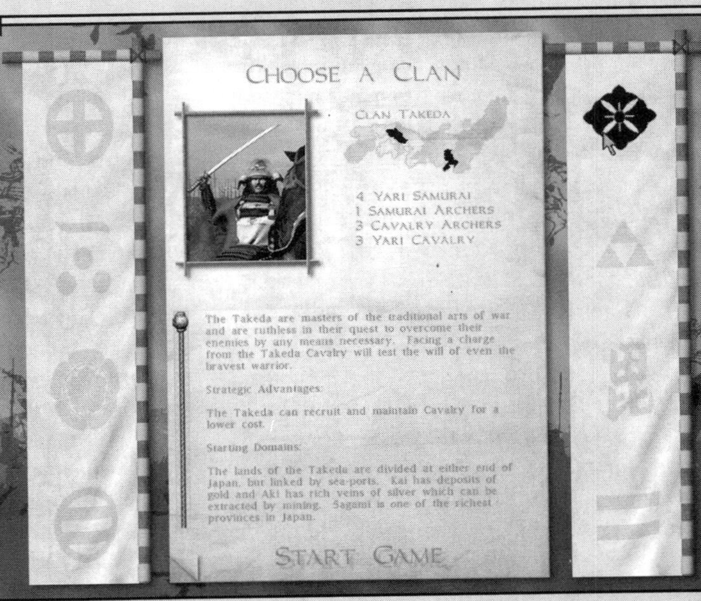

The ruthless Takeda dynasty is known for its deadly Cavalry units.

ANALYSIS

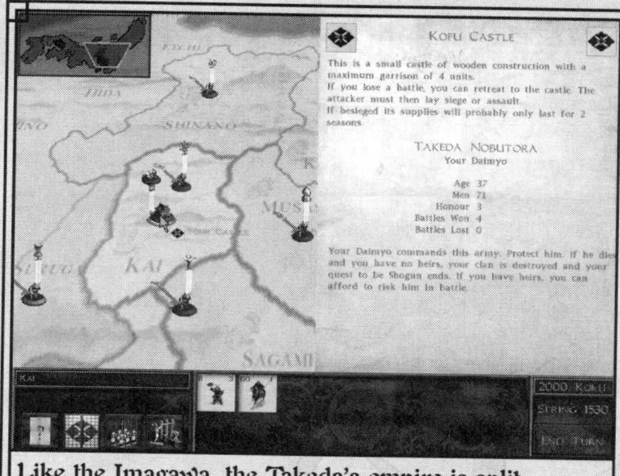

Like the Imagawa, the Takeda's empire is split between lands in the east and west.

Like the Imagawa clan, the Takeda empire is also split into two separate parts. The main, troop-producing lands are located in the fiercely contested centre of Japan, where the Uesugi, Imagawa, Hojo and Oda families jostle for supremacy. Here, the Takeda Daimyo holds onto Kai, Izu and the fertile Sagami, which contributes most to the Black lord's treasury. Farther to the west, the provinces of Aki, Bitchu and Bingo infest the belly of the Mori empire. Like the Imagawa, Takeda commanders face the prospect of a two-pronged strategy if they want to hold onto the 1527 Koku per year income. If Aki is invaded and its Port destroyed, this falls to a woeful 1327 Koku. The Imagawa situation may seem the same, but the Cyan forces have substantially more resources to play with.

It's not all doom and gloom, however. The Takeda's main troop-producing province is Kai, and in addition to the standard trio of Spear Dojo, Archery Dojo and Tranquil Garden, it also boasts a Horse Dojo for instant Cavalry production. Thus, while its rivals need to invest in a Large Castle before they can even start to build a Horse Dojo, the Takeda clan can start training Yari Cavalry and Cavalry Archer units immediately. Of course, it's still slightly more expensive to create a large force of mounted units. But it is this advantage that holds the key to the Takeda clan's survival and expansion. To the east of Kai and Sagami lie the weakly defended lands of the Hojo. Across the other side of the country, the thinly spread Mori forces are trying to hold onto all eight of their provinces. There is ample opportunity to strike quickly before neighbouring clans have the forces to defend their lands properly.

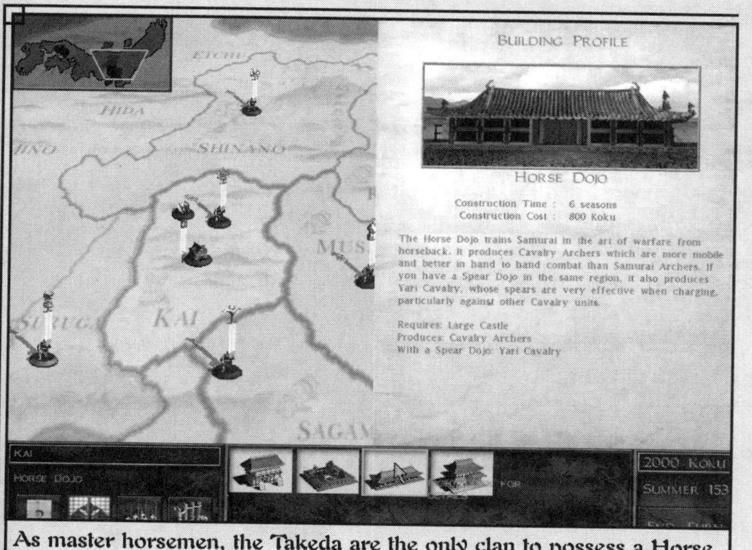

As master horsemen, the Takeda are the only clan to possess a Horse Dojo at the start of the game.

Difficulty Level:
Medium

CLAN HOJO (PURPLE)

INTELLIGENCE

General Information: The name of the Hojo has a long and proud history. They were once Shoguns of Japan, remembered for driving away the Mongol Hordes, and they plan to return to their former glory. They do not trust rivals or strangers, but prefer to rely on their fighting prowess, the great wealth of their lands and their mighty fortresses.

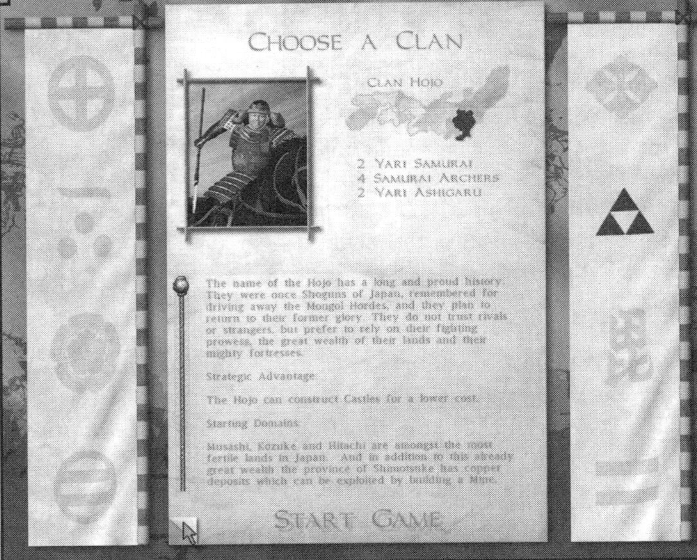

The Hojo are famed for their ability to build strong Castles and Fortresses.

Daimyo Information: Diplomacy and stealth, backed up by unassailable fortifications are this Daimyo's main strategies. He prefers to let a foe exhaust himself against his Castle walls before taking the battle to him. It makes him more trustworthy than most, but still a difficult foe to defeat.

Resources: 6 provinces yielding an average of 2360 Koku per year.

Kozuke	410 Koku
Shimotsuke	210 Koku
Musashi	640 Koku
Hitachi	620 Koku
Shimosa	290 Koku
Kazusa	190 Koku

Military Strength: Initial standing army of 491 men.

Yari Ashigaru:	120
Yari Samurai:	120
Samurai Archers:	240
Daimyo and Guard:	11

Strategic Advantages: The Hojo can construct castles for a lower cost.

Special Units: 1x Emissary.

Buildings: Spear Dojo, Archery Dojo, Tranquil Garden.

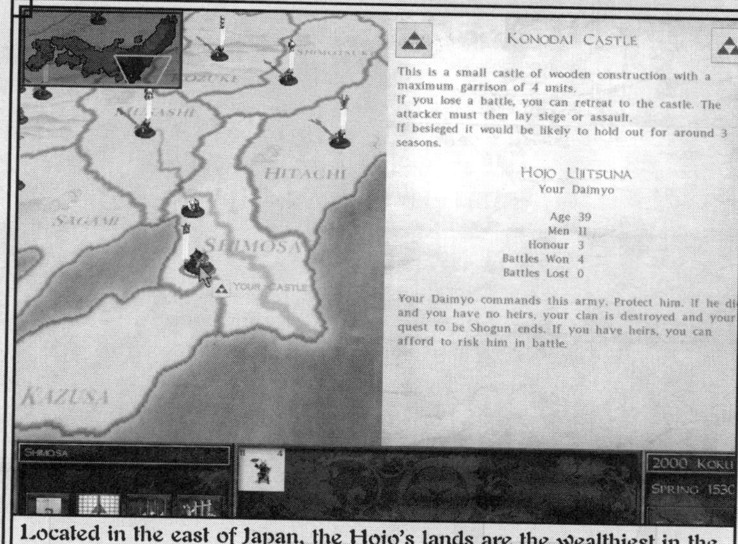

Located in the east of Japan, the Hojo's lands are the wealthiest in the entire country.

ANALYSIS

Of all the seven clans in the Campaign mode, the Hojo have the greatest annual income. Raking in 2360 Koku (and that's just in an average year), the samurai who follow the Purple banner have the resources to reinforce their borders and hide out within them. In fact, considering the Hojo's small standing army, this clan is not in a position to attack anybody. It's all it can do to hold onto its own six provinces, greedily eyed by the Takeda and Uesugi empires that border them. With only 480 regular troops to defend their lands, the Hojo need to pour their starting capital into training extra soldiers. This clan is vulnerable from day one.

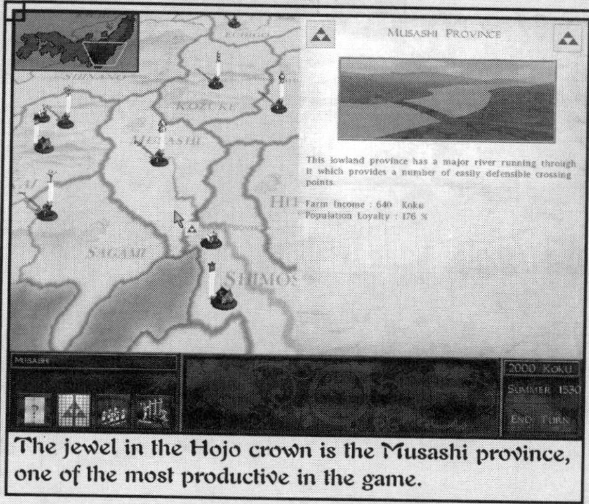

The jewel in the Hojo crown is the Musashi province, one of the most productive in the game.

In the early stages of a new Campaign game, Hojo strategy should revolve around protecting the important provinces of Musashi and Hitachi. These rich lands, yielding an average of 640 and 620 Koku respectively, provide the Hojo with the majority of their wealth. Consequently, when playing against the Hojo, the computer AI will do everything that it can do hold onto them; it's a strategy that human players would do well to emulate. Thanks to the bonus it receives for Castle building, the Hojo has the money to seal themselves off behind a ring of Border Forts and Fortresses, biding their time until they can develop better troop types (i.e. No-Dachi, Warrior Monks). It's also worth noting that the southern province of Kazusa is famous for its Emissaries. Shame that while the Uesugi can be tempted into an alliance, the Takeda are just waiting for the right moment to sweep into Hojo with Cavalry units and Footsoldiers.

Difficulty Level: Medium

CLAN UESUGI (DARK BLUE)

INTELLIGENCE

General Information: The Uesugi have spent much time, effort and blood in their quest to claim the title of Shogun for their clan. The experience has made their warriors tough and their generals wise.

Daimyo Information: New methods, new technology and new approaches to old problems are this Daimyo's strength. They are also possibly his weakness, as he tends to put too much into development at the expense of troop numbers. A quick attack may catch him outnumbered, but eventually his troops will be so superior that numbers mean nothing.

Resources: 6 provinces yielding an average of 2022 Koku per year.

Hida	120
Shinano	340
Echigo	402
Sado	160
Dewa	400
Mutsu	600

Military Strength: Initial standing army of 551 men.

Yari Ashigaru:	120
Yari Samurai:	180
Samurai Archers:	240
Daimyo and Guard:	11

Strategic Advantages: The Uesugi can recruit and maintain Archers for a lower cost.

Special Units: 1x Emissary.

Buildings: Spear Dojo, Archery Dojo, Tranquil Garden.

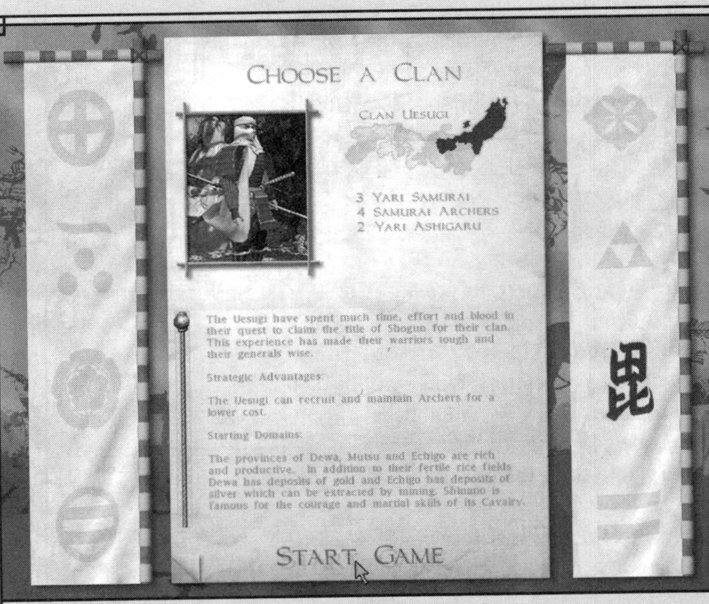

The Uesugi are renowned for the skill of their Archers.

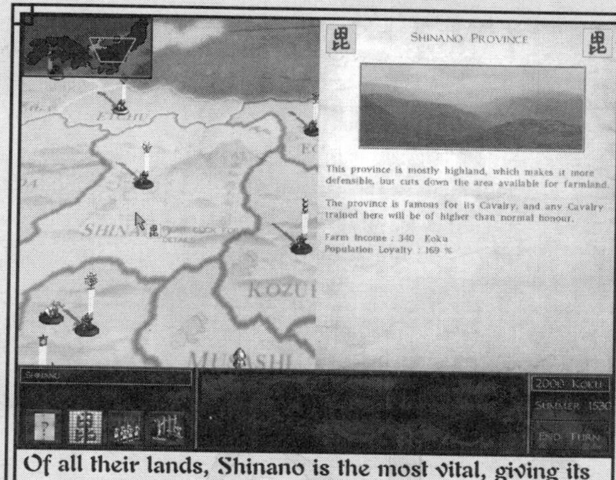

Of all their lands, Shinano is the most vital, giving its owner a bonus when Cavalry are trained here.

ANALYSIS

Although the Uesugi empire contains only six individual territories—a sprawl of lands that stretch from Hida in the west to Dewa and Mutsu on the eastern edge of the Japanese mainland. Like the Hojo clan nearby, the Uesugi Daimyo has only a small standing army with which to marshal a defence of this stretched-out realm. And, bordered as they are by the Oda, Imagawa, Takeda and Hojo clans, not to mention three Rebel-held provinces, the Dark Blue forces will face a battle to retain their homelands before the first year is out. While the rebellious Echizen, Kaga and Etchu initially stay quiet, the Shinano province (famous for its Cavalry units) is a tempting early target for the other clans. Worse still, Shinano is almost the farthest away from the troop-producing buildings in Mutsu. If an enemy launches an attack, the Uesugi will be hard pressed to hang onto it.

It's conceivable that both Hida and Shinano could be abandoned in order to reinforce and consolidate the Uesugi position in the east. Even with the loss of those two lands, the Dark Blue samurai can fall back to Echigo, Dewa and Mutsu. The latter two provinces contribute 400 and 600 Koku respectively to clan resources, while Dewa also contains gold deposits which, when mined, will add an extra 600 to the yearly harvest. While the other clans fight it out amongst themselves for mid-Japan dominance, the Uesugi can pursue a Shimazu-style strategy of isolationism. With the ability to recruit and maintain samurai Archer units more cheaply than its rivals, the Uesugi can reinforce and hide behind their borders until their wealth has bought them the power to retake what was once rightfully theirs.

The strategic and economic importance of Echigo, Mutsu and Dewa make the Uesugi's smallest territory, Sado, seem almost useless. But even this will come in useful later, when used as a stepping stone for invading armies as they push back into central Japan.

Difficulty Level: Hard

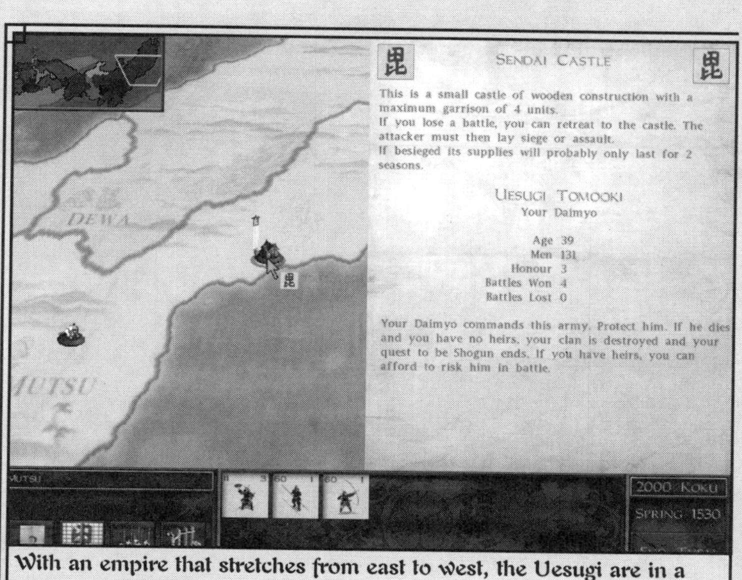

With an empire that stretches from east to west, the Uesugi are in a vulnerable position.

REBELS & RONIN (SILVER)

INTELLIGENCE

General Information: In addition to the seven main clans, there are also 12 Rebel-controlled provinces on the Campaign map. Their growth is initially coordinated from five base Castles—Tosa, Tajima, Yamashiro, Ise and Kaga. While these Ronin ("masterless samurai") keep to themselves at first, if left unchecked they can develop into fierce independent forces that are difficult to conquer. The lands they control are detailed here:

In addition to the seven main clans, a band of Rebels hold several key provinces in Japan.

The small island of Shikoku is home to a small, fiercely-protected Rebel empire.

IYO

Average Yield: 220 Koku
Supply Castle: Tosa
Initial Buildings: None
Initial Troops: 60 Samurai Archers, 60 Ashigaru

SANUKI

Average Yield: 380 Koku
Supply Castle: Tosa
Initial Buildings: None
Initial Troops: 60 Samurai Archers, 60 Ashigaru

AWA

Average Yield: 180 Koku
Supply Castle: Tosa
Initial Buildings: None
Initial Troops: None

TOSA

Average Yield: 242 Koku
Supply Castle: Tosa
Initial Buildings: Castle, Spear Dojo, Archery Dojo
Initial Troops: None

AWAJI

Average Yield: 60 Koku
Supply Castle: Tosa
Initial Buildings: None
Initial Troops: 120 Ashigaru

TAJIMA

Average Yield: 95 Koku
Supply Castle: Tajima
Initial Buildings: Castle, Spear Dojo,

Archery Dojo
Initial Troops: None

YAMASHIRO

Average Yield: 150 Koku
Supply Castle: Yamashiro
Initial Buildings: Castle, Archery Dojo, Buddhist Temple
Initial Troops: 180 Warrior Monks, 120 Archers

ISE

Average Yield: 440 Koku
Supply Castle: Ise
Initial Buildings: Castle, Archery Dojo, Buddhist Temple
Initial Troops: 180 Warrior Monks, 120 Archers

ECHIZEN

Average Yield: 280 Koku
Supply Castle: Kaga
Initial Buildings: None
Initial Troops: 60 Warrior Monks, 60 Archers

KAGA

Average Yield: 200 Koku
Supply Castle: Kaga
Initial Buildings: Castle, Archery Dojo, Buddhist Temple
Initial Troops: 120 Warrior Monks, 60 Archers

NOTO

Average Yield: 100 Koku
Supply Castle: Kaga
Initial Buildings: None
Initial Troops: None

ETCHU

Average Yield: 220 Koku
Supply Castle: Kaga
Initial Buildings: None
Initial Troops: 60 Warrior Monks, 60 Archers

NOTE

Further details regarding the terrain of these 12 Rebel-held provinces and the tactics required to conquer them are described in the Provinces section later in this guide. By destroying the key supply Castles (and therefore the buildings attached to them), players can limit and delay the Rebel expansion. Consequently, before new troops can be trained, a new Castle and troop-producing facilities need to be reconstructed by the surviving Rebel forces.

The province of Yamashiro, which contains the Emperor's palace, is also plagued with Rebels.

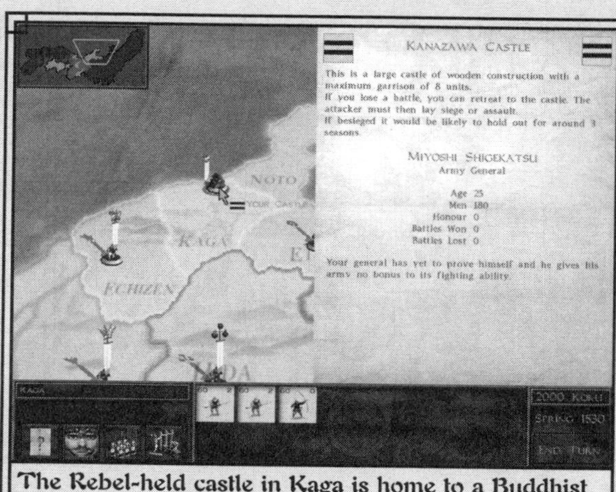

The Rebel-held castle in Kaga is home to a Buddhist Temple and the fearsome Warrior Monks.

BUILDING TYPES

THE SHOGUN

Total War Campaign mode splits its gameplay between the clash of armies on 3D battlefields and a resource-based strategy wargame. The map of Japan used in the game is split into 60 different provinces, each one with its own terrain types, features and agricultural yield. Three basic building types (Watchtower, Castle, Improved Farmland) can be constructed in each one of the 60 provinces using money from a clan's Koku treasury. Once built, these buildings allow players to build further buildings, which, in turn, enable players to access even more facilities. Each new building or facility either allows new troop types to be built, better troops to be trained, or more Koku to be generated. The buildings and facilities available in the Campaign mode are detailed on the following pages:

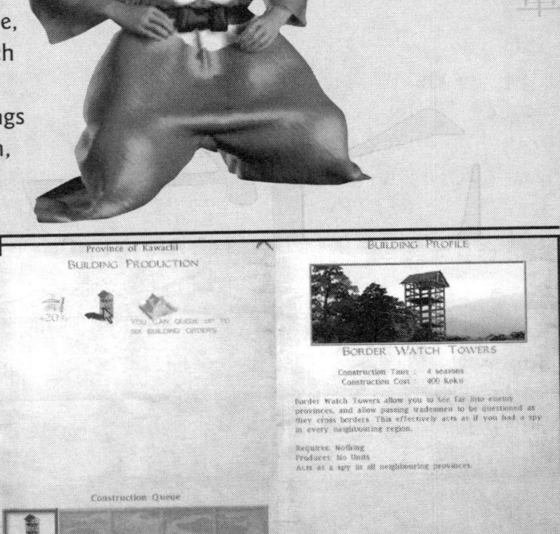

Border Watch Towers

Border Watch Towers

Produces: Acts as spy in neighbouring provinces.
Requires: Nothing
Cost to build: 400 Koku
Time to build: 4 seasons

Border Forts

Produces: Acts as spy in neighbouring provinces, counterspy in home province.
Requires: Border Watch Tower
Cost to build: 800 Koku
Time to build: 4 seasons

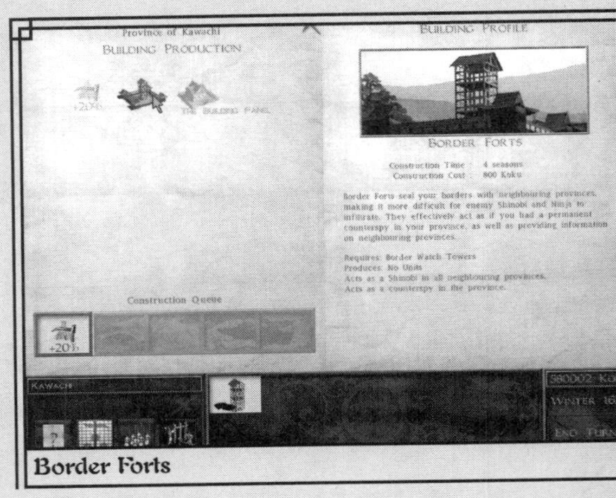

Border Forts

Castle
Capacity: 4 units
Requires: Nothing
Cost to build: 500 Koku
Time to build: 4 seasons

Large Castle
Capacity: 8 units
Requires: Castle
Cost to build: 1000 Koku
Time to build: 8 seasons

Fortress
Capacity: 12 units
Requires: Large Castle
Cost to build: 1500 Koku
Time to build: 10 seasons

Citadel
Capacity: 16 units
Requires: Fortress
Cost to build: 3000
Time to build: 14 seasons

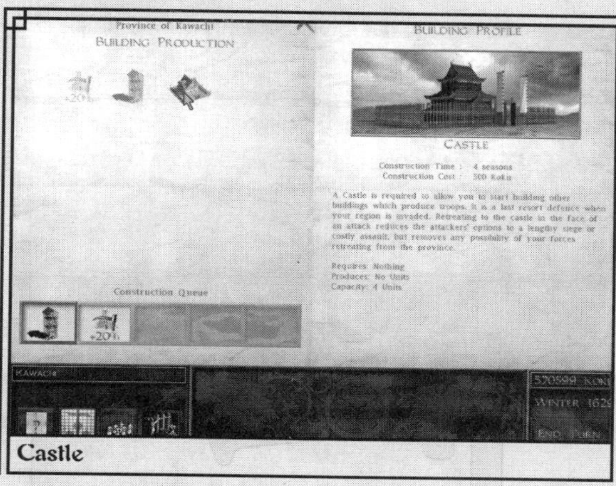

Castle

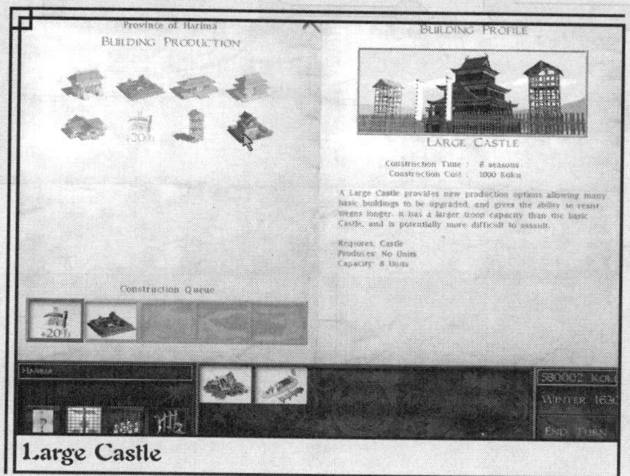

Large Castle

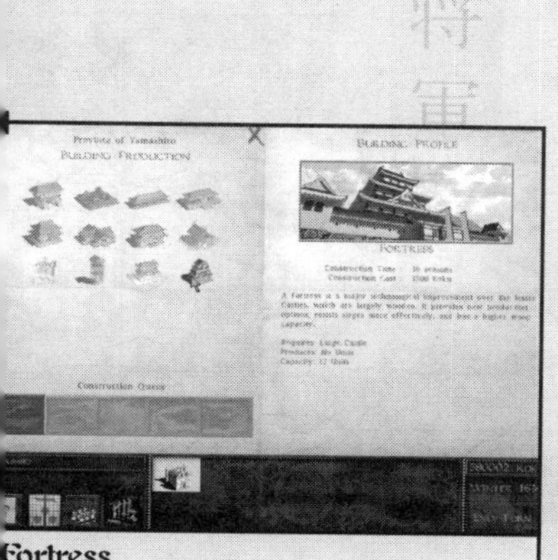

Fortress

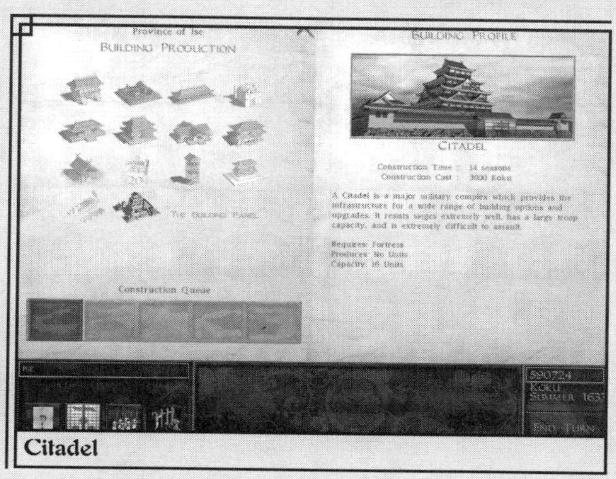

Citadel

Archery Dojo
Produces: Samurai Archers
Requires: Any Castle
Cost to build: 800 Koku
Time to build: 4 seasons

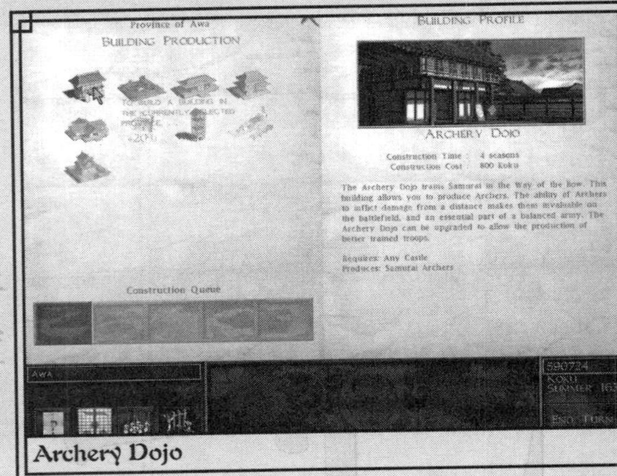

Archery Dojo

Famous Archery Dojo
Produces: Superior Samurai Archers (+1 Honour)
Requires: Large Castle
Cost to build: 800 Koku
Time to build: 4 seasons

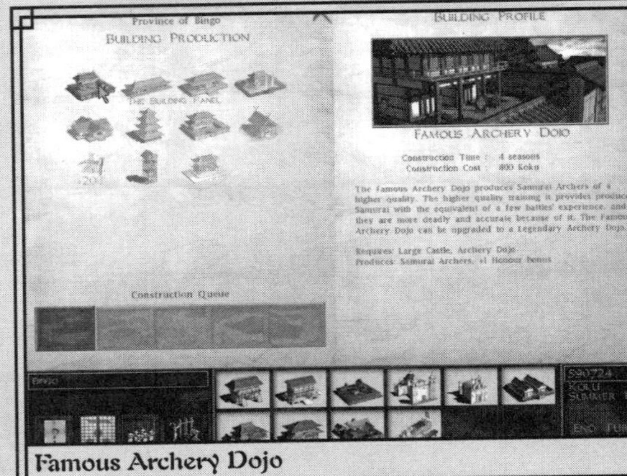

Famous Archery Dojo

Legendary Archery Dojo
Produces: Exceptional Samurai Archers (+2 Honour)
Requires: Fortress
Cost to build: 800 Koku
Time to build: 4 seasons

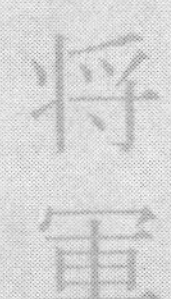

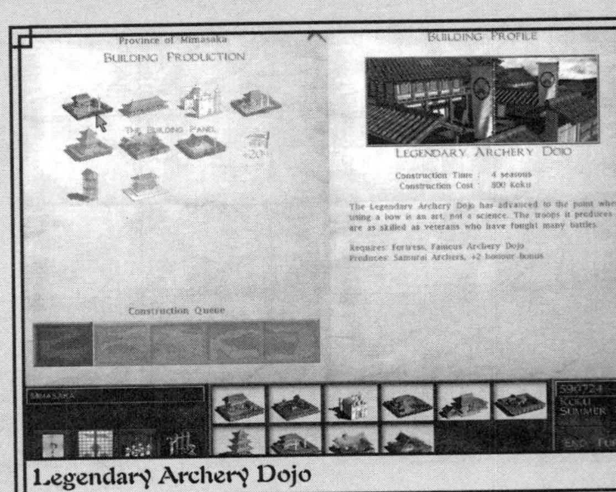

Legendary Archery Dojo

Spear Dojo
Produces: Yari Ashigaru, Yari Samurai
Requires: Any Castle
Cost to build: 500 Koku
Time to build: 4 seasons

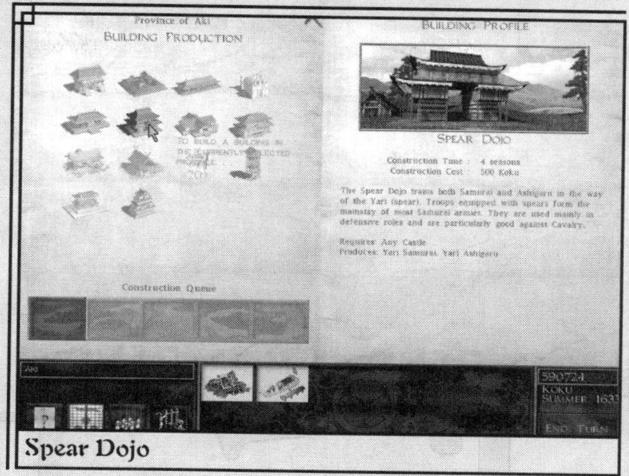

Spear Dojo

Famous Spear Dojo
Produces: Superior Yari Ashigaru (+1 Honour), Superior Yari Samurai (+1 Honour)
Produces with Armoury: Naginata
Requires: Large Castle
Cost to build: 500 Koku
Time to build: 4 seasons

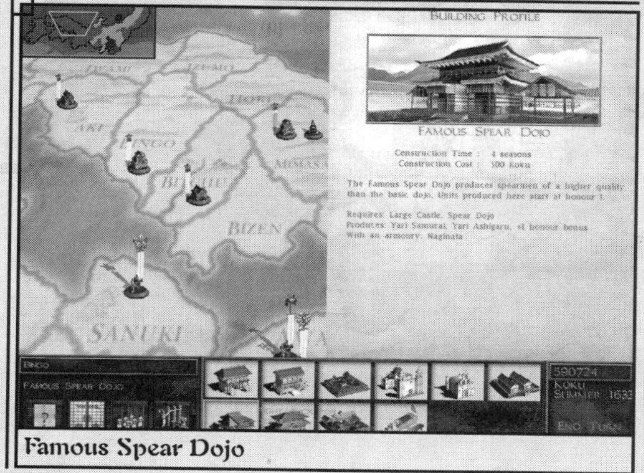

Famous Spear Dojo

Legendary Spear Dojo
Produces: Exceptional Yari Ashigaru (+2 Honour), Exceptional Yari Samurai (+2 Honour)
Produces with Armoury: Superior Naginata (+1 Honour)
Requires: Citadel
Cost to build: 500 Koku
Time to build: 4 seasons

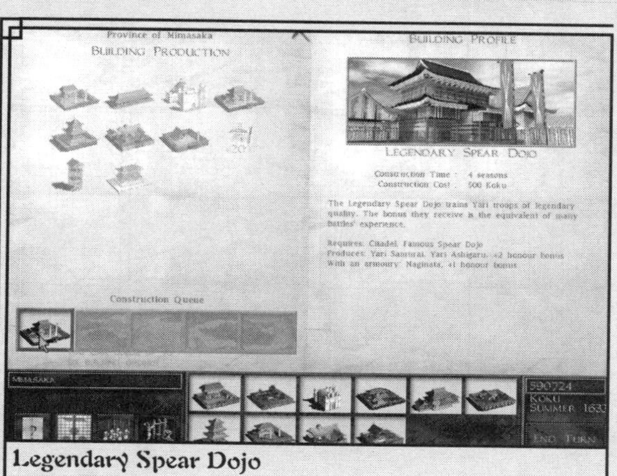

Legendary Spear Dojo

Sword Dojo
Produces: No-Dachi Samurai
Requires: Large Castle, Legendary Swordsman event
Cost to build: 1000 Koku
Time to build: 8 seasons

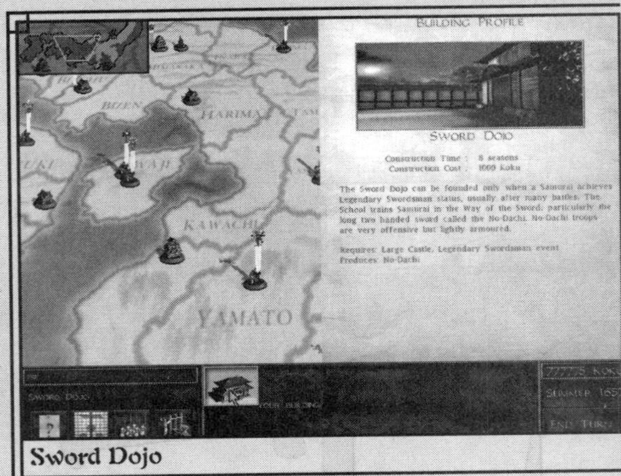
Sword Dojo

Famous Sword Dojo
Produces: Superior No-Dachi Samurai (+1 Honour)
Requires: Fortress, Sword Dojo
Cost to build: 1000 Koku
Time to build: 8 seasons

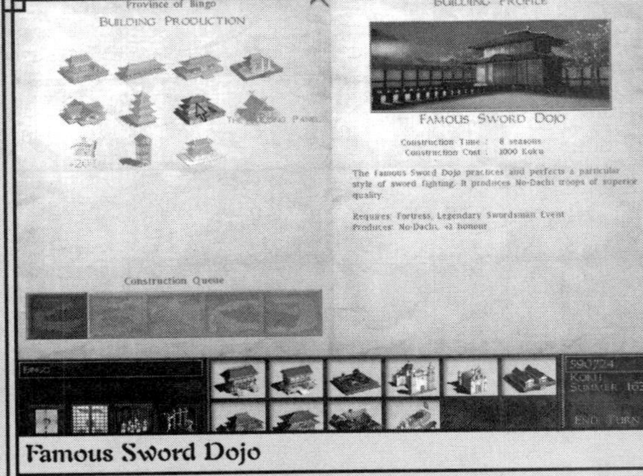
Famous Sword Dojo

Legendary Sword Dojo
Produces: Exceptional No-Dachi Samurai (+2 Honour)
Requires: Citadel, Famous Sword Dojo
Cost to build: 1000 Koku
Time to build: 8 seasons

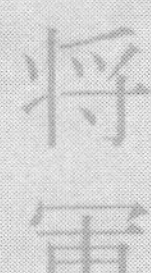

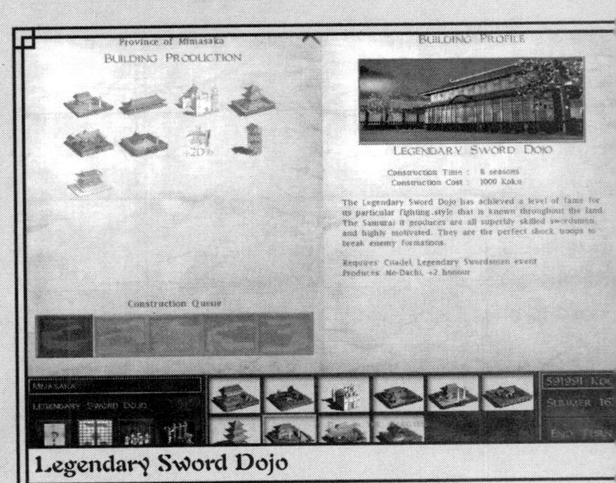
Legendary Sword Dojo

Horse Dojo
Produces with Spear Dojo: Yari Cavalry
Produces with Archery Dojo: Cavalry Archers
Requires: Large Castle
Cost to build: 800 Koku
Time to build: 6 seasons

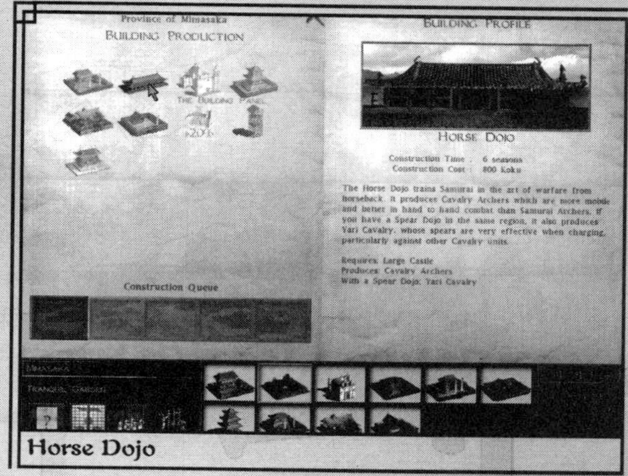

Horse Dojo

Famous Horse Dojo
Produces with Spear Dojo: Superior Yari Cavalry (+1 Honour)
Produces with Archery Dojo: Superior Cavalry Archers (+1 Honour)
Produces with Armoury: Heavy Cavalry
Requires: Fortress, Horse Dojo
Cost to build: 800 Koku
Time to build: 6 seasons

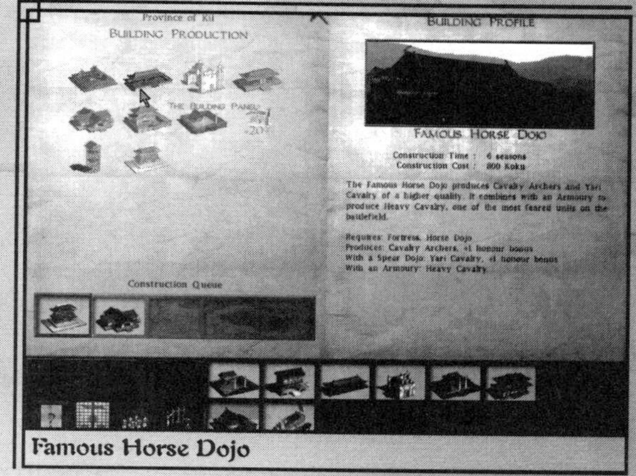

Famous Horse Dojo

Legendary Horse Dojo
Produces with Spear Dojo: Exceptional Yari Cavalry (+2 Honour)
Produces with Archery Dojo: Exceptional Cavalry Archers (+2 Honour)
Produces with Armoury: Superior Heavy Cavalry (+ 1 Honour)
Requires: Citadel, Famous Horse Dojo
Cost to build: 800 Koku
Time to build: 6 seasons

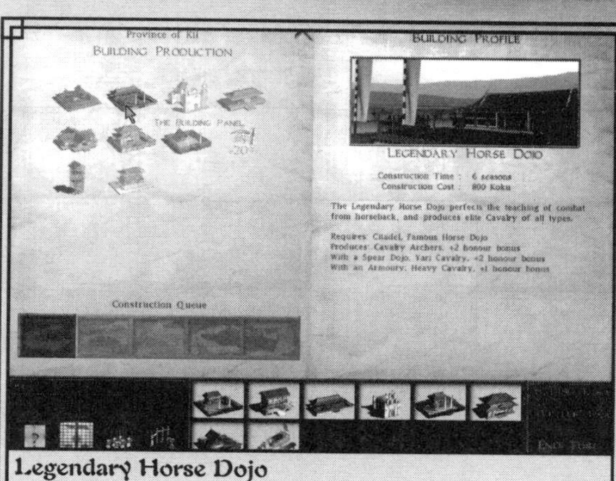

Legendary Horse Dojo

Swordsmith
Produces: +1 attack for all units produced in the province.
Requires: Large Castle
Cost to build: 1200 Koku
Time to build: 8 seasons

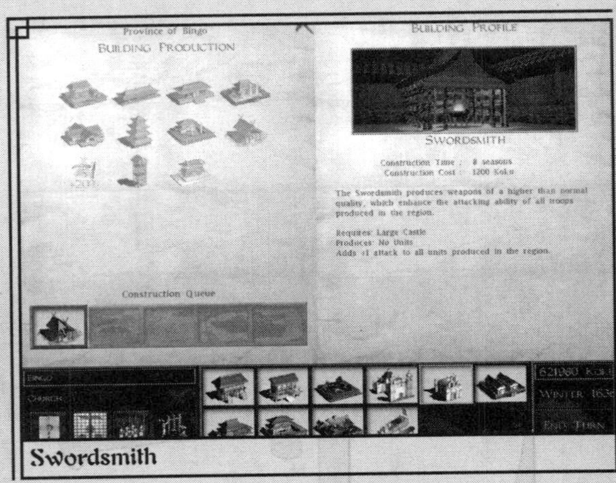

Swordsmith

Famous Swordsmith
Produces: +2 attack for all units produced in the province.
Requires: Fortress, Swordsmith
Cost to build: 1200 Koku
Time to build: 8 seasons

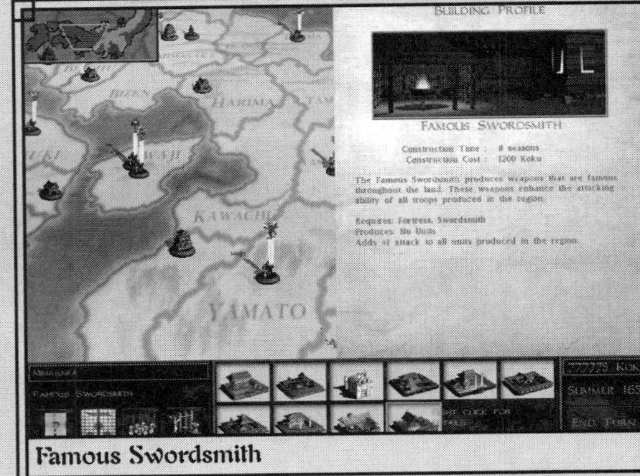

Famous Swordsmith

Legendary Swordsmith
Produces: +3 attack for all units produced in the province.
Requires: Citadel, Famous Swordsmith
Cost to build: 1200 Koku
Time to build: 8 seasons

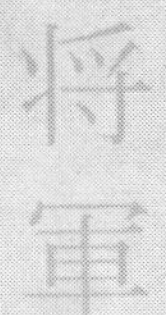

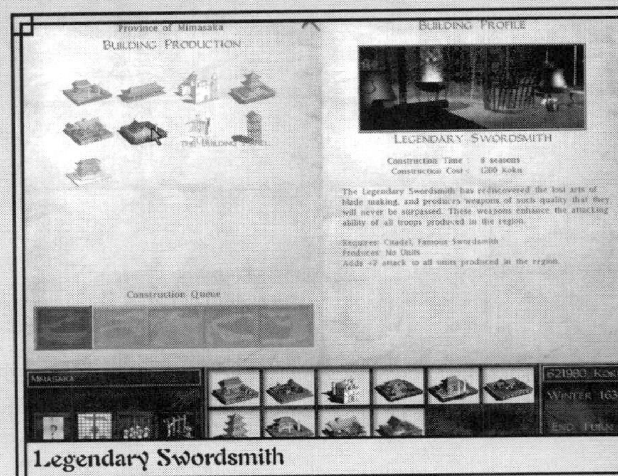

Legendary Swordsmith

Armoury
Produces: +1 armour for all units produced in the province.
Requires: Any Castle, Iron and Sand deposits
Cost to build: 1200 Koku
Time to build: 8 seasons

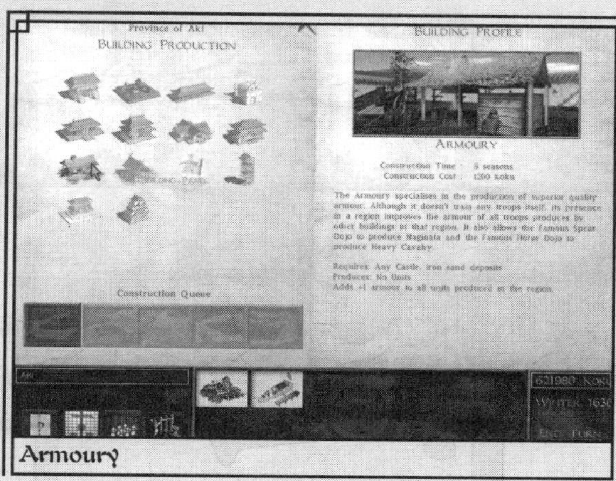
Armoury

Famous Armoury
Produces: +2 armour for all units produced in the province.
Requires: Large Castle, Iron and Sand deposits, Armoury
Cost to build: 1200 Koku
Time to build: 8 seasons

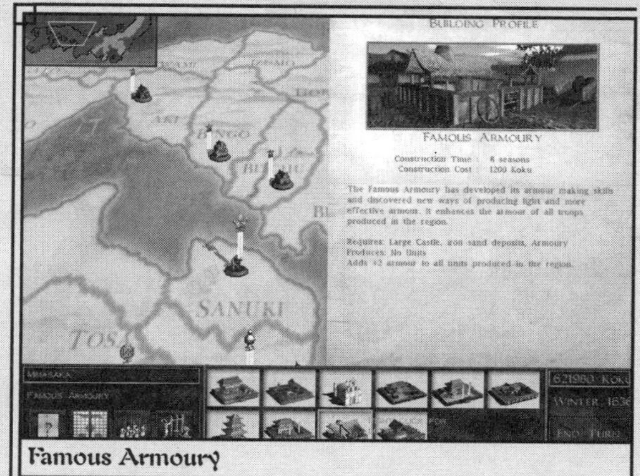
Famous Armoury

Legendary Armoury
Produces: +3 armour for all units produced in the province.
Requires: Fortress, Iron and Sand deposits, Famous Armoury
Cost to build: 1200 Koku
Time to build: 8 seasons

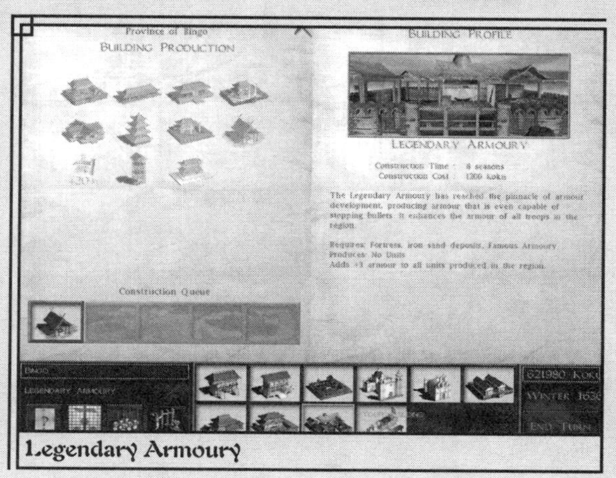
Legendary Armoury

Tranquil Garden
Produces: Emissary
Requires: Any Castle
Cost to build: 500 Koku
Time to build: 4 seasons

Buddhist Temple
Produces: Warrior Monks
Requires: Large Castle, Tranquil Garden
Cost to build: 1500 Koku
Time to build: 10 seasons

Famous Buddhist Temple
Produces: Superior Warrior Monks (+1 Honour)
Requires: Fortress, Buddhist Temple, Tranquil Garden
Cost to build: 1500 Koku
Time to build: 10 seasons

Temple Complex
Produces: Exceptional Warrior Monks (+2 Honour)
Requires: Citadel, Famous Buddhist Temple, Tranquil Garden
Cost to build: 1500 Koku
Time to build: 10 seasons

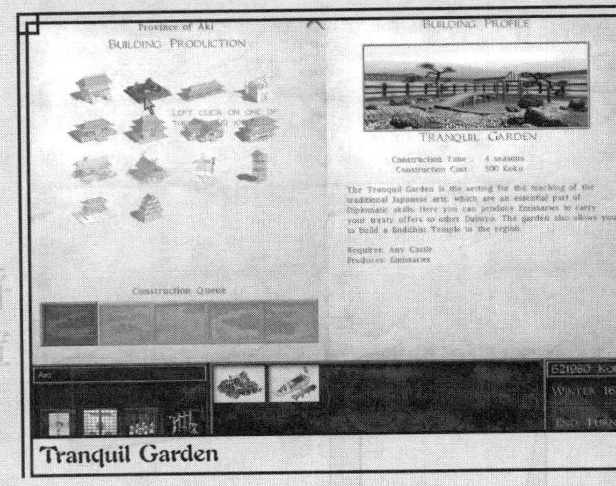

Tranquil Garden

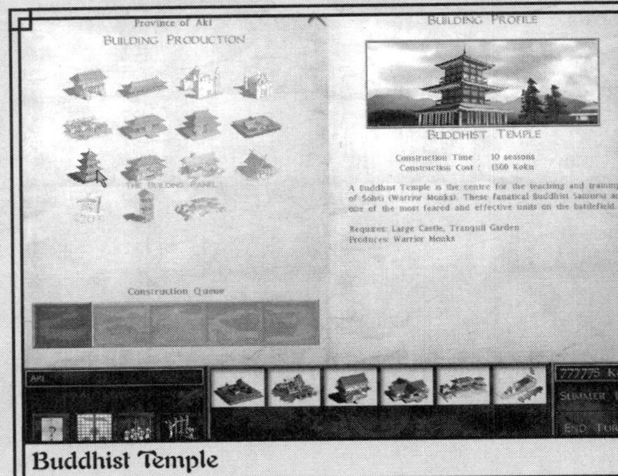

Buddhist Temple

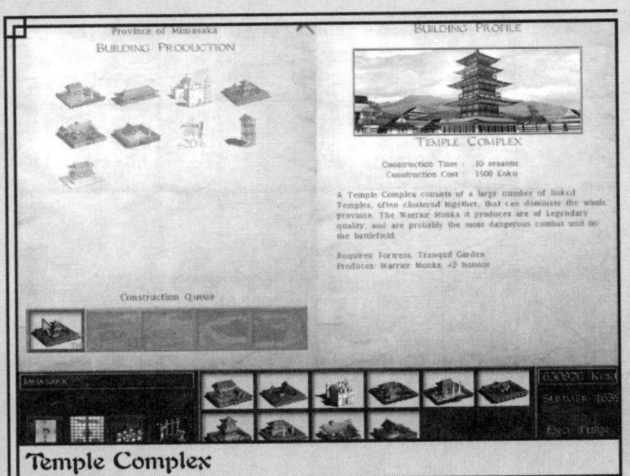

Temple Complex

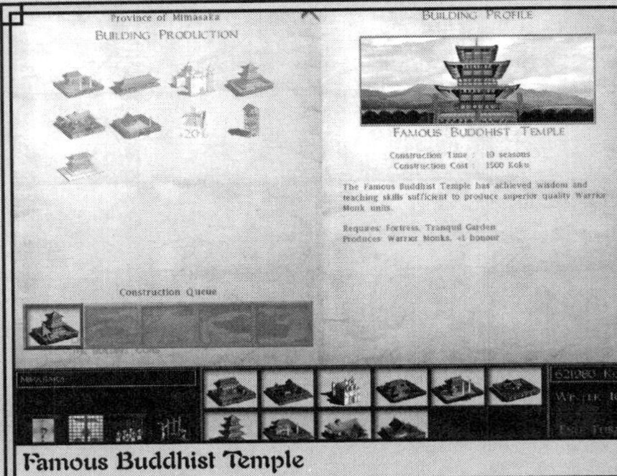

Famous Buddhist Temple

Church
Produces: Priest
Requires: Large Castle, Portuguese Traders
Cost to build: 800 Koku
Time to build: 6 seasons

Cathedral
Produces: Musketeers (with Portuguese Trading Post and Gun Factory), financial bonus to Daimyo (100 Koku per Church)
Requires: Citadel, 6 Churches anywhere within empire
Cost to build: 2000 Koku
Time to build: 12 seasons

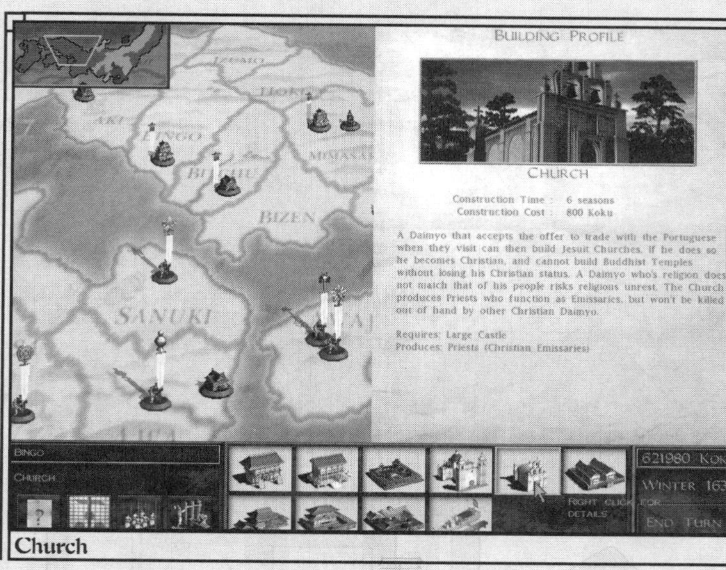

Church

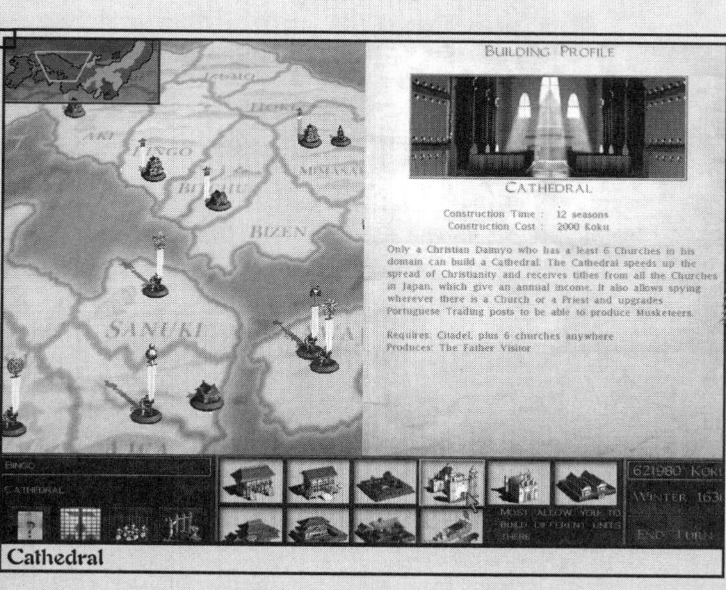

Cathedral

Ninja House
Produces: Ninja
Requires: Any Castle
Cost to build: 800 Koku
Time to build: 6 seasons

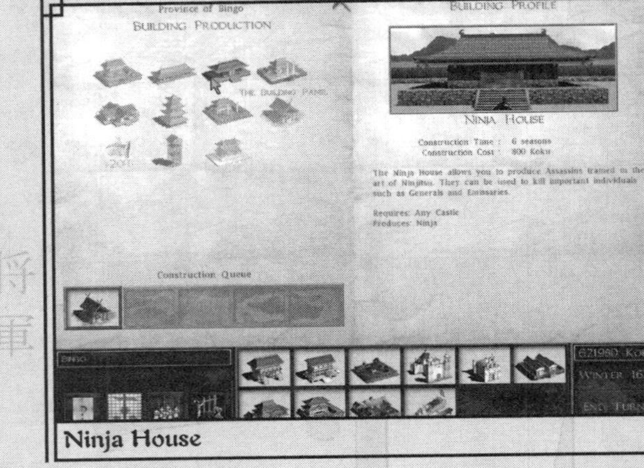

Ninja House

Infamous Ninja House
Produces: Ninja (+1 Kills)
Requires: Fortress, Ninja House
Cost to build: 800 Koku
Time to build: 6 seasons

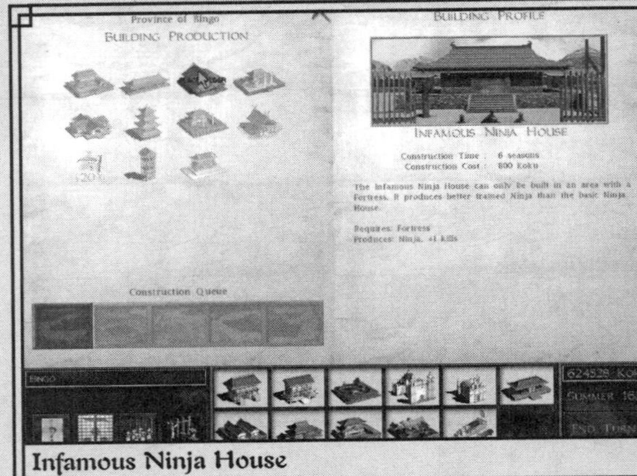

Infamous Ninja House

Geisha House
Produces: The Legendary Geisha, Ninja (+2 kills)
Requires: Citadel, Tranquil Garden, Legendary Tea House
Cost to build: 1000 Koku
Time to build: 8 seasons

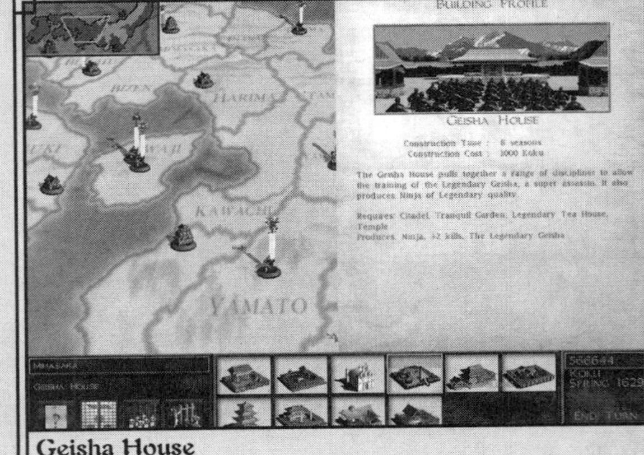

Geisha House

Palace
Produces: +1 morale for all units produced in the province.
Requires: Large Castle
Cost to build: 1000 Koku
Time to build: 8 seasons

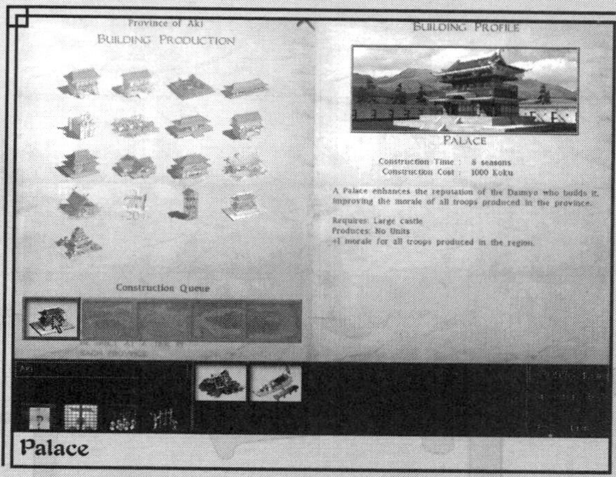

Palace

Golden Palace
Produces: +2 morale for all units produced in the province.
Requires: Fortress, Palace
Cost to build: 2000 Koku
Time to build: 10 seasons

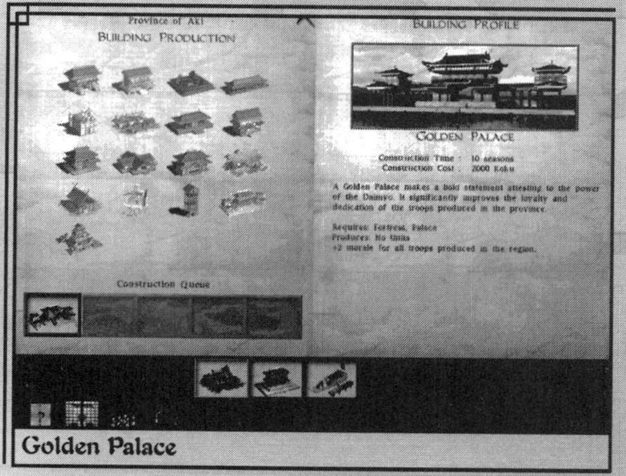

Golden Palace

Legendary Palace
Produces: +3 morale for all units produced in the province.
Requires: Citadel, Golden Palace
Cost to build: 3000 Koku
Time to build: 12 seasons

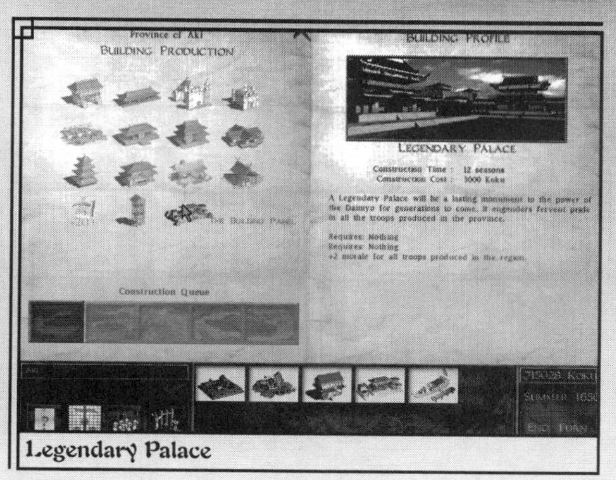

Legendary Palace

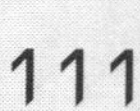

Tea House
Produces: Shinobi
Requires: Any Castle
Cost to build: 500 Koku
Time to build: 4 seasons

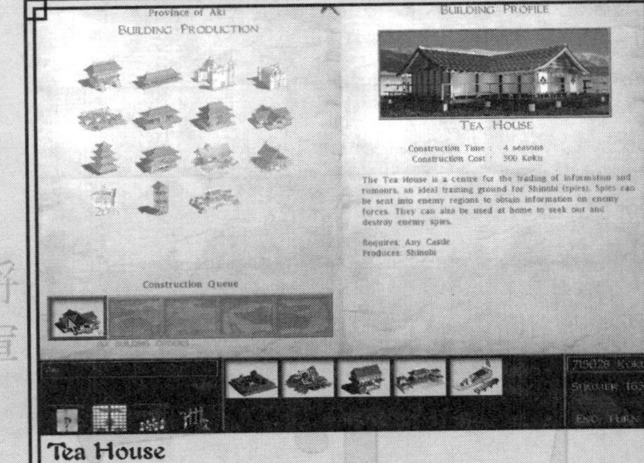

Tea House

Famous Tea House
Produces: Superior Shinobi (+1 Honour)
Requires: Large Castle, Tea House
Cost to build: 500 Koku
Time to build: 4 seasons

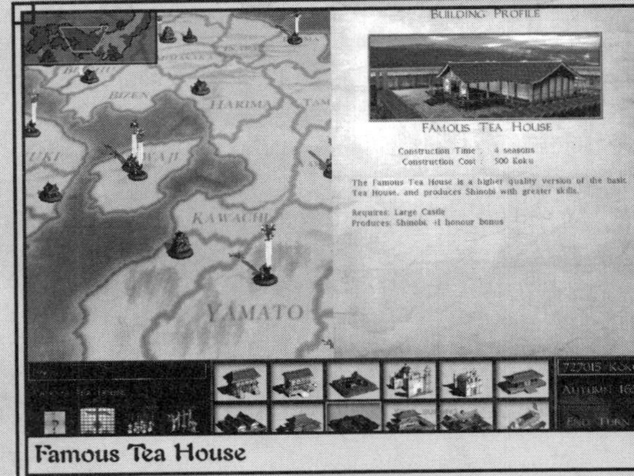

Famous Tea House

Legendary Tea House
Produces: Exceptional Shinobi (+2 Honour)
Requires: Fortress, Famous Tea House
Cost to build: 500 Koku
Time to build: 4 seasons

Legendary Tea House

Port
Produces: +200 Koku trade bonus. Allows units to move to another province with a Port.
Requires: Any Castle, Coastal province
Cost to build: 1500
Time to build: 10 seasons

Portuguese Trading Post
Produces: Arquebusiers
Requires: Any Castle, Port, Portuguese Traders
Cost to build: 1000 Koku
Time to build: 8 seasons

Dutch Trading Post
Produces: Arquebusiers
Requires: Large Castle, Port, Dutch Traders
Cost to build: 1000 Koku
Time to build: 8 seasons

Gun Factory
Produces: Arquebusiers, Musketeers
Produces with Armoury: Musketeers
Requires: Citadel, Trading Post
Cost to build: 1500 Koku
Time to build: 8 seasons

Port

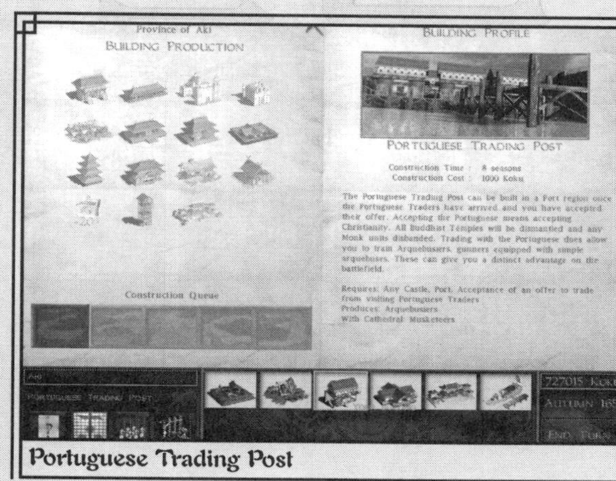

Portuguese Trading Post

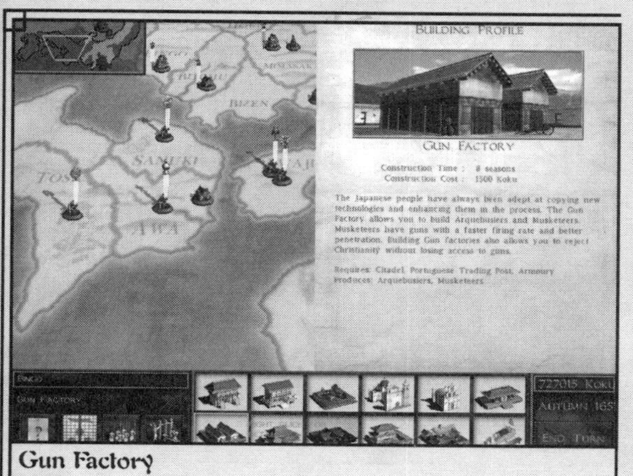

Gun Factory

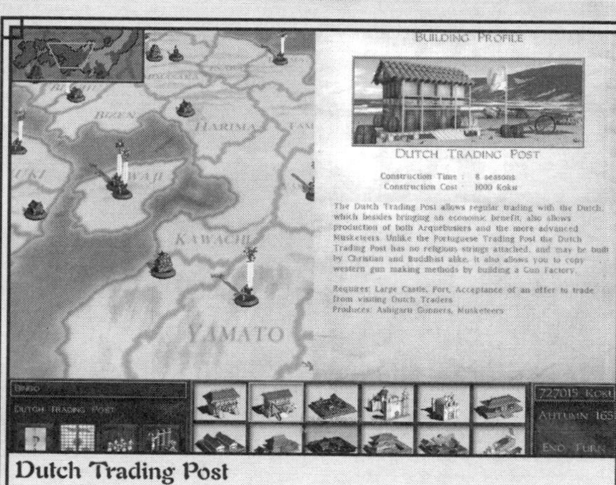

Dutch Trading Post

Improved Farmland
Produces: +20% Koku yield
Requires: Nothing
Cost to build: 500 Koku
Time to build: 8 seasons

Superior Farmland
Produces: +40% Koku yield
Requires: Improved Farmland
Cost to build: 700 Koku
Time to build: 10 seasons

Exceptional Farmland
Produces: +60% Koku yield
Requires: Superior Farmland
Cost to build: 900 Koku
Time to build: 12 seasons

Legendary Farmland
Produces: +100% Koku yield
Requires: Exceptional Farmland
Cost to build: 1000 Koku
Time to build: 12 seasons

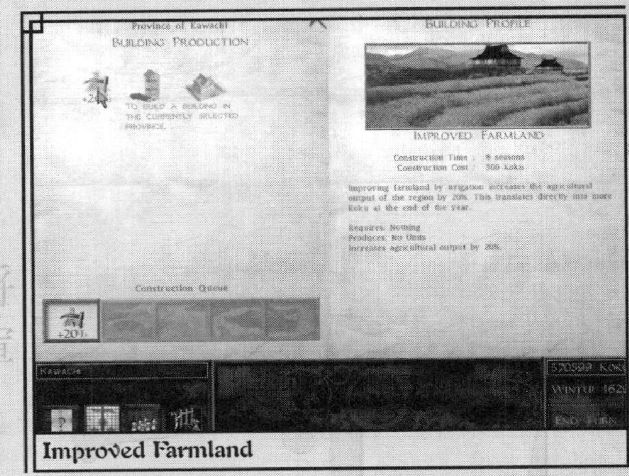

Improved Farmland

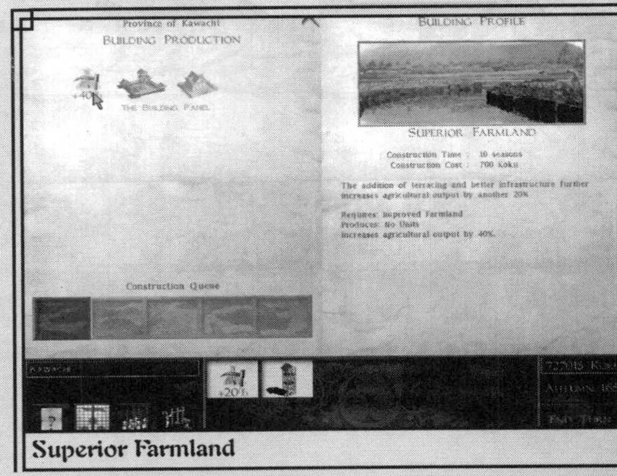

Superior Farmland

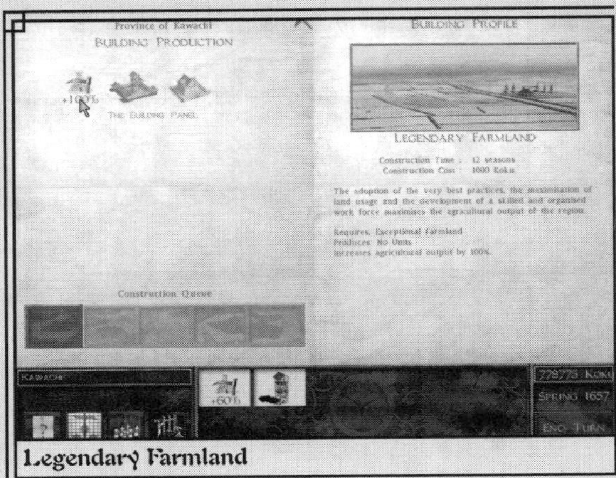

Legendary Farmland

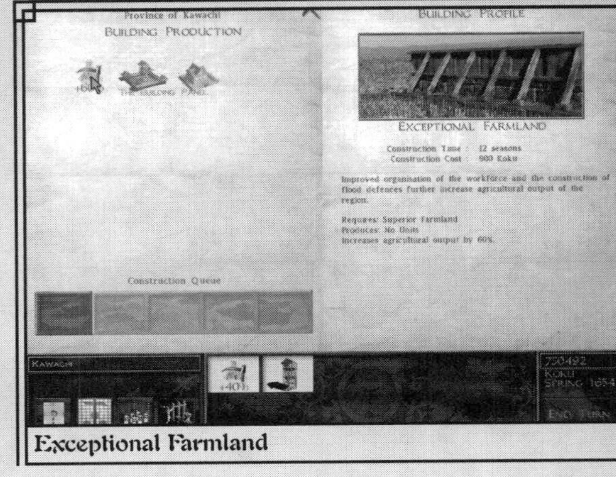

Exceptional Farmland

Mine
Produces with Copper deposits: +200 Koku per year
Produces with Silver deposits: +400 Koku per year
Produces with Gold deposits: +600 Koku per year
Requires: Mineral deposits (see above)
Cost to build: 1000 Koku
Time to build: 8 seasons

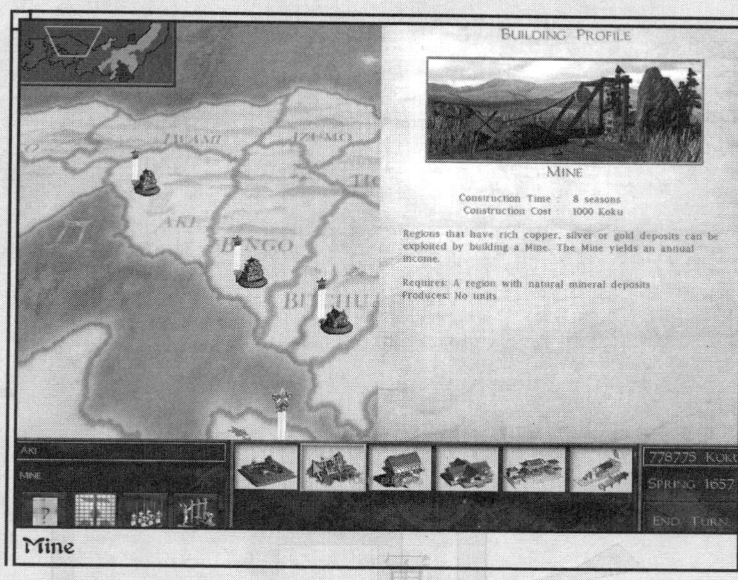

Mine

Mine complex
Produces with Copper deposits: +400 Koku per year
Produces with Silver deposits: +800 Koku per year
Produces with Gold deposits: +1200 Koku per year
Requires: Fortress, Mine, Mineral deposits (see above)
Cost to build: 1000 Koku
Time to build: 8 seasons

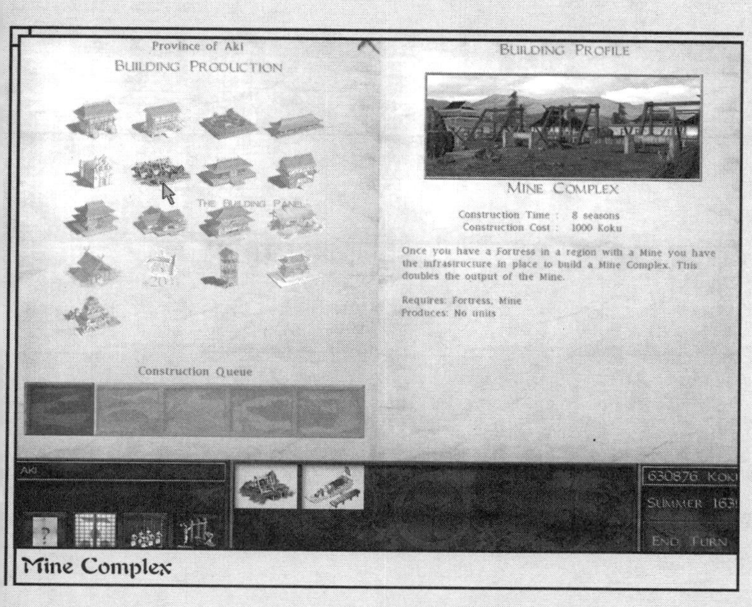

Mine Complex

BUILDING DEVELOPMENT

Knowing what building types to construct and what other building options they open up is a key part of the Campaign game. The following pages outline which buildings are required before setting up other structures or improvements that are available in the game. Most of the improvements and buildings require the presence of one of the Castles. Those that don't are listed here...

NO CASTLE REQUIRED:

Gold/Silver/Copper Mine

↓

Gold/Silver/Copper Mine Complex

Border Watch Towers

↓

Border Forts

Improved Farmland

↓

Superior Farmland

↓

Exceptional Farmland

↓

Legendary Farmland

CASTLE REQUIRED BEFORE YOU CAN BUILD:

Archery Dojo

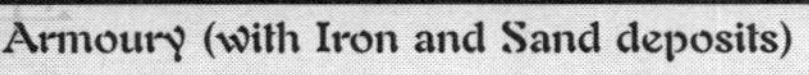

Armoury (with Iron and Sand deposits)

Tea House

Spear Dojo

Ninja House

Tranquil Garden

Port

LARGE CASTLE REQUIRED BEFORE YOU CAN BUILD:

Famous Archery Dojo

Famous Spear Dojo

Sword Dojo

Swordsmith

Horse Dojo

Famous Armoury

Buddhist Temple

Palace

Church

Portuguese Trading Post

Famous Tea House

FORTRESS REQUIRED BEFORE YOU CAN BUILD:

Famous Sword Dojo

Famous Horse Dojo

Legendary Archery Dojo

Legendary Armour

Famous Swordsmith

Golden Palace

Famous Buddhist Temple

Infamous Ninja House

Legendary Tea House

Dutch Trading Post

CITADEL REQUIRED BEFORE YOU CAN BUILD:

Legendary Spear Dojo

Legendary Horse Dojo

Legendary Sword Dojo

Legendary Swordsmith

Temple Complex

Cathedral

Geisha House

Legendary Palace

Gun Factory

SPECIAL UNIT TYPES

The Campaign mode in *Shogun: Total War* features several extra unit types that don't appear anywhere else in the game. These troops are "special units", employed on the Campaign mode's strategy map to spy on other clans, to broker alliances or to assassinate enemy generals. Any analysis of the Campaign is incomplete without knowing the capabilities of the Emissary, Shinobi, Ninja, Legendary Geisha and Priest.

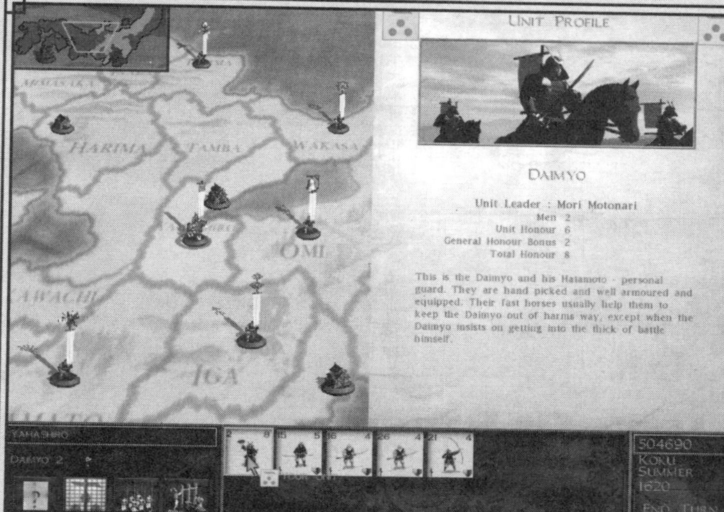

The Daimyo (which translates to "Big Name") is the leader of a family or clan.

DAIMYO

The Daimyo is the head of a clan, the physical embodiment of the player within Campaign mode. Protected by a small group of bodyguards, the Daimyo has an influence on all units under his direct command on the battlefield. This advantage must be weighed against the prospect of losing the Daimyo in battle whereupon, if no heir is present, the game ends. The Daimyo can fall victim to swords and arrows on the battlefield and is also vulnerable to Ninja attacks. Your Daimyo must be protected at all costs. Lose him and you lose the game.

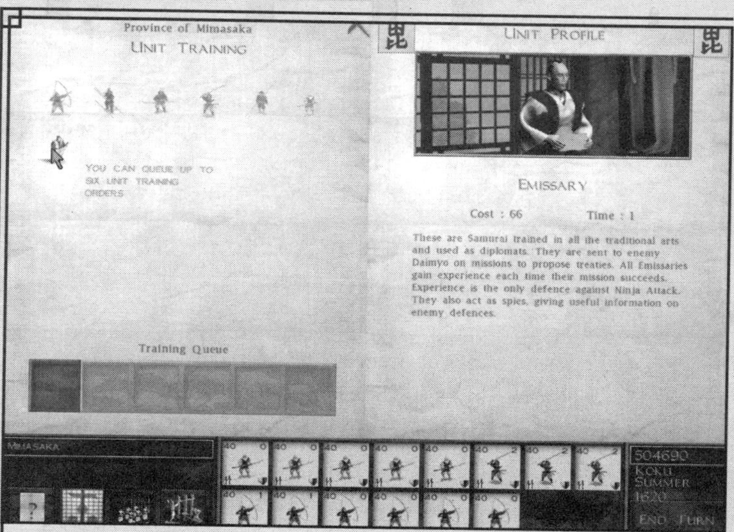

Produced via the Tranquil Garden building, Emissaries are able to broker alliances and spy on enemy clans.

EMISSARY

Only by building a Tranquil Garden can a Daimyo begin to recruit and train samurai skilled in the diplomatic arts. Such Emissaries are primarily used to offer alliances or peace treaties to other Daimyo and players can do this by moving the Emissary unit onto a rival Daimyo. In addition to their peacemaking skills, Emissaries can also be used to spy on troop numbers and province facilities. Emissaries gain experience by successfully brokering an alliance, making them slightly less vulnerable to Ninja attacks.

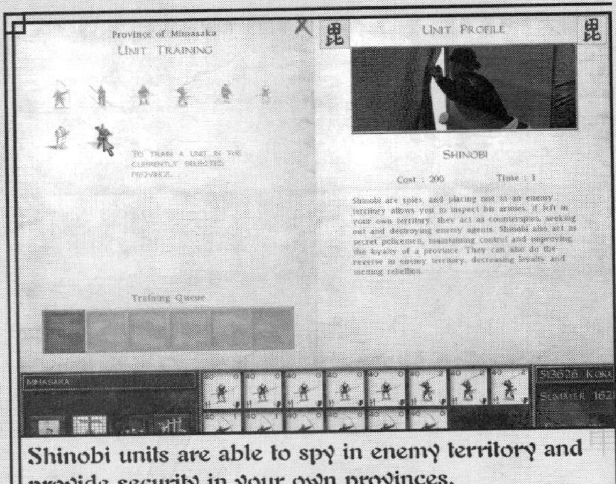

Shinobi units are able to spy in enemy territory and provide security in your own provinces.

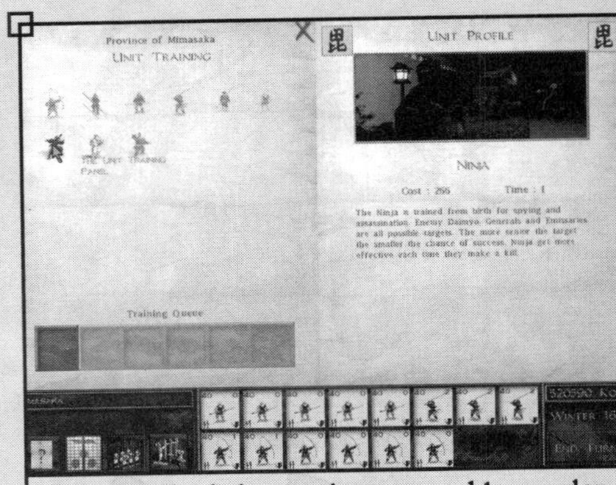

These black-clad assassins are used to murder spying Emissaries or experienced generals.

SHINOBI

By constructing a Tea House, a Daimyo gives himself the power to recruit and train Shinobi, samurai skilled in spying and intelligence gathering. Like an Emissary, Shinobi units can be used to reveal enemy troop numbers, troop types and province facilities. Better still, however, Shinobi units can be used in counter-intelligence roles, acting as security forces within your own boundaries (some protection against Ninja and enemy Shinobi), and as insurgents in enemy territories. Unrest created by Shinobi units decreases population loyalty.

NINJA

Once a basic Castle has been constructed, a Ninja House can be established, giving Daimyo the opportunity to develop a cadre of assassins. Like Shinobi, Ninja can operate as spies, but are best used to assassinate enemy Emissaries, Priests or generals. Ninja gain experience and honour according to the number of kills they have achieved. The more experience and honour a Ninja has gained, the easier it will be for the black-clad assassin to strike at prominent and well-protected targets.

LEGENDARY GEISHA

If you thought that the Shinobi was redundant next to the Ninja, think again. By developing the Tea House to Legendary status, Daimyo have the opportunity to build a new building type: the Geisha House. This facility produces the Legendary Geisha, a combination of the skills possessed by the Emissary, Shinobi and Ninja units. In the Daimyo's own Castle, the Legendary Geisha acts as a counterspy, while in an enemy Castle she can act as both spy and assassin. Unlike Ninja and Shinobi who can be caught, the only way to rid yourself of a Geisha is through assassination.

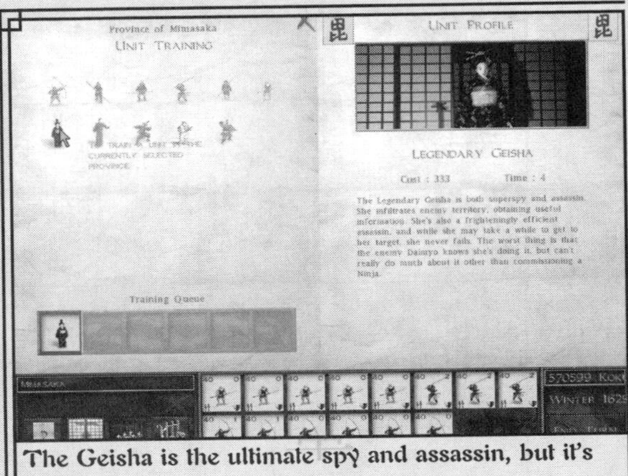

The Geisha is the ultimate spy and assassin, but it's difficult to access.

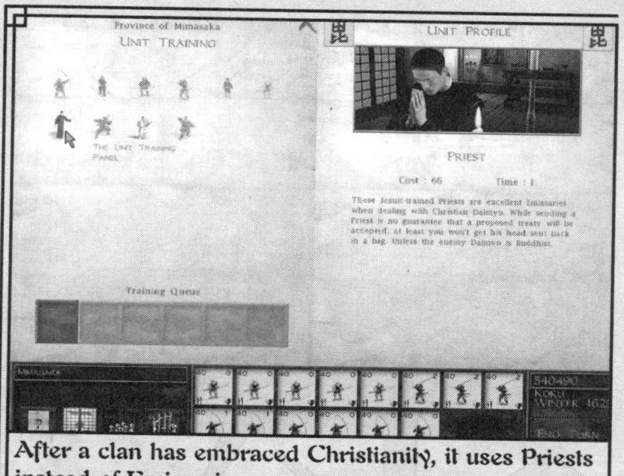

After a clan has embraced Christianity, it uses Priests instead of Emissaries.

PRIEST

Once the Portuguese have landed, a successful alliance with these Europeans allows a Daimyo to construct a new building type: the Church. Erecting a Church signals a Daimyo's conversion to Christianity (thereby causing Buddhist Temples to be dismantled) and allows the wannabe-Shogun to produce Priests. The Priest unit is much like the Buddhist Emissary. However, unlike the Buddhist Emissary, the Priest cannot be killed by another Christian Daimyo. Buddhist Daimyo, unfortunately, don't have to adhere to this rule.

Note: Priest units can only be created by first accepting an offer of trade from either Portuguese or Dutch visitors. In a Campaign game, the Portuguese will always arrive first offering new building types (Trading Post, Church, Cathedral, Gun Factory) and new weapons (Arquebusiers, Musketeers). Remember, however, that although the Dutch allow a Daimyo access to firearms, the development of Musketeers requires a Gun Factory and a Cathedral, while the rival Dutch only require the Gun Factory. However, one of the bonuses associated with a conversion to Christianity is that a Cathedral gives a financial bonus to the clan that builds it—100 Koku per year, per church, in Japan. This means that a Daimyo receives a cash bonus for every church in Japan, even if it is a church that they do not own.

CAMPAIGN MAP

SIXTY PROVINCES MAKE UP THE 16TH CENTURY LANDSCAPE OF JAPAN. AS DAIMYO, YOU MUST CONQUER THEM ALL.

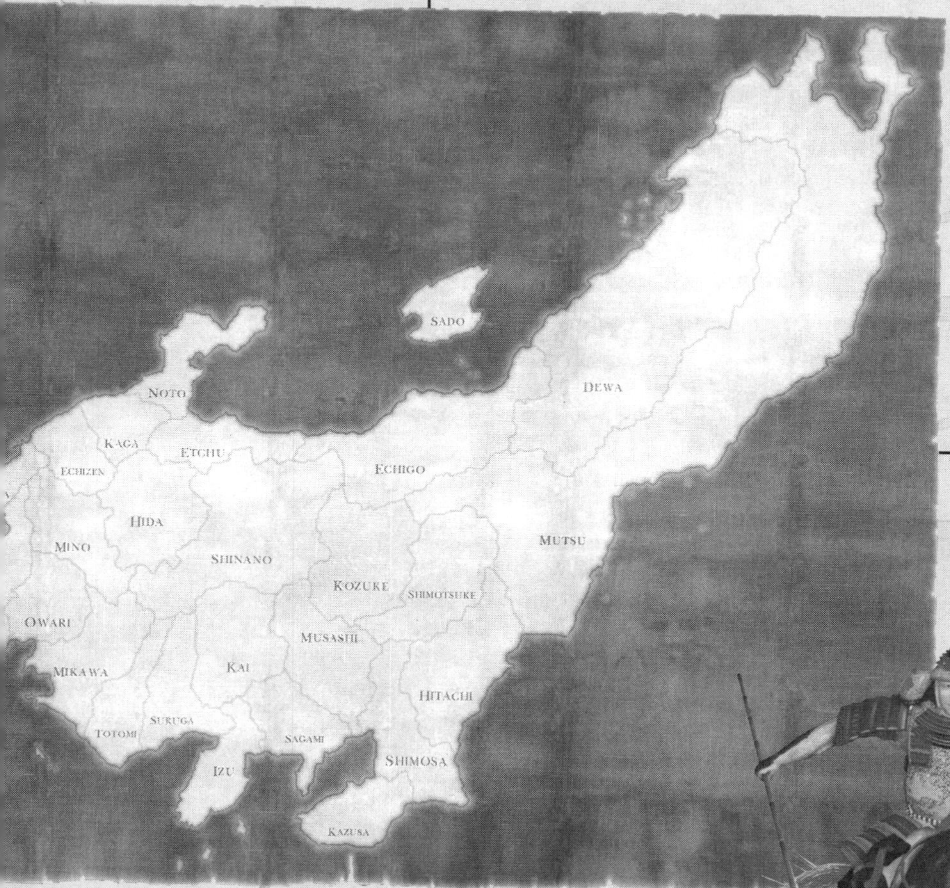

将軍

SADO
NOTO
DEWA
KAGA
ETCHU
ECHIZEN
ECHIGO
HIDA
MUTSU
MINO
SHINANO
KOZUKE
SHIMOTSUKE
OWARI
MUSASHI
KAI
MIKAWA
HITACHI
SURUGA
TOTOMI
SAGAMI
IZU
SHIMOSA
KAZUSA

将軍

CAMPAIGN PROVINCES

By looking at the map in the Throne Room, you can see which territories belong to which clans...

Considering that the average size of a clan's empire at the beginning of a Campaign game is six provinces, this means that there are 54 left for the ambitious Daimyo to conquer. It's a tall order, requiring a lengthy, methodical and patient campaign of positioning, diplomacy and aggressive expansion. If you take command of the Green Shimazu clan, you face the prospect of trying to sweep east across the Japanese mainland. If you control the Gold Oda clan, you must plan a strategy that permits you to expand from your central position without losing the territories you already have. For each Daimyo and for each clan, strategies will be different.

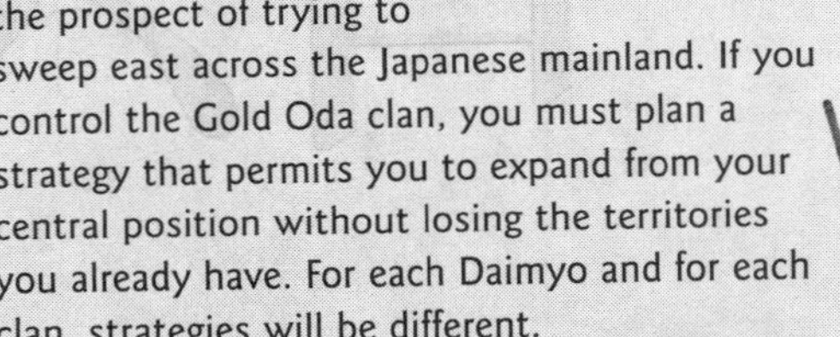

Likewise, for each clan certain provinces will be more important than others. The Mori, for example, guard Harima fiercely as it contains Silver deposits vital for boosting the clan's treasury. On the other side of the Japanese mainland, the Hojo clan are rightly protective of both Hitachi and Musashi, which between them contribute an average of 1,260 Koku annually to the Purple war effort. On the following pages, we've detailed the value, features and strategic importance of each of the 60 Campaign provinces. Also included is an extra section called Battle Notes, which gives you some idea of what to expect in a territory should you want to invade or defend it. After all, the Daimyo who prosper know in detail the territory that they own.

AKI

VALUE: 153 KOKU
FEATURES: SILVER DEPOSITS
(MINE: +400 KOKU PER YEAR)
IRON AND SAND DEPOSITS (ARMOURY)
PORT (+200 KOKU FOR TAKEDA)
BONUS: NONE
HELD BY: REBELS (SILVER)

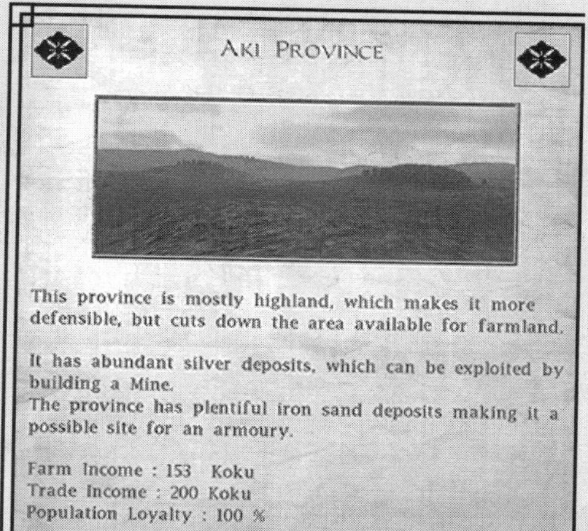

STRATEGIC IMPORTANCE

Part of the Takeda clan's western lands, Aki is the most valuable of the three provinces that hug the coast here surrounded by the Mori empire. For Black, Aki not only contributes an extra 200 Koku per year via its pre-built Port, but it also has abundant silver deposits which can be mined for an extra 400 Koku (800 with a Mine Complex). Of course, it's precisely this feature that makes Aki a tempting target for the Mori, who are in a strong position at the start of a Campaign game to invade not only Aki, but neighbouring provinces Bingo and Bitchu as well. While Aki's agricultural return is poor (due to the lack of good farmland), the loss of Aki to the Takeda is not only the loss of a potential Mine, but of a Port that links these fragile states to Kai, Sagami and Izu to the east.

BATTLE NOTES

Aki is a bleak land, gently undulating and dotted with woodland. Surrounded by steep hills, it's a good defender's province—generals are able to sit and wait for an opposing force on a steep incline, knowing that the enemy must attack uphill to reach them. Any attacker trying to invade Aki will have to face troops that are typically dug on this raised ground, often taking advantage of tree cover. As ever, you can combat the enemy's height advantage by gaining height of your own, pressing the enemy into retreating from his position or into an attack, thereby allowing you to draw him down toward you.

PROVINCES

AWA

VALUE: 180 KOKU
FEATURES: NONE
BONUS: NONE
HELD BY: REBELS (SILVER)

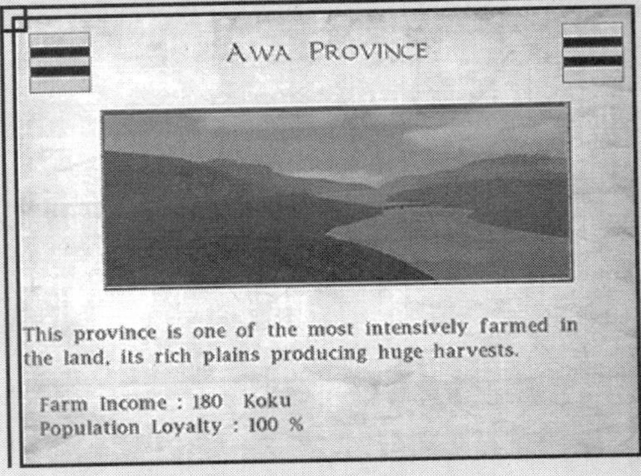

STRATEGIC IMPORTANCE

One of the four territories that make up the isle of Shikoku, while Awa begins every Campaign game in the hands of the silver-liveried rebels, it's rarely garrisoned with any troops. Attention instead is focused on the more interesting (and more valuable) lands of Iyo, Tosa and Sanuki, because Awa is neither a strategic nor an economic prize. Despite the fact that it is an intensely farmed lowland area, the average annual harvest of 180 Koku is disappointing compared to the yields of the provinces nearby. That said, thanks to its river, Awa is at least a province where a defender can make a brave military stand. Threatened by the expansionist Mori to the north, the peaceful Shimazu to the west and the restless Oda to the East, it's only a matter of time before one of the three decides that the average 1,022 Koku harvest available on this island is too good to ignore.

BATTLE NOTES

Awa is the least important of the four provinces that make up Shikoku island. Like many of the other provinces that feature a river, Awa only has one bridge, making a swift, bloodless invasion of this Rebel land something of an impossibility. Even if an opposing force makes it across the bridge and onto the land beyond, defending forces can still retreat to the spectacular high ground immediately behind the crossing point. With a landscape that is steeply sloping and difficult to march across without tiring your troops, generals should attempt to conquer this land with superior numbers thereby forcing the enemy to retreat without ever resorting to a fight.

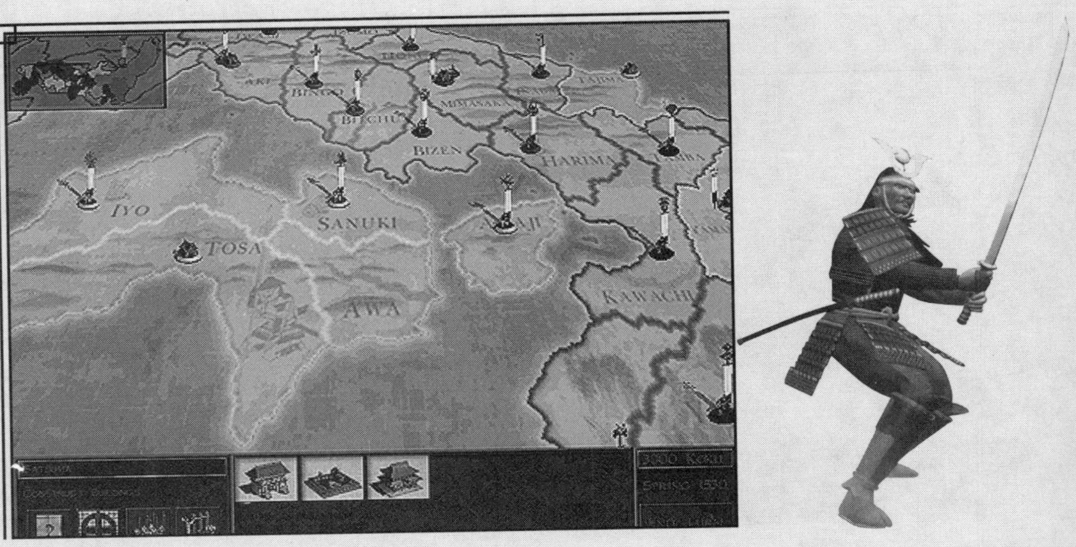

AWAJI

VALUE: 60 KOKU
FEATURES: NONE
BONUS: NONE
HELD BY: REBELS (SILVER)

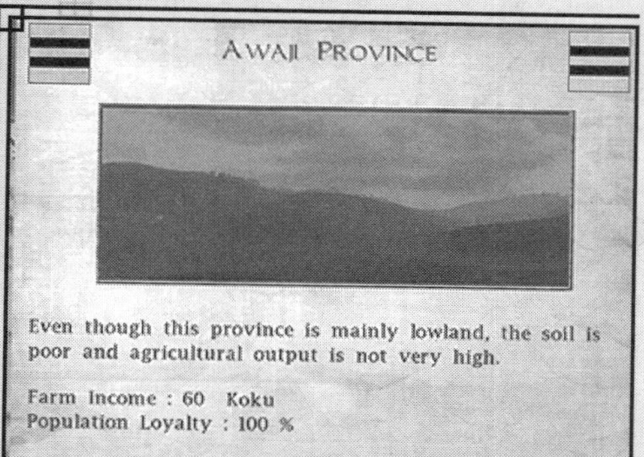

STRATEGIC IMPORTANCE

With an average agricultural yield of just 60 Koku per year, Awaji is a strategic prize rather than an economic one. Located between the mainland and the resource-rich isle of Shikoku, this tiny island is a two-way stepping stone—Red and Gold forces can use it to move west, while Rebels will need it if they plan to strike east to the mainland. Garrisoned by a small force, Awaji is arguably more important to the Oda clan. Without it, Gold doesn't have a hope of trying to conquer the Shikoku lands of Iyo, Tosa, Sanuki and Awa. Together this quartet of territories boasts an average annual harvest of 1,022 Koku—a tempting pool of resources that will prove crucial for the Oda and Mori if they decide to push east. And don't forget the Green Shimazu clan; they have their own back-door route to Shikoku, and will need to travel via Awaji to avoid a costly confrontation with the Mori when they push eastward.

BATTLE NOTES

There's barely a flat stretch of land anywhere on Awaji. Aiding the defending force more than the attacking one, this strategically important isle can prove a tough, unforgiving battleground. If playing the attacker, the enemy forces will camp on the clifftop that's in the distance. From here they gain an unparalleled field of fire over the valley below. Whichever way you decide to attack, it's an uphill battle. As a result, ranged weaponry tends to work better than the sword and spear, and you should aim for an operation of attrition, slowly wearing down the enemy. As the defender, however, pick the same mountainside and rain constant arrow-fire down onto any attackers brave enough to approach.

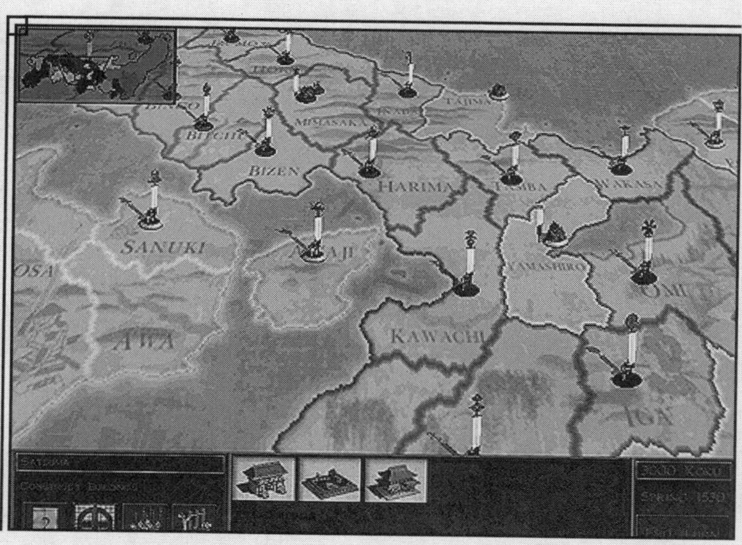

BINGO

VALUE: 130 KOKU
FEATURES: IRON AND SAND DEPOSITS (ARMOURY)
BONUS: NONE
HELD BY: CLAN TAKEDA (BLACK)

STRATEGIC IMPORTANCE

Due to its highland terrain, Japanese farmers have a hard time squeezing more than 130 Koku out of Bingo's unsuitable soil. Like the Mori-controlled lands that surround it to the north, what Bingo lacks in the way of economic strength, it makes up for with the Iron and Sand required to build an Armoury. Ruled by the Takeda clan, the armies that follow the Black banner desperately need to hang onto Bingo despite its poor statistics. With only six provinces making up its empire at the beginning of a Campaign game, the Takeda can't afford to lose any of its territories. The situation, however, looks bleak. For the Mori, who surround Bingo and the neighbouring Black states of Bitchu and Aki, this trio of provinces is an obvious early target. In fact, unless Black significantly bolsters its defences within the first year, Red can sweep into Aki to capture the Port link, before conquering Bitchu and Bingo at their leisure.

BATTLE NOTES

With a low agricultural yield, you should expect the Bingo landscape to consist of undulating highlands. It doesn't disappoint, and fighting a battle there reveals a dramatic vista of rolling hills and shallow valleys, perfect for attackers and defenders alike. Attackers will start on the southern edge of this province, just to the left of a large hill. By marching up this incline and then north, the enemy will usually be spotted arranged on the high ground opposite. To attack, a force must attempt to move into the valley to engage the defenders. However, as Sun Tzu taught that an army should never fight uphill, by manoeuvring "around" the defending army, an attacker can force the defender to alter position. If defending the province, camp your army at the very top of the map, using the high ground and tree cover to your advantage.

BITCHU

VALUE: 114
FEATURES: NONE
BONUS: NONE
HELD BY: CLAN TAKEDA (BLACK)

STRATEGIC IMPORTANCE

Although it's the least exciting of the Takeda clan's western colonies, Bitchu is arguably the easiest to defend thanks to the river that splits it in two. The poor soil quality of this lowland area means that farmers regularly break their backs trying to improve on the average 114 Koku harvest. It's an uphill struggle and Bitchu is hardly a prize asset for either the untrustworthy Mori or the Takeda themselves. But with only six territories to their name, the Black forces can't be choosy. As each new Campaign game begins, Bitchu faces an uncertain future alongside the weakly defended Bingo and Aki. Unless reinforced quickly, not even the Takeda's mounted cavalry units will be enough to stop the Mori clan rolling over the provinces one by one. Within a year, the Takeda can go from six provinces to only three.

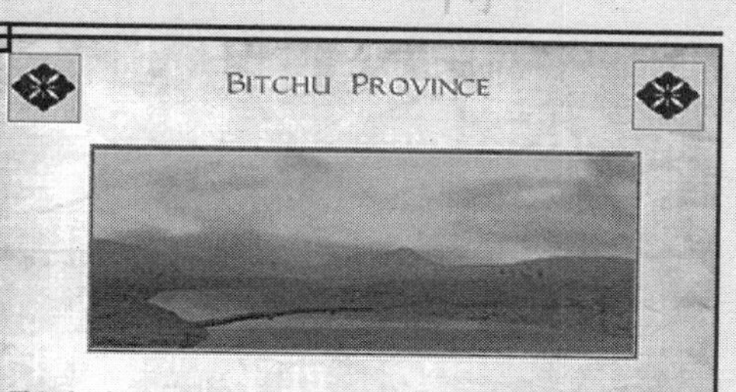

BATTLE NOTES

Bitchu is one of those rare lands split into two by an impassable river. For attackers to get from one side to the other, they are forced to cross a single bridge (typically defended by hordes of bow- or gun-wielding enemies). There are numerous ways to minimise your casualties during these risky operations, including attacking with superior numbers (thereby forcing the enemy to retreat before you get there), and crossing first with heavily armoured Naginata (who stand up better to ranged weapon fire). Beyond the bridge crossing the flat landscape gives way to gently sloping hills. As a defender you can use these hills to mount a do-or-die defence. As the attacker, beware pursuing fleeing enemy forces in case you are drawn into an uphill melee.

BIZEN

VALUE: 190 KOKU
FEATURES: NATURAL HARBOUR (CHEAPER TO BUILD A PORT)
BONUS: NONE
HELD BY: CLAN MORI (RED)

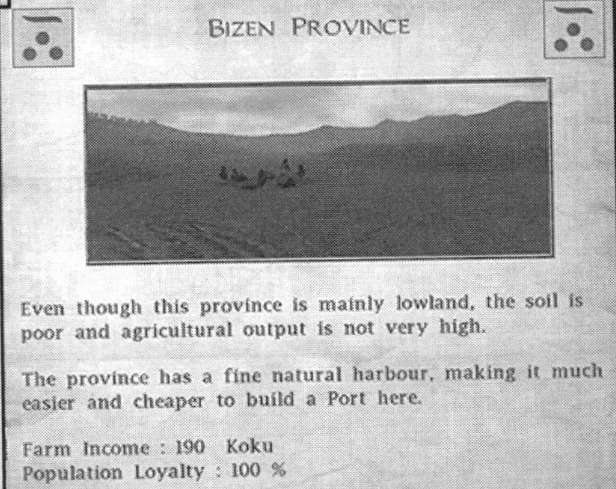

STRATEGIC IMPORTANCE

Fiercely protected by Mori forces, Bizen's lowland terrain still manages to contribute an average of 190 Koku to the Red war effort. For its rulers, Bizen is not just important because it has a handy natural harbour (allowing a Port to be constructed quicker and cheaper than usual). Bordering Bitchu to the west, it's a good staging point for an invasion of the poorly defended Takeda province. With supplies from the Castle in neighbouring Mimaska, the Mori clan can also strike into the Koku-rich lands of Sanuki and Iyo. Unless, Black forces are left unchecked, Bizen is safe from Rebel raids to the south, and separated from the Red/Gold front line by the strategically important land of Harima.

BATTLE NOTES

Half lowland plains, half steep mountain range, Bizen has a few hills and slopes to aid both the attacking and defending force. To triumph here, either take up a defensive position on the raised ground that you start the battle on, tempting the enemy forces to come to you. Or, if you decide to march quickly towards the defending force, it will most likely retreat to the high, tree-covered hill in the north of the map. Providing you have been thoughtful enough to include some sort of ranged weapon units in your attacking (or indeed your defending) forces, you should have the strength to invade or repel your opponent depending on the situation.

BUNGO

VALUE: 120 KOKU
FEATURES: NONE
BONUS: NONE
HELD BY: CLAN SHIMAZU (GREEN)

STRATEGIC IMPORTANCE

While the highland nature of the Bungo landscape severely cuts back the agricultural yield, this province is a vital piece in Green's defensive plans. For starters, a well garrisoned Bungo prevents the Rebels in Iyo from mounting raids across the sea. Admittedly, the renegades who are slowly establishing a mini-empire spanning Tosa, Iyo, Sanuki, Awa and Awaji are not likely to pose a threat to Shimazu interests. Instead, Bungo needs to be reinforced to check Imagawa expansion in the northwest. To take complete control of the Kyushu island, Green needs to contain the three Cyan provinces until such time as it is strong enough to defeat them. For the Imagawa, they have to strike out at Bungo, Higo or Buzen at some point, or remain trapped in that tight corner until Green attacks them.

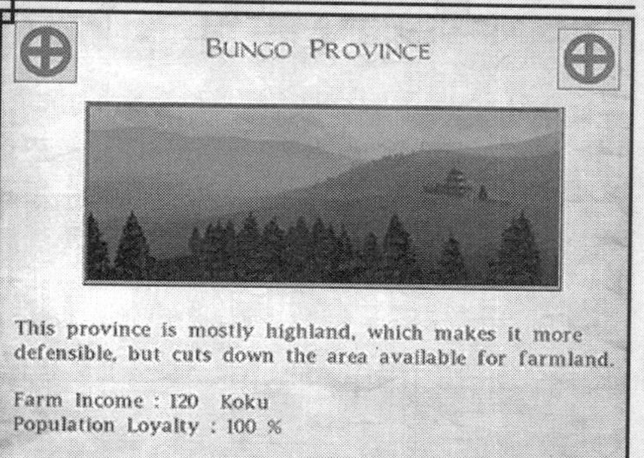

BATTLE NOTES

A long, low valley with steep sides, it's vitally important when fighting in the Bungo region not to get caught on the valley floor. As soon as you gain control of your forces, whether you are attacking or defending, you need to gain as much height as possible. Once you are happy that you have established a good vantage point from which to survey the battlefield, you need to locate the enemy and plan how best to approach him. The type and number of forces that you have under your command will ultimately determine the reaction of the defending troops. If you have a light force, expect the enemy to bring the fight to you. But for those of you with a giant, lumbering war machine, the computer AI will do exactly what you would do in a situation like this: find the steepest hill it can and hope that you are reckless enough to fight uphill.

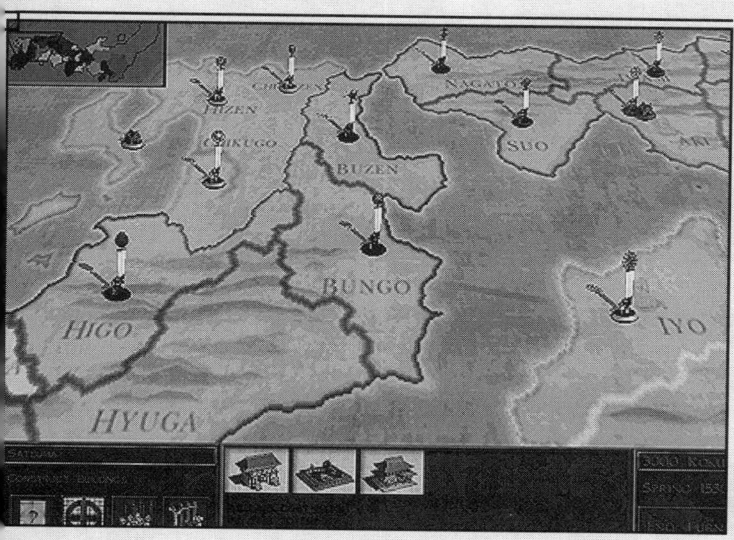

BUZEN

VALUE: 228 KOKU
FEATURES: NONE
BONUS: NONE
HELD BY: CLAN SHIMAZU (GREEN)

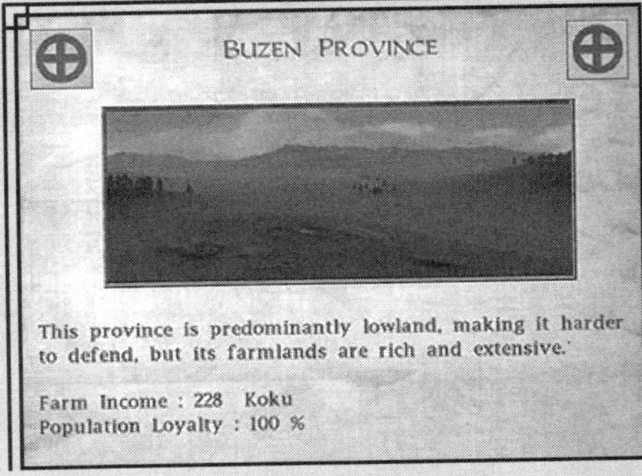

STRATEGIC IMPORTANCE

As its 228 Koku yield suggests, Buzen is a predominantly lowland area dominated by farmland. Lacking useful features or unit bonuses (like the majority of the Shimazu lands), it's only when you look closely at the Campaign map that you see just how strategically valuable Buzen is. Initially, three clans have an interest in this Green-held territory—the Shimazu, the Mori and the Imagawa. For the Green forces, Buzen is a vital border province guarding one of the only two entrances to the island. Should Nagato on the mainland fall to the advancing Mori, then Buzen is where the Shimazu can regroup to fight again. The Cyan-coloured Imagawa, meanwhile, will eventually need to break out of their corner of the island, while the Mori will be looking for a foothold on the Shimazu's home patch just as the Shimazu have Nagato on theirs.

BATTLE NOTES

Unlike Bungo to the south, Buzen is a wide, bowl valley dotted with small but defendable hills. Around the edges, the land rises just enough to provide a number of good defensive positions, but the one that stands out is a tree-covered hill directly opposite the start point for the attacking force. Quite obviously, by camping an army here, the defending forces get a good view of the battlefield, a height advantage, plus cover for their more vulnerable units in the trees. But, due to the fact that Buzen is a lowland region, this position can be attacked from the side by an enemy who is prepared to march toward the village in the centre, east along the track and then north to outflank it.

As usual, height is the most important weapon here, and with it you can inflict a great deal of damage.

CHIKUZEN

VALUE: 304 KOKU
FEATURES: NONE
BONUS: NONE
HELD BY: CLAN IMAGAWA (CYAN)

STRATEGIC IMPORTANCE

Boasting rich farmland that yields an average of 304 Koku, Chikuzen is one of three valuable lands that make up the western half of the Imagawa empire. Like the Black Takeda clan, which can't afford to lose any of its six provinces, the Samurai in Cyan need to reinforce and consolidate before they expand. Initially receiving its supplies from the Castle at Hizen, Chikuzen is a tempting target for the neighbouring Green forces, the first step in its planned domination of the entire island. For the Imagawa, the resources that Chikuzen, Chikugo and Hizen provide help to ensure the clan's survival on the map. The Red Mori clan might make a determined effort to reach westwards, tempted by the Imagawa's rich lands.

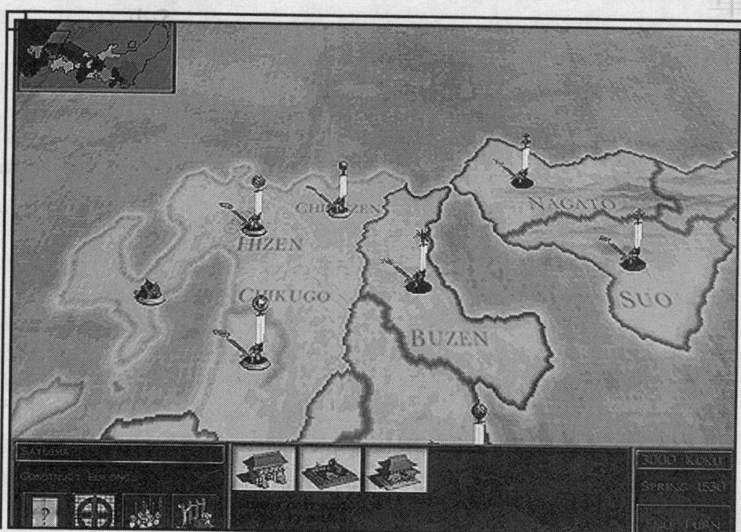

BATTLE NOTES

A rich, low-lying land cut in two by a river, the tactics required to invade Chikuzen are similar to those required to attack the Bitchu province. The main obstacle here is getting over the single bridge—usually guarded by a mixture of Footsoldiers and ranged weapon specialists (Archers, Arquebusiers, Musketeers). As has been mentioned before, to attack or defend a river province *without* any ranged weapon units makes the job much harder. As the attacker, you require Archers to wear down the enemy's own Footsoldiers; as the defender, you'll rely on ranks of bowmen to ruthlessly cut down the attacking forces as they file over the bridge. Beyond this initial battleground, Chikuzen features a series of low hills.

CHIKUGO

VALUE: 320 KOKU
FEATURES: NONE
BONUS: NONE
HELD BY: CLAN IMAGAWA (CYAN)

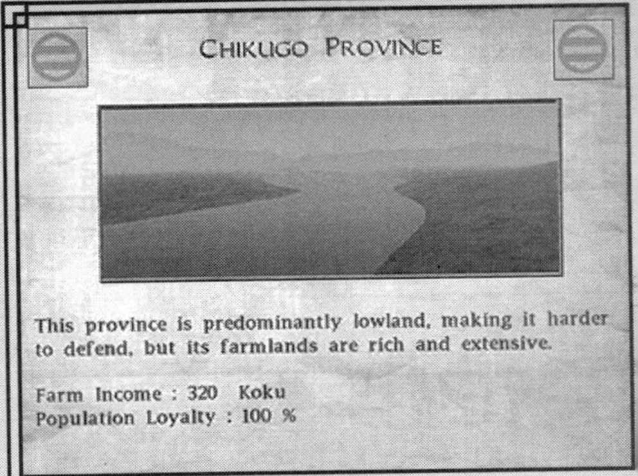

STRATEGIC IMPORTANCE

Like Hizen and Chikuzen, the land of Chikugo on Kyushu is one of the Imagawa's most important provinces. Bordered by the Green Shimazu lands of Bungo and Higo, Chikugo is a cash-rich lowland area with farmland irrigated by the natural river that runs through it. Producing an average of 320 Koku per annum, Chikugo can be further developed with land improvements and by the construction of a Port. If lost by the Cyan forces, the Imagawa treasury suffers a significant loss, and so it should be fiercely defended at all times. At the start of a Campaign game, only the Green Shimazu armies are in a position to attack Chikugo, desperate to force out the Imagawa from a Kyushu that they believe to be theirs by right.

BATTLE NOTES

Despite the fact that Chikugo is mostly lowland, any defending force should camp itself on the highest hill it can find—it's in the north of the map covered with trees. From here, defenders can watch an attacking army approach and decide how best to engage them. Playing the attacker, and if the two forces are evenly matched, it's possible to draw the computer-controlled enemy down from its position by simply standing on the battlefield doing nothing. The computer will then weigh up the pros and cons of the situation and, even if it's defending the province, will attack with confidence. As they march toward you, rather than the other way around, you then have time to pick a defensive position, letting loose with ranged weapons to soften them up, before hitting their ranks with sword and spear troops.

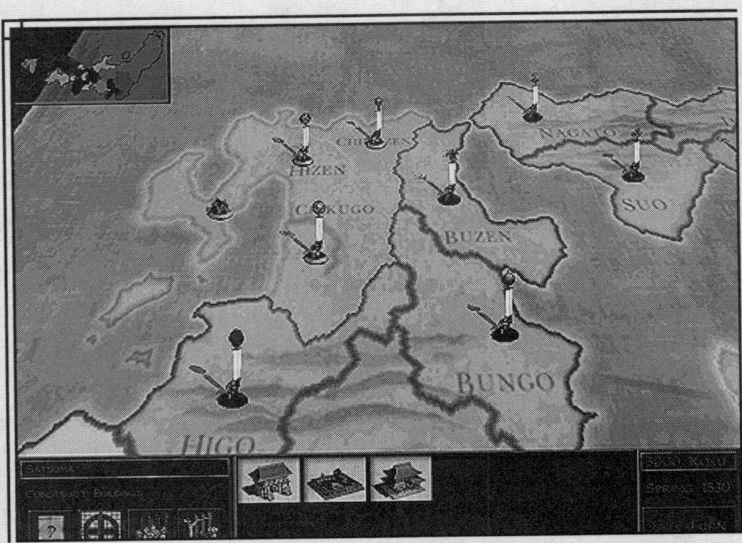

DEWA

VALUE: 400
FEATURES: GOLD DEPOSITS
(MINE: +600 KOKU PER YEAR)
BONUS: NONE
HELD BY: CLAN UESUGI (DARK BLUE)

STRATEGIC IMPORTANCE

Making up the majority of the eastern tip of the Japanese mainland, Dewa is initially isolated from attack by fellow Uesugi lands Echigio, Sado and Mutsu. Contributing an annual average of 400 Koku to the Dark Blue cause, Dewa's enormous size and its fertile valleys make it a must-hold territory for the Uesugi whose mini-empire is threatened almost as soon as a Campaign game begins. Dewa also features extensive Gold deposits and a Mine established here will add an extra 600 Koku annually to the Uesugi treasury. As a result, the Uesugi will do everything that they can to hold onto it, and any expansionist army must first conquer the buffer states of Echigo or Mutsu to be in a position to attack. There is, however, a back door to Dewa via the small island of Sado. But again, any army that wishes to sneak by Dark Blue's heavy defences this way, must first overcome the Rebel-held lands of Noto, Etchu and Kaga.

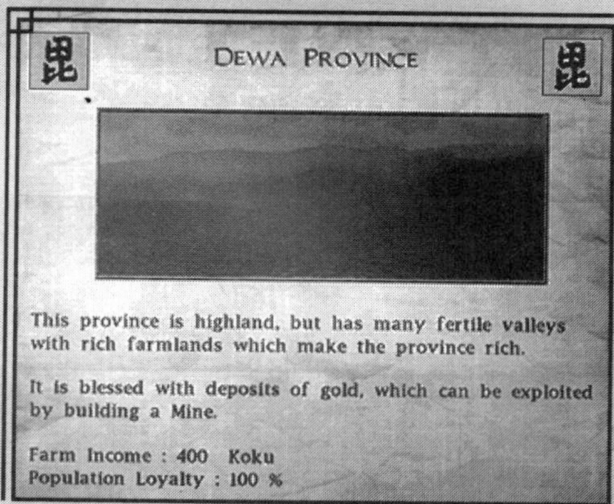

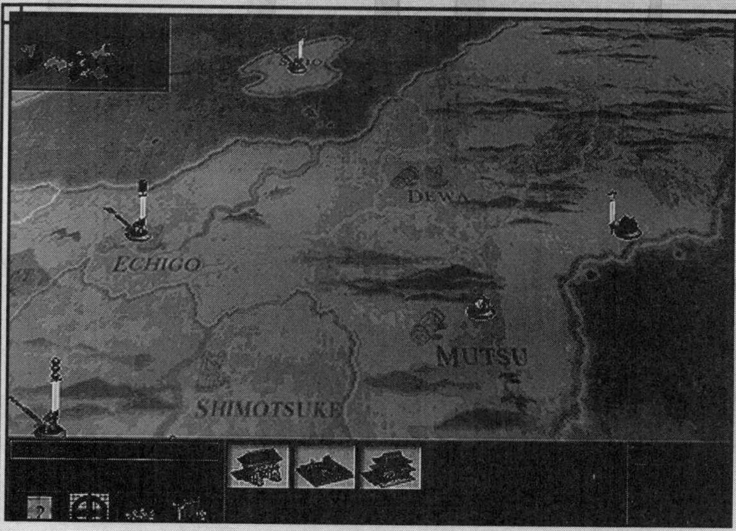

BATTLE NOTES

Dewa is a high land with numerous hills and valleys, so it's hardly surprising that when two armies clash, one hides in the trees to the northwest and the other in the woods to the south. Victory here is a case of keeping the height you have and moving your forces around the edges of the battlefield to engage the enemy with the least amount of penalties (see Battle Strategies on page 42). Don't march boldly *down* into the centre of the valley; you will tire your troops on the journey down and half-kill them on the climb back up again. Keep your soldiers fresh so that they can move across the difficult terrain and still retain the strength to fight (and win) when they encounter the enemy.

ECHIGO

VALUE: 402
FEATURES: SILVER DEPOSITS
(MINE: +400 KOKU PER YEAR)
BONUS: NONE
HELD BY: CLAN UESUGI (DARK BLUE)

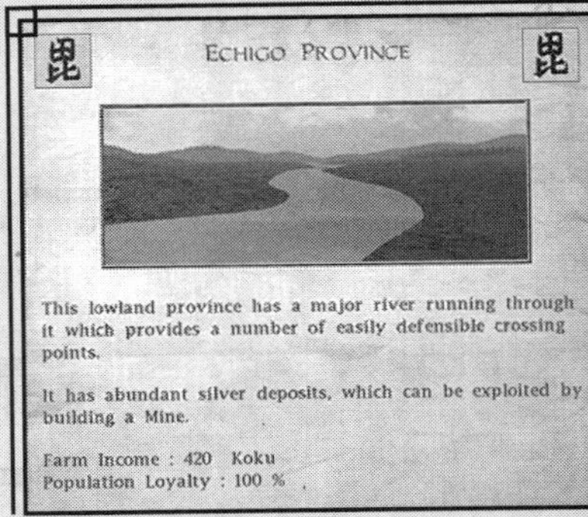

STRATEGIC IMPORTANCE

The Uesugi clan is one of the richest in Japan, and with a basic average yield of 402 Koku per year, Echigo is another land that the Dark Blue forces need to hold to establish themselves early in the game. Bordered by the Rebel-held Etchu to the west and the Purple frontier of Kozuke to the south, Echigo only faces one potential enemy. With its natural river system, this province can be defended more easily than most. But with the Uesugi facing a tough fight for control of Shinano, it should not be weakened to reinforce the neighbouring province. For the first few years, the Rebels in Etchu will pose no threat to Echigo's border. Meanwhile, the Purple Hojo forces to the south will be facing a struggle to hold onto their own lands, let alone attack anybody else's.

BATTLE NOTES

The battle for Echigo involves another risky bridge crossing and some fighting on flat ground with no height advantage for either side.
As usual, if you are the attacking force in this scenario, use your preferred tactic to make the bridge crossing as easy as possible. Meanwhile, defenders should make things as difficult as possible for the attacker to invade their side of the river without paying for it in blood Beyond the river, the attacking army will find little to work with to satisfy Sun Tzu's demand for a height advantage. A bank of trees to the left provide cover for retreating troops, but the slightly sloping edges of the map are a long way away from the main zone of medieval death and destruction.

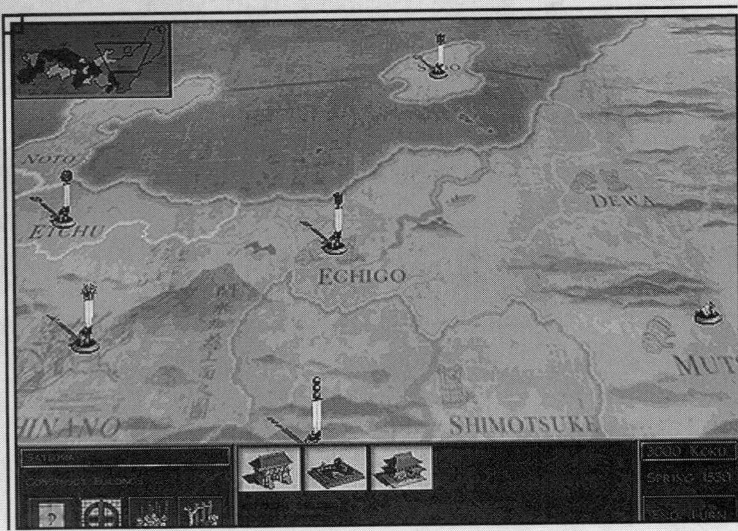

ECHIZEN

VALUE: 280
FEATURES: NONE
BONUS: NONE
HELD BY: REBELS (SILVER)

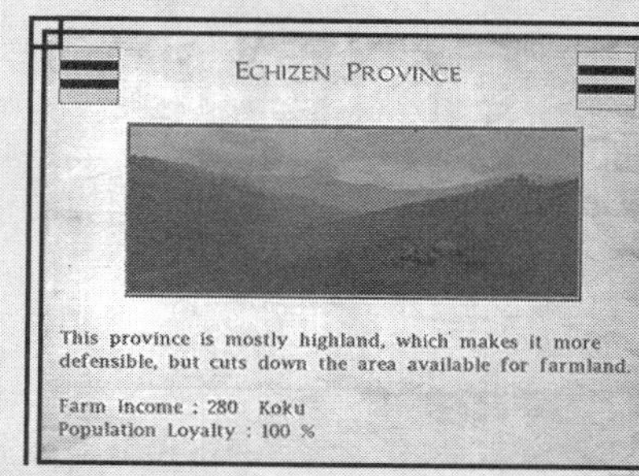

STRATEGIC IMPORTANCE

Located to the east of the golden Oda empire, Echizen is one of four allied states controlled by Rebels and Ronin. Producing an average annual yield of 280 Koku, Echizen represents a possible target for an Oda invasion launched from either Wakasa or Mino. The territory is also bordered by the Uesugi province of Hida, but the Dark Blue forces are stretched as any new Campaign game begins so they will prefer to consolidate what they have rather than risk a prolonged conflict with the Rebels. Significantly, while Echizen is often poorly defended, it can be quickly resupplied from the neighbouring rogue state of Kaga. This advanced territory already has a Castle, Archery Dojo and Buddhist Temple as the game begins. Thus, any army that attacks Echizen should be prepared to do battle with Kaga immediately afterwards.

BATTLE NOTES

A long, spectacular valley, with steeply sloping sides greets invaders of this Rebel-held province. Unsurprisingly, if the computer is controlling the defending force it will start on the highest hill that Echizen has to offer (on the left-hand side as you view the battlefield). From here it will march confidently down the hillside, hoping to draw you into a battle that it is best placed to win. To make things complicated, move your own forces up the side of the steepest slope here and engage the enemy on equal terms. Remember: Echizen is supplied from nearby Kaga where the Buddhist Temple can crank out an endless supply of Warrior Monks. Make sure you have the troops to combat these fanatical fighters.

ETCHU

VALUE: 220 KOKU
FEATURES: NONE
BONUS: NONE
HELD BY: REBELS (SILVER)

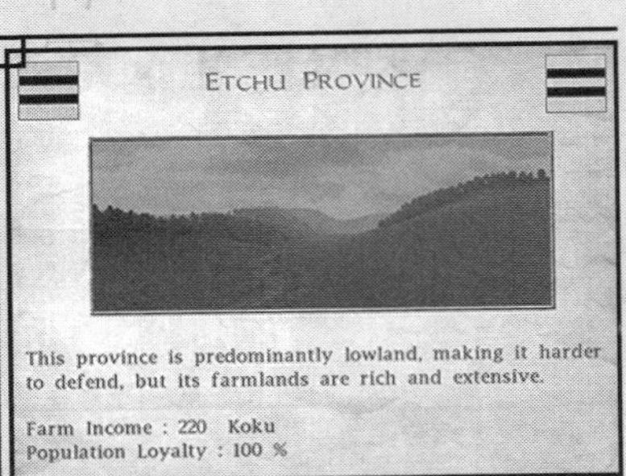

STRATEGIC IMPORTANCE

This large, Rebel-controlled province threatens, and is threatened by, the nearby Uesugi-held lands of Echigo, Shinano and Hida. The Dark Blue forces are unlikely to mount an early offensive, expending their energy and budget on reinforcing the defences in their own lands. For any clan looking to successfully invade Etchu, they must also be aware of the support of the neighbouring Rebel states of Noto and Kaga. Of these, Kaga is the vital link, the troop-producing centre of this independent mini-empire that contains a Castle, Archery Dojo and Buddhist Temple. Uesugi or Hojo generals planning to invade Etchu from the east would do well to remember that unless the facilities in Kaga are destroyed first, they could face a prolonged and costly battle. And as Etchu only yields 220 Koku and has no special bonuses it's not really worth the time or the effort.

BATTLE NOTES

As an attacker, you have a commanding view of the hilly Etchu landscape when you invade this Rebel-held province. With any luck, the Rebel forces will be hiding out in the strip of trees down in the valley, directly ahead of your starting position. Providing you have equipped your forces with ranged weapon units, and have Footsoldiers that are mightier than the basic Yari Samurai, you should be able to hold your position and let the enemy come to you. It's worth noting that Etchu is another Rebel province that can be supplied with Warrior Monks from nearby Kaga. Make sure you have ample resources to counter their religious fervour—they have no fear of death.

HARIMA

VALUE: 220 KOKU
FEATURES: SILVER DEPOSITS (MINE: +400 KOKU PER YEAR)
NATURAL HARBOUR (CHEAPER TO BUILD A PORT)
BONUS: NONE
HELD BY: CLAN MORI (RED)

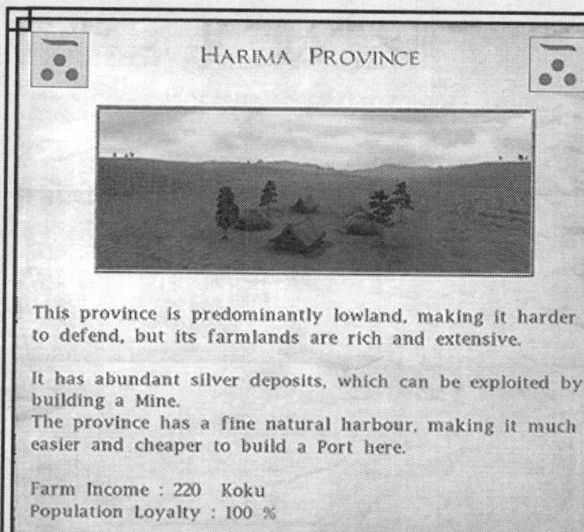

STRATEGIC IMPORTANCE

Unlike the majority of the Mori lands on the eastern tip of the mainland, Harima is a predominantly lowland area with a slightly higher annual yield as a consequence. Better still, the fertile soil of Harima also hides a vein of valuable Silver deposits which can be mined to add an extra 400 Koku per year to Harima's initial 220 Koku total. The province also features a good, natural harbour making it easier and cheaper to build a Port in the region. Harima is undoubtedly the jewel in the Mori crown, second only in importance to Mimaska, which is home to the clans Castle plus its Archery and Spear Dojos. As a result, Harima is not only vital for the Mori's future expansion, but is a tempting target for the Oda who sit waiting for an opportunity to strike from both Kawachi and Tamba.

BATTLE NOTES

Harima is a strange battleground consisting of two raised plains split by a shallow valley. With only a few trees to use as cover and hills that are barely bumps on the landscape, you have to make use of the high ground to repel or defeat an enemy. The key is to catch the enemy on the valley floor, enabling you to use the height advantage to inflict damage before they get into hand-to-hand combat range. If you are the attacking army facing an AI-controlled defender, the computer will wait patiently for you to make the first move. Respond to this inaction by marching your army into a position where it threatens to outflank the defending army. This may force the defenders to alter their defensive stance. On the other hand, when defending, stay clear of the valley floor and stubbornly defend your chosen high spot.

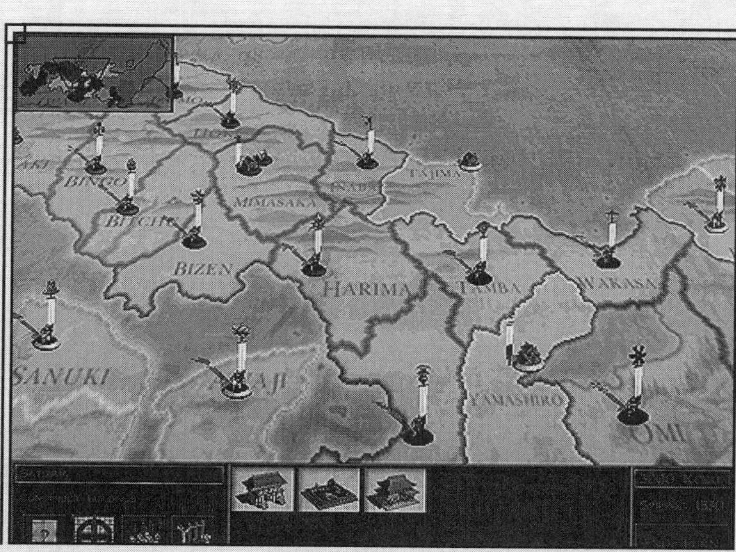

HIDA

VALUE: 120
FEATURES: NONE
BONUS: NONE
HELD BY: CLAN UESUGI (DARK BLUE)

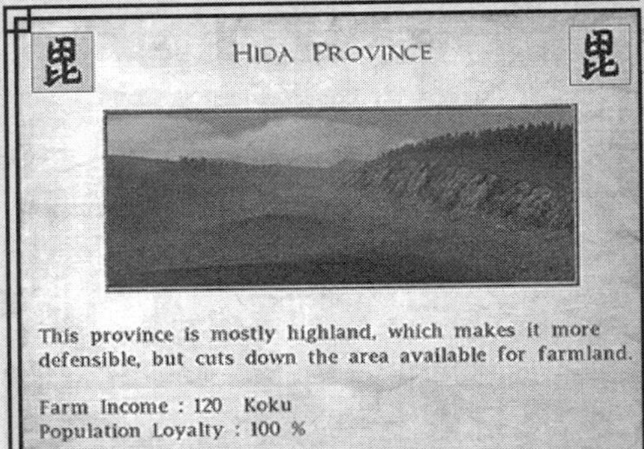

STRATEGIC IMPORTANCE

This highland area is one of the poorest of the Uesugi lands and it's almost worth abandoning to reinforce the vital and weakly garrisoned province of Shinano to the east. So rather than being strategically "important" to the Uesugi, Hida is strategically "unimportant". Its loss will hardly dent a treasury boosted by 400 Koku from Dewa, 600 Koku from Mutsu and 402 Koku from Echigo. So while the Dark Blue forces can do without Hida, it's debatable whether the Oda clan to the west can spare enough forces to capture and hold it. As the Imagawa clan to the south has an empire comprising of only six provinces, the Cyan generals may be tempted to move in for an extended stay. With only an initial 120 Koku harvest per year and no bonuses or special features, Hida is barely worth the cost in blood to invade it.

BATTLE NOTES

The Hida province is dominated by a steep cliff, but while this impressive natural feature would make a good defensive position, it's too close to the attacker's start point to be of any real use. What you must not do in this region is march down onto the valley floor. Typically, defending forces will set up their formations to the northeast of the start point and you can move into range by skirting around the edge of the map, retaining your height advantage as you march. In trying to defend this region, however, there are numerous steep slopes and tree-covered hills that provide plenty of opportunities for ambushes and heroic rear-guard actions.

HIGO

VALUE: 178 KOKU
FEATURES: NONE
BONUS: NONE
HELD BY: CLAN SHIMAZU (GREEN)

STRATEGIC IMPORTANCE

Part of the Green empire on Kyushu to the far west, Higo initially acts as a buffer to the expansionist aspirations of the Cyan-liveried Imagawa who control Hizen, Chikugo and Chikuzen. As a highland area, Higo is more defensible than most, but it pays for this strategic plus with a poor agricultural yield of around 178 Koku per year. For the Shimazu forces, Higo is both a border fortification and a staging post for operations across the border in Chikugo. For the opposing Cyan troops, Higo is often less well defended than Buzen and Bungo nearby, but offers a reasonable resource reward if captured. Lastly, as a coastal region, whoever holds Higo can boost its value by adding a Port and therefore +200 Koku trade points per year. Unless the Red-clad Mori have made a dramatic push westward, Cyan and Green will battle for overall control of it.

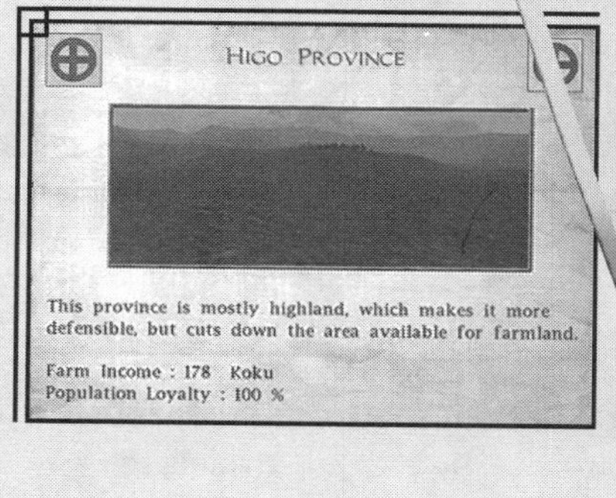

BATTLE NOTES

Bleak but blessed with an abundance of low hills, Higo can prove a tricky battleground. Starting as the attacking force, your view of the landscape is restricted by a hill directly in front of your forces. It's only by marching atop this that you get a commanding view of the province—more low hills to the right, steeper slopes to the left. The enemy meanwhile should be camped in the distance, having chosen a wide slope that gives an effective field of fire and that all-important height advantage.

Naturally, the farther away you position the defending force, the more energy the attacker has to expend to reach you. If you make sure that a series of strength-sapping hills lies between you and the enemy, your opponent's fighting efficiency will have lessened by the time he finally reaches you.

HITACHI

VALUE: 620 KOKU
FEATURES: IRON AND SAND DEPOSITS (ARMOURY)
BONUS: NONE
HELD BY: CLAN HOJO (PURPLE)

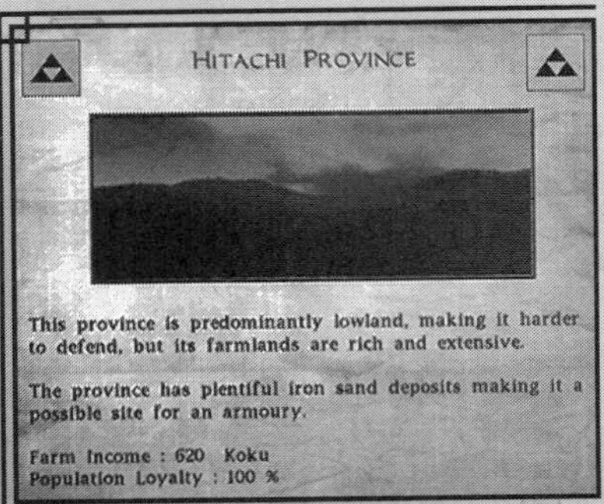

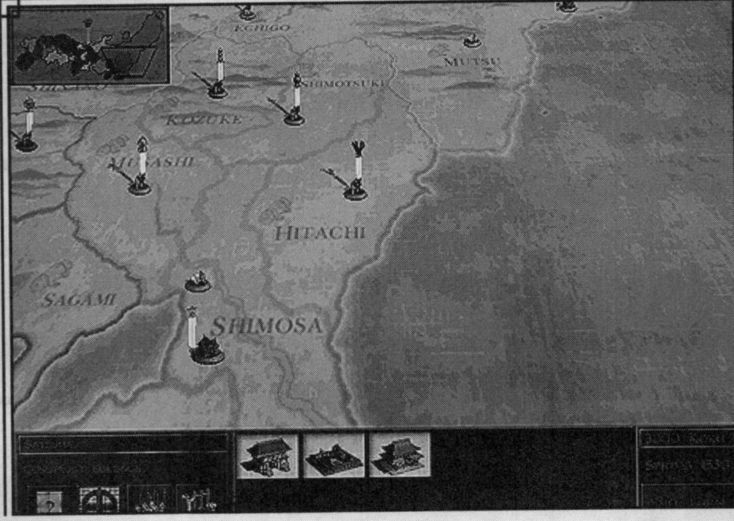

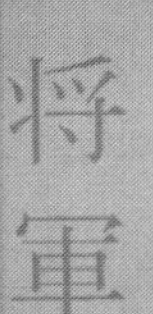

STRATEGIC IMPORTANCE

This lowland coastal province is one of the most productive in the game, and together with Musashi, it provides a substantial amount of the Hojo's wealth. Any army approaching from the west, needs to overcome at least two Purple-controlled lands before getting a crack at this Koku-rich state. At the start of the game the only threat Hitachi faces is from the Uesugi province of Mutsu to the north. As the capital of the Dark Blue empire and the early centre of troop production, the Hojo need to consolidate their position before even entertaining the notion of expansion. As they start with a weak standing army, whether you play the Hojo clan or plot against them, you can be sure that remaining secure within their borders is their highest priority. Note that extensive Iron and Sand deposits also allow the construction of an Armoury.

BATTLE NOTES

There's little to take advantage of when fighting in Hitachi, for this area of Japan consists of a wide, shallow valley with gently sloping sides. If you are defending the province (and most clans will want to invade it), there are high hills to the left and right that can provide a good, steep defensive position. When attacking, try to move your forces around the sides of the map, retaining any height that you initially started with. Remember to "walk" rather than "charge" to your destination and in so doing you can attempt to keep your troops fresh and able for the battle ahead.

HIZEN

VALUE: 408 KOKU
FEATURES: NATURAL HARBOUR (CHEAPER TO BUILD A PORT)
PORT (+200 KOKU FOR IMAGAWA)
BONUS: NONE
HELD BY: CLAN IMAGAWA (CYAN)

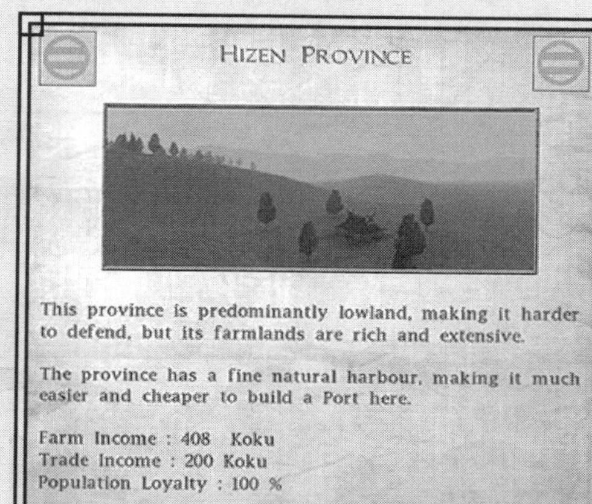

STRATEGIC IMPORTANCE

Protected from Shimazu aggression by the allied provinces of Chikuzen and Chikugo, Hizen is the most valuable of all the Imagawa states. Connected to the eastern lands of Totomi, Mikawa and Suruga via its Port, Hizen contributes an average total of 608 Koku (including the 200 Koku bonus from the Port) to the Cyan war effort each year. If Chikuzen and Chikugo are vital to the Imagawa's continued prosperity (and survival) in the game, then Hizen is doubly so. Not only is it the richest of the six Cyan-controlled regions, but it's also the richest plot of land on the whole Kyushu landmass. As a result, Green will want to acquire it to further its own plans of Japanese domination. And don't rule out a quick do-or-die attack from the Red forces to the east. Sun Tzu taught that triumph often lies in unexpected actions.

BATTLE NOTES

Hizen is a tricky province to mount an attack against, especially if it has a Castle. While the defending force has the advantage of starting on high-ground, the attacking contingent begins the battle on a low plain. Thus, for the attacker, the first objective is to gain some height so it's not vulnerable to the defending force should it decide to sweep down into hasty combat.

There are numerous areas of woodland here too, and attacking generals should take care not to focus on a visible enemy at the expense of those that it can't yet see (i.e. hidden in the trees). Good generals will survey and familiarise themselves with the battlefield before combat takes place. Whether you are attacking or defending, make sure you do the same.

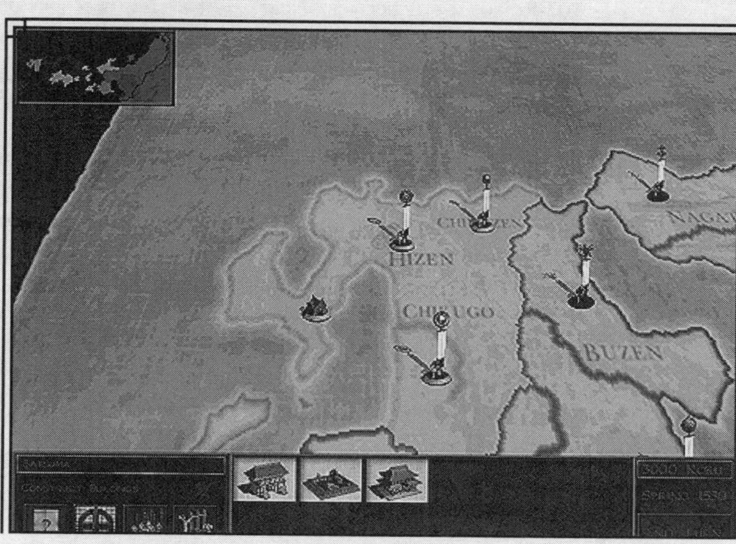

HOKI

VALUE: 103 KOKU
FEATURES: IRON AND SAND DEPOSITS (ARMOURY)
BONUS: NONE
HELD BY: CLAN MORI (RED)

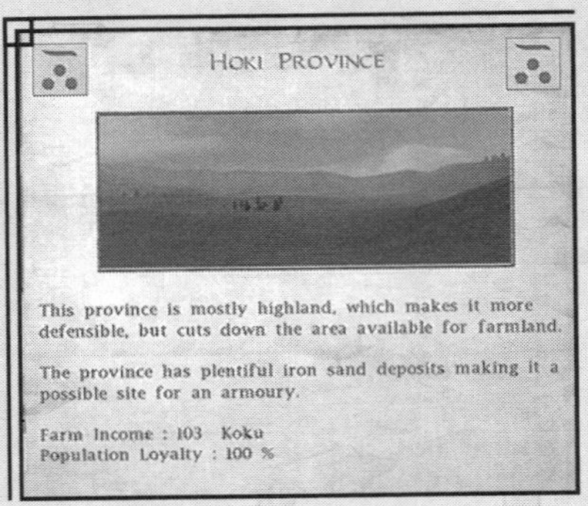

STRATEGIC IMPORTANCE

Like many of the Mori lands, Hoki is a highland area that is of little strategic value since its farmland is relatively poor. Producing a meagre 103 Koku harvest per year, Hoki is not even in a position to halt the charge of an aggressor attacking from the east or west—enemies can simply "go around it" by attacking Bitchu to the south. Nevertheless, considering that the majority of the Mori empire consists of low-yield land, the Red forces need to hold on to every one of them to keep their annual income as high as possible. At the start of a Campaign game, Hoki is useful for mounting attacks against the Takeda-held Bitchu. But once the Mori has wiped out the Black presence here, it becomes an irrelevant state as Red needs to move its forces to defend its western (Suo and Iwami) and eastern (Harima, Inaba) frontiers.

BATTLE NOTES

Like many of these Mori lands, Hoki is a wildly undulating landscape, blessed with several strategic hills even if they are hardly big enough to support an army with more than four units. Wherever you begin the battle for Hoki, the key to success is to position yourself on the biggest hill that you can find. Due to the lowland nature of the ground here, highly mobile units such as cavalry can be particularly effective. As ever, ranged weapon troops can turn the tide of battle, especially if they can make use of the higher points of the battlefield to cause maximum damage.

HYUGA

VALUE: 174 KOKU
FEATURES: NONE
BONUS: NONE
HELD BY: CLAN SHIMAZU (GREEN)

STRATEGIC IMPORTANCE

Contributing 174 Koku in an average year to the Green imperialist cause, Hyuga is a relatively isolated province on the island of Kyushu. Protected from attack by the Green-held states of Higo and Bungo, generals can safely develop this province by building a Castle and subsequently the troop-producing facilities that come with it. Like Osumi to the south, Hyuga is a defensible highland area that makes a good staging point for Shimazu troops. For any opposing armies seeking to conquer the whole of the Kyushu isle, Hyuga is just another stepping stone on the road to Green's total annihilation. Its resources can be boosted by the addition of a Port (as it's a coastal region), but experience suggests that a constant troop presence is rarely needed and forces should be directed elsewhere.

BATTLE NOTES

Hyuga is basically one, long valley with shallow sides. As the attacking force, your units start on the valley floor facing an enemy who is positioned on the hillside directly ahead of you. As usual, by gaining some height for your own troops, you lessen the severity of the combat penalties suffered for fighting uphill. As the defending force, however, you should use the features of the landscape to suit the type of units you are fighting with and against. For example, if the enemy possesses Cavalry units, hide your forces in the trees to break up their formation (there are an abundance of woodland areas for you hide in here).

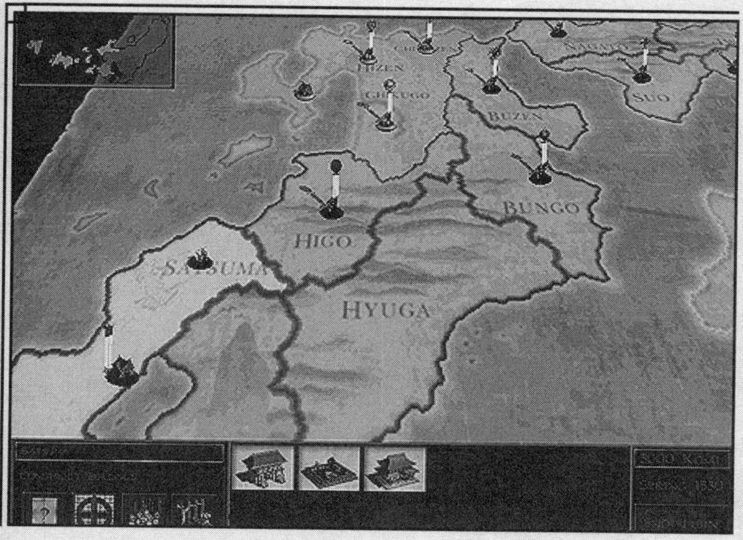

PROVINCES

IGA

VALUE: 120 KOKU
FEATURES: IRON AND SAND DEPOSITS (ARMOURY)
BONUS: THIS PROVINCE IS FAMOUS FOR ITS NINJA; ANY NINJA TRAINED HERE RECEIVE +1 HONOUR
HELD BY: CLAN ODA (GOLD)

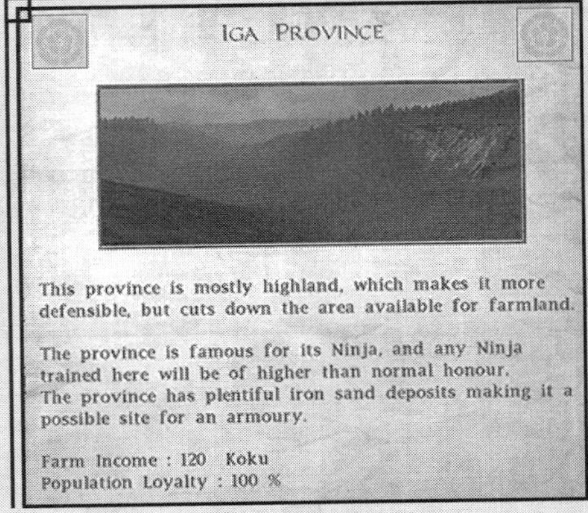

STRATEGIC IMPORTANCE

Again, as this is a predominantly highland area, Iga's agricultural yield ranks amongst the worst in the game. Yet it does, however, have several advantages that make it a vital part of the Oda empire and difficult to conquer. Located in the heart of the Gold zone, Iga faces potential trouble from the two Rebel-held states of Ise and Yamashiro. Close to the Oda supply centre at Owari, Iga not only has Iron and Sand deposits (allowing construction of an Armoury), but it is a region that is also famed for the skills of its Ninja. Thus, once a player has built a Castle and a Ninja House here, any assassins trained within its borders automatically receive +1 to their honour level. For these reasons, Iga represents an attractive target for any would-be invading army. But it should mostly be used by the Oda to funnel new troops from Owari to the western frontiers of Kawachi and Tamba.

BATTLE NOTES

Sun Tzu talked about the importance of height in his military essay, *The Art of War*, and using height to your advantage is crucial. Iga, therefore, is a joy to fight on, a highland area blessed with the sort of open plains and generous hills that make attacking and defending that little bit easier. If you are playing the role of the attacker in this province, you'll hardly be astonished to learn that the enemy will find a good hill and sit on it in anticipation of your arrival. The usual rules of hill-storming therefore apply. As the defender, you have a wide choice of slopes (some with trees, some without) to arrange your forces on. Arguably, the composition of your forces is much more important than whether one hill is better to fight on than another.

INABA

VALUE: 125 KOKU
FEATURES: IRON AND SAND DEPOSITS (ARMOURY)
BONUS: NONE
HELD BY: CLAN MORI (RED)

INABA PROVINCE

This province is mostly highland, which makes it more defensible, but cuts down the area available for farmland.

The province has plentiful iron sand deposits making it a possible site for an armoury.

Farm Income : 125 Koku
Population Loyalty : 100 %

STRATEGIC IMPORTANCE

Like Iwami, Izumo and Hoki, Inaba is another highland province, its farmland limited by the undulating terrain. So while defending forces can make use of its high ground to win battles with less troops than their opponents, Inaba contributes a measly 125 Koku on average to the Mori treasury. Similar to many of the other Red-held lands, Inaba features extensive Iron and Sand deposits, the raw materials required to construct an Armoury. Initially, Inaba is only threatened by the presence of the self-contained rogue enclave of Tajima. The Rebels and Ronin that control this coastal province, however, will rarely trouble the Mori borderland. Instead, Mori commanders should reinforce Inaba to protect Mimaska, the Mori's troop-producing centre, from the ruthless and often chaotic plans of the Oda to the east.

BATTLE NOTES

By pausing for a few minutes as each battle begins, you can determine (a) where the enemy is, (b) what he's doing (i.e. holding position or advancing), and (c) what tactic you should use to combat the situation. Inaba, for example, is a wide bowl-valley and by tracing the mouse cursor over the visible hilltops, it's fairly easy to locate the enemy forces. If you're playing the attacker here and you spot the defenders advancing, then you should set up a defensive position while you have the time. Similarly, if you are defending the Inaba province, you should watch the enemy approach from a safe vantage point and then adjust your defensive stance appropriately.

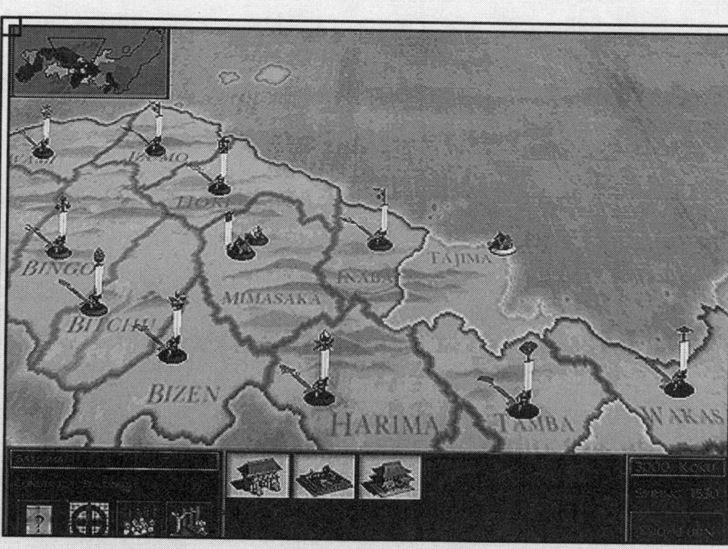

ISE

VALUE: 440 KOKU
FEATURES: NONE
BONUS: NONE
HELD BY: REBELS (SILVER)

STRATEGIC IMPORTANCE

Infesting the belly of the golden Oda empire, Ise is yet another one of the well protected, self-contained Rebel states that are dotted across ancient Japan. Predominantly lowland, the agricultural yield in Ise (440 Koku) is temptingly high. If this can be boosted by investment in the farmland and by building a Port, Ise can become a very wealthy province. The big test for any invading army, however, is whether they are strong enough to attack and conquer it. Even as a new Campaign game begins, Ise boasts its own Castle, Archery Dojo and Buddhist Temple allowing it to produce Samurai Archers and Warrior Monks by the cartload. Strong enough to withstand an early Oda attack, Ise should not be left to expand its defensive forces. Because once the Castle capacity has been exceeded, the extra troops will look to make trouble in neighbouring lands.

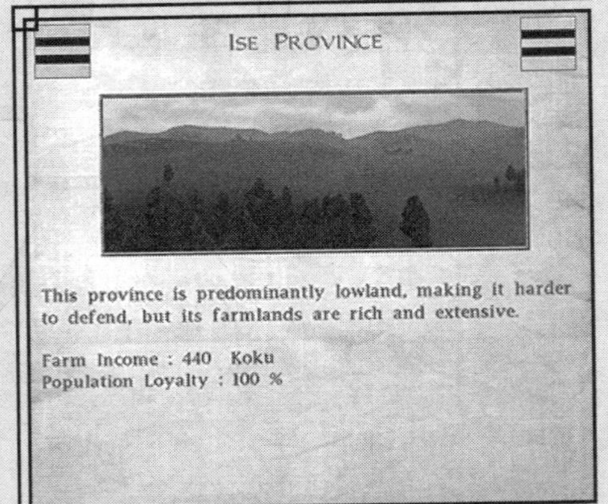

BATTLE NOTES

Because of its 440 Koku yield, Ise's landscape is predominantly lowland, with gentle (often useless) undulations and larger, strategically placed hills. Playing the attacker in Ise, you start on the raised ground to the south, while the enemy occupies the raised ground to the north. What you don't want to do is to get caught on the valley floor, but even this advice will depend on what sort of units you are using. If you have Cavalry Archers, for example, you can use them to harry the advancing enemy, while Heavy Cavalry operates better on flat ground than they do on hillsides. As the defender, have faith in your ranged weapon units. But make sure you have sufficient Footsoldiers to counterattack any attacking sword- or spearmen who get too close.

IWAMI

VALUE: 120 KOKU
FEATURES: IRON AND SAND DEPOSITS (ARMOURY)
BONUS: NONE
HELD BY: CLAN MORI (RED)

STRATEGIC IMPORTANCE

Located on the western frontier of the Red Mori empire, Iwami initially acts as a buffer against the expansionist intentions of the Shimazu who stubbornly hold Nagato nearby. For Red, continued possession of Iwami is vital if it wants to hold back a Green advance to the west and a Black advance to the south. With Iron and Sand deposits (allowing the construction of an Armoury), the meagre 120 Koku yield doesn't seem quite so poor. To make best use of it, Red should mount a lightning raid into Aki (aided by troops from Suo), swiftly capturing the Black-held state and taking control of the Port that links the Takeda colonies to Izu and Kai to the east. If undertaken during the first season of the first year, Red can have captured Aki, destroyed its Castle, and be moving onto Bingo and Bitchu before the end of 1530.

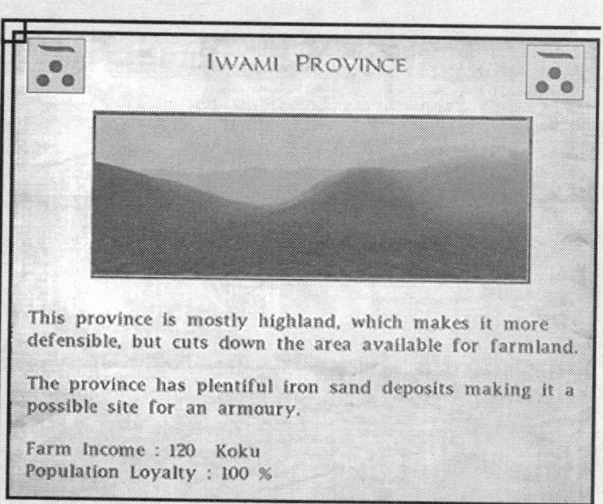

BATTLE NOTES

The low Koku yield indicates the presence of some varied terrain and Iwami's bleak landscape features everything from flat plains to high hills covered with dense forest. Starting as the attacker, your view of the battlefield is limited due to a huge hill. Chances are, you may not be able to march to and up this particular feature before the enemy are upon you. So instead, turn right and climb the steep hill nearby, marching your forces slowly toward the high wooded area. From here, you should be able to locate the enemy and defend yourself if necessary. To pursue a wounded foe, take care to keep to the high ground just in case the AI is faking a retreat; such a tactic has been programmed in by the designers.

IYO

VALUE: 220 KOKU
FEATURES: COPPER DEPOSITS
(MINE: +200 KOKU PER YEAR)
BONUS: NONE
HELD BY: REBELS (SILVER)

STRATEGIC IMPORTANCE

This highland province is one of five that make up the rebellious mini-empire that spans the isles of Shikoku and Awaji. Supplied with troops from the Rebel Castle in Tosa, Iyo proves to be an attractive target thanks to a reasonable yearly harvest (220 Koku) and Copper deposits that can add an extra 200 Koku per year to the total. While the Rebels will rarely attack any of the seven clans (unless a clan land is weakly defended), they will stockpile troops to rebuff any raids from the Green-held Bungo to the west. For the Shimazu, Iyo represents a much less costly route eastward than fighting across the Mori-held peninsula to the north. It's worth noting, however, that only by destroying the Castle in Tosa, can the Rebel threat be damaged and defeated.

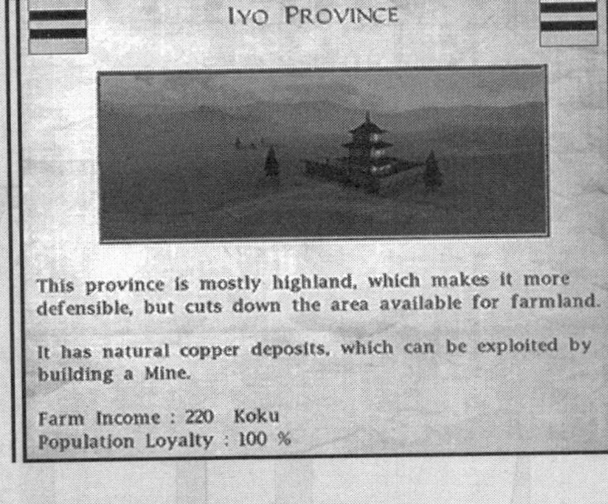

BATTLE NOTES

Iyo gives you the chance to fight in a wide valley, its gentle, sloping sides slowly rising to much steeper hillsides. As the attacker, your forces start on the flat plain, while the defending force has picked a low-lying hill nearby. If you decide to stay true to Sun Tzu's poetic ideals (i.e. sprint for higher ground), then your actions will undoubtedly cause a rethink in the enemy's strategy. If the AI thinks that it can beat you, the defending army will march boldly forward without a care for ancient Chinese tactics. If, however, the odds don't look favourable, the AI will attempt to fall back and regroup somewhere a little higher.

IZU

VALUE: 70 KOKU
FEATURES: NONE
BONUS: NONE
HELD BY: CLAN TAKEDA (BLACK)

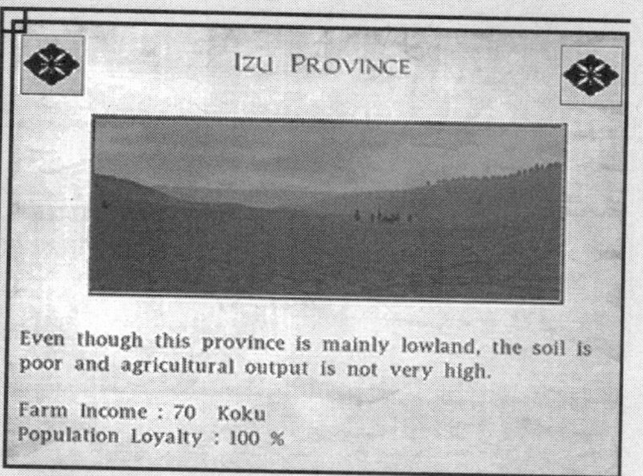

STRATEGIC IMPORTANCE

As one of the six Takeda provinces, Izu is arguably the least important. Although mostly a lowland region, the soil has been over-farmed and it barely manages to contribute more than 70 Koku to fund the Black armies. Located on its own at the foot of the western Takeda realm, Izu is the perfect place to establish a Castle and troop-producing facilities. Unlike Kai that faces the Hojo to the east, Imagawa to the west, and the Uesugi to the north, Izu isn't threatened with immediate invasion. Take advantage of its isolation to establish a strong defensive province, especially if a stronger army rolls over both Kai and Sagami (cutting off links to the three lands—Aki, Bitchu and Bingo—in the west).

BATTLE NOTES

As a lowland region, Izu's terrain is a combination of flat plains and small hills. This province also features two main areas of woodland—one to the left, one to the right. He who climbs highest shoots the farthest, and you can bet that the computer AI has arranged the enemy soldiers in ordered ranks on a nearby hillside. It expects you to march straight toward its forces, so make it shift position by marching in an unexpected direction—straight up the nearest hill, for example. Even when you are the attacker, if you can force the enemy to come to you, you'll have more control over how the battle unfolds.

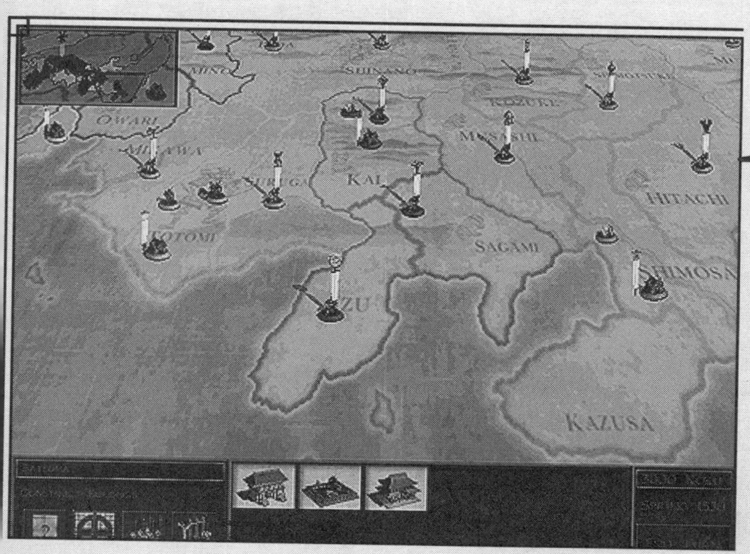

IZUMO

VALUE: 143 KOKU
FEATURES: IRON AND SAND DEPOSITS (ARMOURY)
BONUS: NONE
HELD BY: CLAN MORI (RED)

STRATEGIC IMPORTANCE

Part of the Red empire that borders the Takeda colonies in the west, Izumo is a region of harsh highland with little room for farmland. Consequently, farmers find it difficult to eke out more than 143 Koku from the soil per year, although good harvests can boost this amount by up to 50 percent. Facing Bingo, Aki and Bitchu to the south, Izumo is of little strategic importance beyond its basic agricultural contribution. Later in the game, however, whoever controls this bleak region can make use of the extensive Iron and Sand deposits to construct an Armoury. Such a building will thereby improve the defensive might of any units that are produced there.

IZUMO PROVINCE

This province is mostly highland, which makes it more defensible, but cuts down the area available for farmland.

The province has plentiful iron sand deposits making it a possible site for an armoury.

Farm Income : 143 Koku
Population Loyalty : 100 %

BATTLE NOTES

Faced with a long, thin valley (otherwise known as a "death trap"), the best way to locate the enemy in Izumo is to trudge up the steep hill immediately to the left of the attacker's start position. The best defensive location on the map is in the southwest corner—a steep incline with a strip of trees at the top. Whether you play the defending force or the invaders, the battle will probably take place across a valley with both sides stubbornly perched on hilltops waiting for the other to make the first move. As ever, don't get drawn into a melee on the valley floor.

KAGA

VALUE: 200 KOKU
FEATURES: NONE
BONUS: THIS PROVINCE IS FAMOUS FOR ITS SHRINES AND WARRIOR MONKS. ANY MONKS TRAINED HERE RECEIVE +1 HONOUR.
HELD BY: REBELS (SILVER)

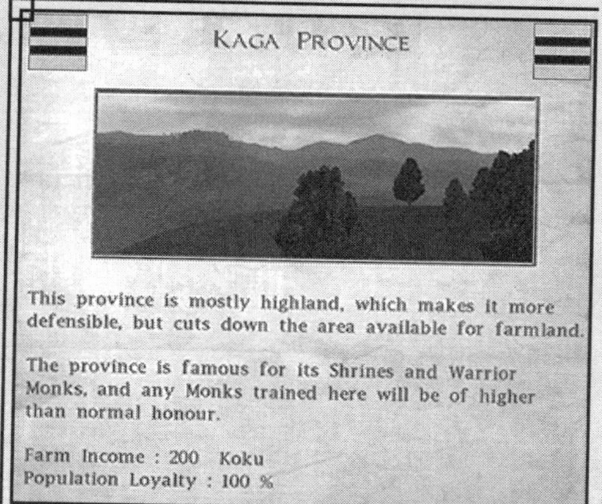

STRATEGIC IMPORTANCE

One of a quartet of rebellious provinces that includes Echizen, Noto and Etchu, Kaga is the troop-producing core of this rogue mini-empire. As such, it may not be the most Koku-rich province in central Japan (yielding 200 Koku in an average year), but it has some significant advantages to the Rebels that are camped there. Most importantly, Kaga is a region that is famous for its Warrior Monks and any that are produced here automatically receive a +1 honour bonus. It's depressing news, therefore, that Kaga already possesses a Castle, Archery Dojo and Buddhist Temple as a Campaign game begins. And while it can only be attacked directly via Hida (initially owned by the Uesugi), any attempt to invade Echizen or Etchu will not be tolerated by the Kaga renegades. It's also worth noting that, if you plan to attack Dewa via the back door (i.e. through Sado), you have to conquer the fiercely defended Kaga first.

BATTLE NOTES

Kaga is a harsh landscape, a chaotic mix of low hills and towering cliff faces. The defending force will start on the highest point of the terrain—by waiting a few moments you should be able to spot them "coming round the mountain" in the distance. By remembering the simple, but effective rules of combat, you should easily be able to engage and defeat the force sent against you. Obviously, this won't work if you throw 25 Ashigaru against 560 Warrior Monks. As usual, the type of forces you use determine how you handle the combat.

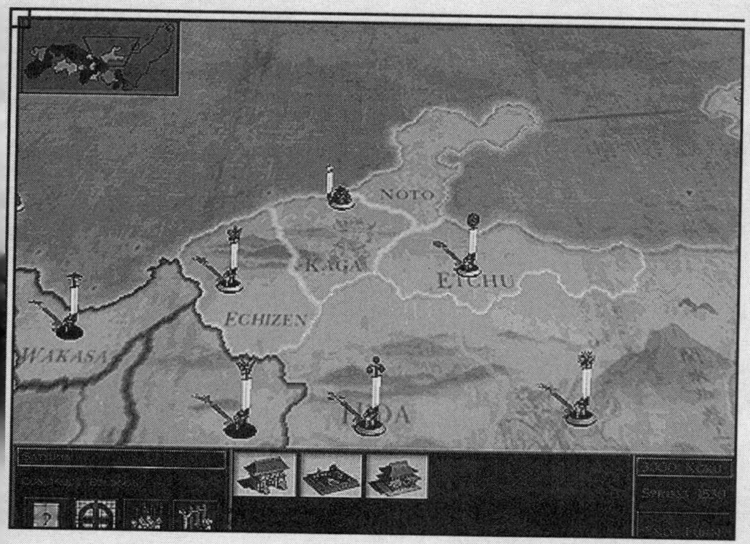

KAI

VALUE: 200 KOKU
FEATURES: GOLD DEPOSITS
(MINE: +600 KOKU PER YEAR)
BONUS: NONE
HELD BY: CLAN TAKEDA (BLACK)

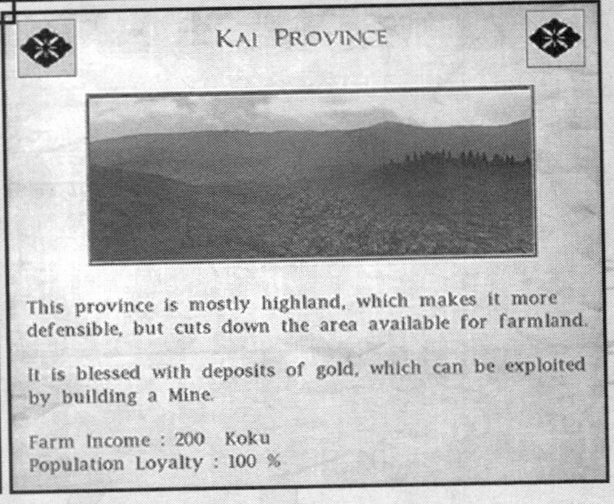

STRATEGIC IMPORTANCE

As the cornerstone of the Takeda empire, Kai sits precariously between the Imagawa land of Suruga, the Uesugi province of Shinano and the Hojo territory of Musashi. Predominantly a highland region, the lack of extensive farmland means that the average agricultural yield is limited to 200 Koku per year. But it's not all doom and 16th Century gloom for these Japanese men in Black. Kai is home to the Takeda Daimyo and features the basic Castle, Archery Dojo, Spear Dojo and Tranquil Garden. In addition, the Black-clad Samurai are famed for their cavalry units and to offset the fact that Takeda only have six provinces, Kai begins the game with a Horse Dojo. Add to all this the fact that there's Gold in them thar Kai hills, and it's no wonder that the Takeda will fight to the death to defend this territory.

BATTLE NOTES

There's barely a stretch of flat land in Kai province and so it's a race to see who can claim the high ground first—the attackers or the defenders. Usually it's no contest as the computer AI will have already set out its forces on the most defensible mountain top. While it's suicide to approach and attack from the front, a flanking manoeuvre (i.e. creeping around the side) ensures that you remain in control and retain a height advantage until battle is joined. Again, the most effective form of attack is also the most effective form of defence. Employ a mix of ranged weapon and hand-to-hand forces so that the enemy can be attacked from a variety of angles and distances.

KAWACHI

VALUE: 220 KOKU
FEATURES: NONE
BONUS: NONE
HELD BY: CLAN ODA (GOLD)

STRATEGIC IMPORTANCE

This lowland Oda territory is in a prime strategic position. In the hands of the Golden armies, it serves as a front-line outpost for operations against both the Mori in Harima and the Rebels on Awaji. Contributing an average of around 220 Koku per year to the Oda treasury, Kawachi is typical of this sort of province that makes up the Gold empire. Blessed with a river system, which makes the territory more defendable than most, a strong Kawachi can block both expansion via Shikoku to the west, and from the Mori-held lands to the north. If the Mori want to push southward, lured perhaps by Kii's reputation for Warrior Monks, it must invade Kawachi or head south via the Rebel-held Yamashiro. If neither of these appeal, a well-fortified and garrisoned Kawachi will force enemy troops to go around the lake via Tamba, Wakasa and Omi. If Kawachi falls, the Oda's hopes of expansion go with it.

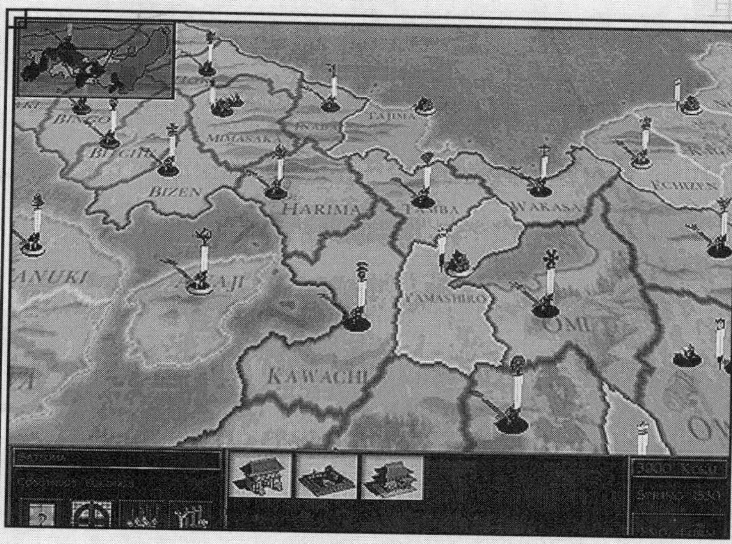

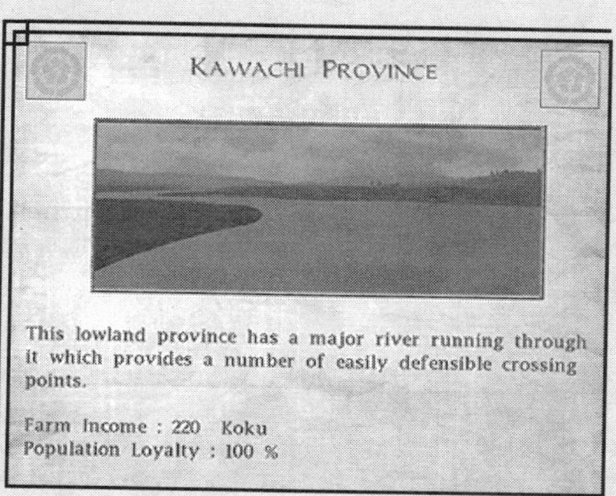

BATTLE NOTES

With only a single bridge spanning the river here, it helps to customise your forces before you send them into attack. For example, as the attacker you can attempt to limit your casualties during the crossing by sending heavily armed Naginata over the narrow bridge first. While as the defender, the more ranged weapon units you have, the more damage you can inflict as the enemy crosses. By instructing an Ashigaru unit to hold the bridge, you can keep an attacking force pinned down on it while Archers decimate their numbers with volleys of arrows.

KAZUSA

VALUE: 190 KOKU
FEATURES: NONE
BONUS: THIS PROVINCE IS FAMOUS FOR ITS EMISSARIES. ANY EMISSARIES TRAINED HERE RECEIVE +1 HONOUR.
HELD BY: CLAN HOJO (PURPLE)

STRATEGIC IMPORTANCE

An invading army has to fight through two Hojo lands before it can conquer Kazusa, no matter which direction it approaches from. It's a shame then that this far-flung province isn't a little more exciting. Admittedly, it has a reputation for producing highly trained Emissaries, but its average harvest (190 Koku) hardly makes it a tempting target for an aggressive power. If you're commanding the Hojo clan, so much the better. Like Satsuma to the west and Dewa to the northeast, Kazusa is safe from enemy aggression, the perfect place to build another Large Castle and extra troop-producing facilities. In the early stages of a new Campaign game, the Hojo will not need to garrison Kasuza and can move any troops stationed there to bolster the defences in other parts of the empire.

BATTLE NOTES

Half lowland plain, half highland hills, Kazusa is weighted toward the defending army which has the advantage of starting on the higher ground to the south. For the attacker, there's little natural cover to make use of and, dependent on the actions of the defending army, it may be worth retreating to the edge of the map and digging in on the slight rise there. Otherwise, march either left or right and attempt to approach the defenders' position from the side.

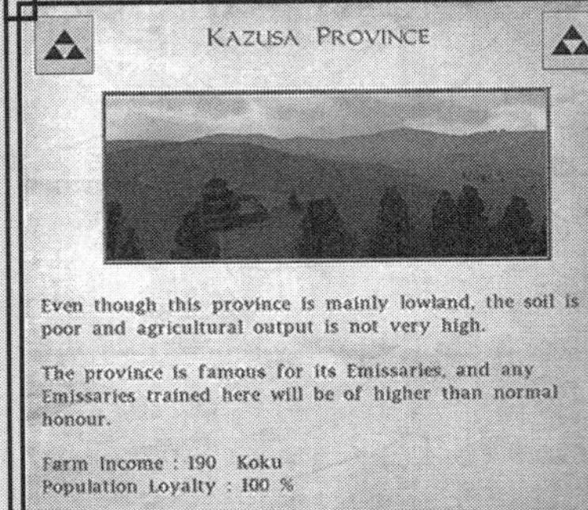

KII

VALUE: 270 KOKU
FEATURES: NONE
BONUS: FAMOUS FOR ITS SHRINES AND WARRIOR MONKS. ANY MONKS TRAINED HERE RECEIVE +1 HONOUR.
HELD BY: CLAN ODA (GOLD)

STRATEGIC IMPORTANCE

Located deep within the heart of the Oda empire, Kii faces only a distant threat of invasion from the Rebel-held province of Ise to the east. Contributing a reasonable 270 Koku per annum to the Oda's Golden war machine, its strategic importance is boosted significantly by the fact that it produces Warrior Monks who are even more fanatical than usual. Specifically, any Warrior Monks produced in this region (requires Tranquil Garden, Large Castle and Buddhist Temple) will automatically receive a +1 honour bonus. The Oda can rest easy with the fact that, due to its geographical location, Kii should not require a heavy garrison as long as Kawachi, Yamato, Omi and Iga resist invasion around it.

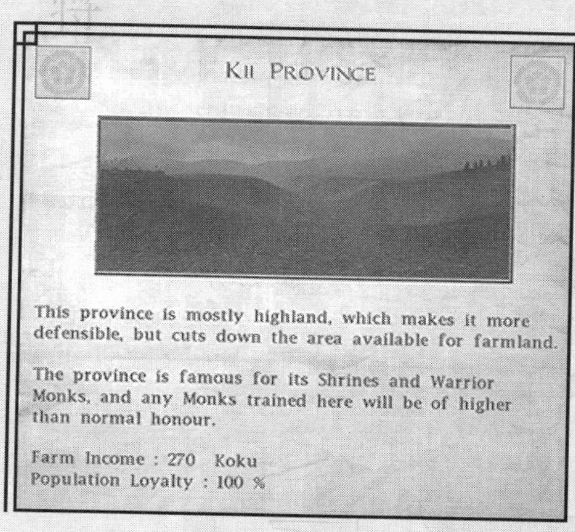

BATTLE NOTES

The Kii province is characterised by a small, snaking valley that cuts through the landscape much like an empty river bed. If you are attacking this province, you'll find that the computer AI sets up the defenders at the bottom of the map in front of a circular wooded area. Either approach their location from the side or cross over the valley to advance on them directly, keeping the valley safely between you and them. You might have a little time to order your troops into an appropriate formation before the enemy samurai mass for an attack.

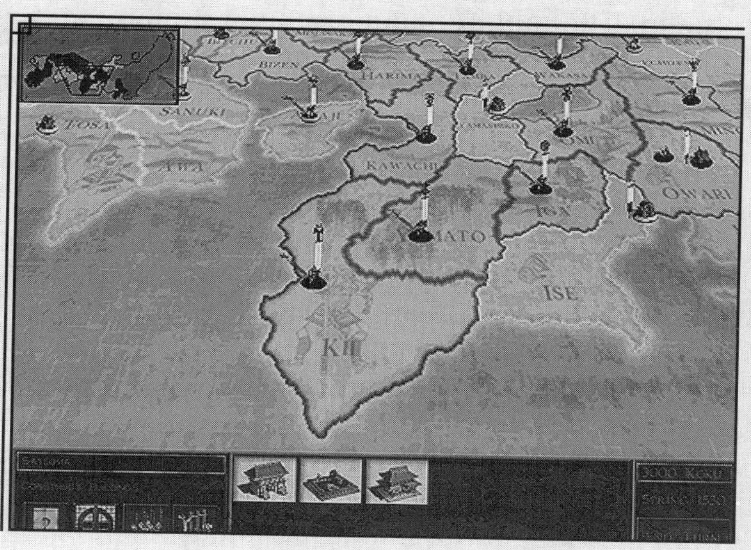

KOZUKE

VALUE: 410 KOKU
FEATURES: NONE
BONUS: NONE
HELD BY: CLAN HOJO (PURPLE)

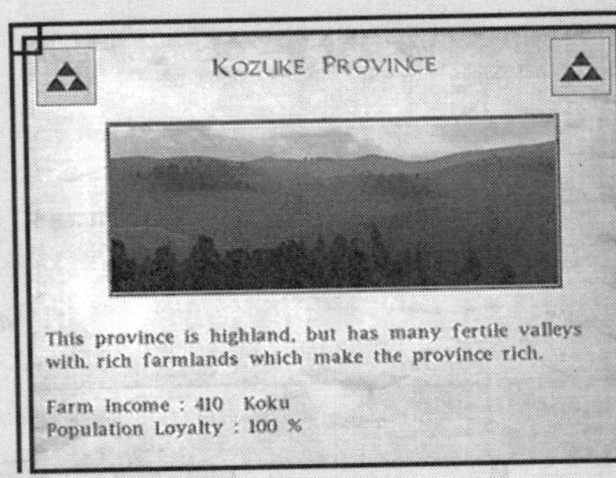

STRATEGIC IMPORTANCE

Of all the Hojo provinces, Kozuke is by far the most vulnerable in the long term. Although Musashi nearby needs to be quickly reinforced to rebuff the attempts of Black to steal it, Kozuke is surrounded by Uesugi states. Bordered by Shinano, Echigo and Mutsu, it could be attacked by any one of them. It's therefore vitally important that Hojo commanders protect the 410 Koku income here just as efficiently as they do the 620 Koku in Hitachi and the 640 Koku from Musashi. If it can retain all of its provinces, even an average harvest brings in 2,360 Koku, more than any other clan in Japan. The Hojo desperately need all this ready cash as they begin the game with one of the smallest and weakest armies. Kozuke, however, should be safe from the Uesugi hordes as they will probably have their hands full defending Shinano, which allows its owner to recruit higher than normal honour Cavalry units.

BATTLE NOTES

In contrast to all the bleak highland provinces in the western part of Japan, the eastern lands are predominantly lowland areas, dotted with small hills and woods. Kozuke is no exception and the key to surviving here, whether you are attacking or defending, is to use what high ground there is to your advantage. Even on the flattest of terrain, there are always slopes and inclines that can be used to maximise the damage that you do to an enemy. Remember, however, to make sure that you have the right combination of units to do the job required. It's no use investing heavily in Archers, for example, if you don't have any Yari samurai or Yari Ashigaru units to charge into the survivors who escape the hail of arrow-fire.

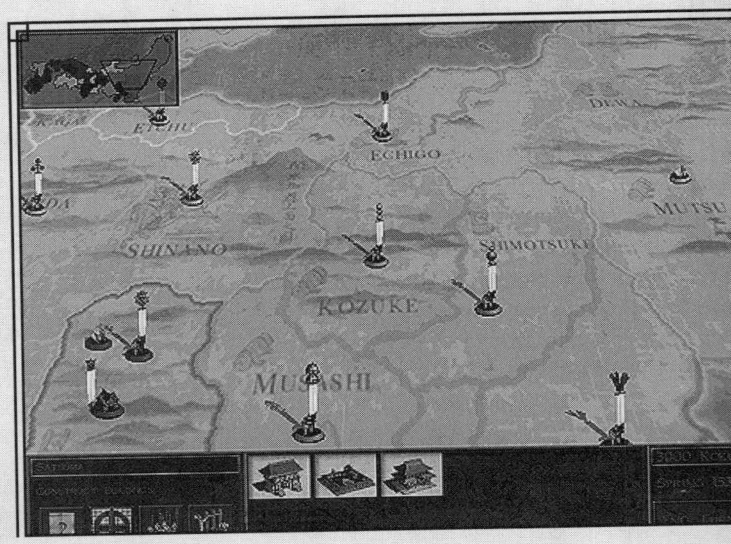

MIKAWA

VALUE: 260 KOKU
FEATURES: NONE
BONUS: NONE
HELD BY: CLAN IMAGAWA (CYAN)

MIKAWA PROVINCE

This lowland province has a major river running through it which provides a number of easily defensible crossing points.

Farm Income : 260 Koku
Population Loyalty : 100 %

STRATEGIC IMPORTANCE

If you're commanding the Imagawa clan, *all* six of your provinces can be deemed strategically important. Mikawa, located on the Japanese mainland divides the Cyan forces from the war-mongering Oda in the west and the stretched forces of the Uesugi to the north. As has been mentioned in the descriptions of Chikugo, Hizen and Chikuzen, the Imagawa cannot afford to lose any of their lands. For even the loss of a province like Mikawa would seriously affect the clan's resources and subsequently its chances of maintaining military parity with its neighbours. Contributing 260 Koku on average per game year, Mikawa is an unremarkable territory. Its position, next to the Oda capital, Owari, makes it instantly vulnerable should troop levels fall. This cannot be allowed to happen, as the Imagawa need Mikawa as a buffer state between the Oda and the clan's troop-producing facilities in Totomi. Fortunately, thanks to the river, the region is well suited to a heroic defence.

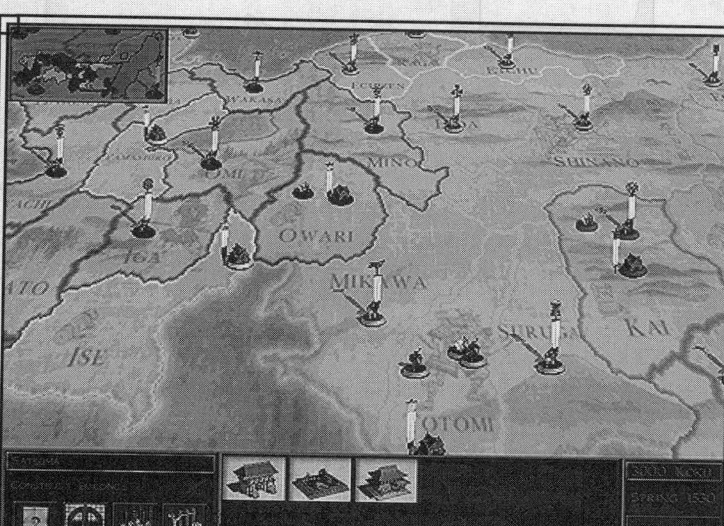

BATTLE NOTES

River crossings are always tricky, especially if you haven't developed some of the stronger units that make the whole thing a little easier. At its most basic level, a mixture of Yari Ashigaru and Yari samurai, supported by samurai Archers is a good combination. The Ashigaru run across to tempt the enemy into attacking, drawing them into the range of the Archers standing safely on the opposite bank. When the Ashigaru have been sacrificed, the Yari samurai can then attack the weakened enemy lines, hoping to force them into a retreat. Once this is achieved, the Archers can move across the bridge and the pursuit can begin. At the other end of the scale, line up Archers to shoot at the enemy force and use armoured Naginata to attack (they are less vulnerable to ranged weapons fire).

MIMASAKA

VALUE: 123 KOKU
FEATURES: IRON AND SAND DEPOSITS (ARMOURY)
BONUS: NONE
HELD BY: CLAN MORI (RED)

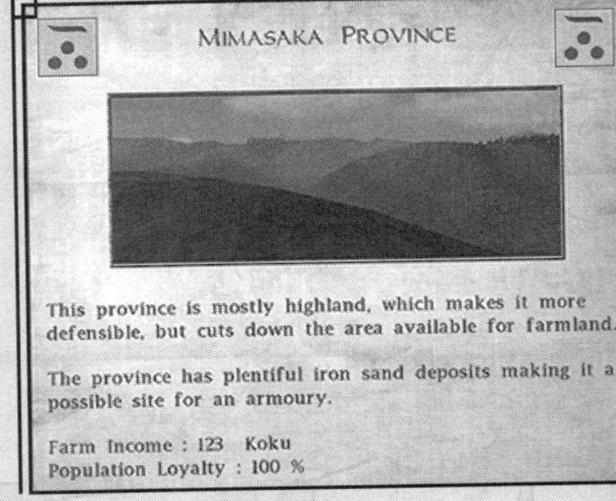

STRATEGIC IMPORTANCE

Despite its poor farmland and the 123 Koku average a year, Mimasaka starts the game as the most important Mori land. In addition to its rich Iron and Sand deposits (making construction of an Armoury possible), the province is home to the main Mori Castle, plus Archery and Spear Dojos. Only Harima to the south has the potential to replace Mimasaka in the long term, but not until the Mori has extended their borders by pushing the Oda from Tamba and Kawachi. As the game begins, Mimasaka is home to the Mori Daimyo, and the troops stationed here are in a good position to launch a surprise attack on Bitchu while forces from Suo and Iwami move into Aki. Once Bingo is secured and the peninsula has been conquered, Mimasaka is in a relatively safe position to expand its facilities.

BATTLE NOTES

Mimasaka is a land of valleys and hills and, as usual, your first strategic decision should be which hill to march up. Experience shows that the nearest hill is often the best, and if it isn't, at least it will give you a good vantage point from which to spot a better one. Here in Mimasaka, expect the computer to defend the highest hill that the landscape has to offer. If this does happen, direct your men to the hill nearest the enemy, whereupon the opposing general will adjust his position to take into account your new location. And if this means marching straight toward you, so be it.

MINO

VALUE: 260 KOKU
FEATURES: IRON AND SAND DEPOSITS (ARMOURY)
BONUS: NONE
HELD BY: CLAN ODA (GOLD)

STRATEGIC IMPORTANCE

As one of the Oda family's more profitable provinces, Mino sits on the eastern frontier, holding back the Uesugi forces that have pushed as far as Hida. Close to Owari, the Oda capital, Mino is also faced with the prospect of having to deal with the renegade territories to the north. Echizen, Kaga, Noto and Etchu may be quiet when the game begins, but the longer these rebellious states are left to their own devices, the harder it is to get rid of them. Notable for its Iron and Sand deposits (allowing the construction of an Armoury), this predominantly highland region is not only important to the Oda's long-term plans for eastward expansion, but it's a target for all those clans who want to invade a profitable territory on their march west.

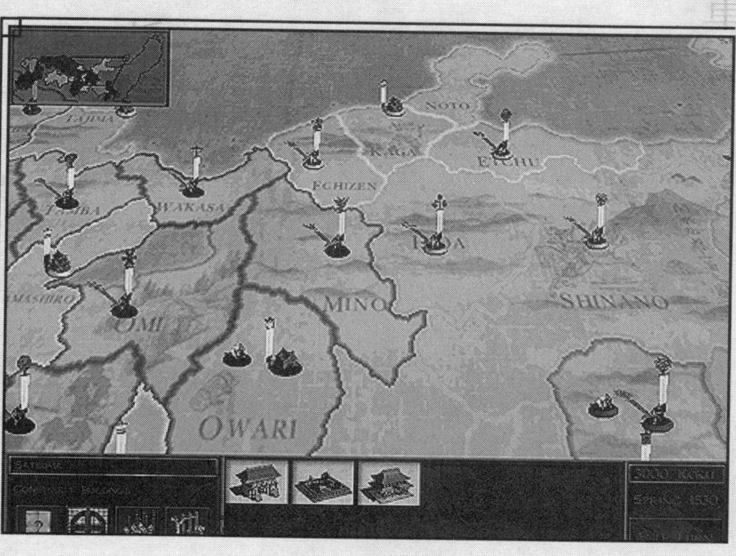

BATTLE NOTES

Mino is a landscape of two halves. At one end the terrain is high and mountainous. But beyond the pass that lies ahead of the attacker's starting position, the landscape levels out and becomes a shallow valley. Obviously, veteran campaigners will realise that using the high ground will make attacks more effective and deadly. Archers have a wider field of view and greater range, while Footsoldiers battle better against an opponent who is forced to fight uphill.

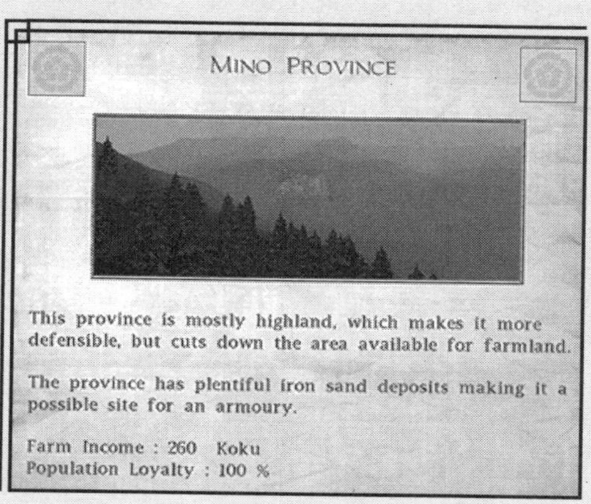

MUSASHI

VALUE: 640 KOKU
FEATURES: NONE
BONUS: NONE
HELD BY: CLAN HOJO (PURPLE)

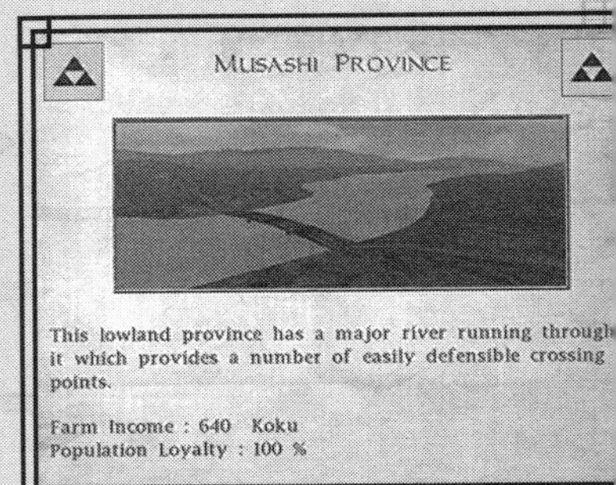

STRATEGIC IMPORTANCE

Musashi generates 640 Koku per year—important enough for you? If you do step into the sandals of the Hojo Daimyo, you won't want to lose Musashi. And if the Black Takeda forces detect the slightest weakness in the first few years, they'll charge in with all of the horse cavalry they've got. The only way to guard against this potential disaster is to move as many troops as you can into the province. In essence, the Hojo's five-year plan is a repetitive period of consolidation, recruiting troops in such numbers that the Takeda can't commit to an attack without leaving some of their other lands vulnerable to a counter-invasion. Like Hitachi to the east, Musashi would benefit from a program of farmland improvement. Even a 20 percent increase boosts the Koku-haul to 768.

BATTLE NOTES

Fighting for Musashi involves mastering the fine art of bridge crossing. As the attacker, you must be able to assault the enemy units defending the bridge, overcome them, before finally crossing the bridge to chase any survivors off of the map. Most importantly, you want to do this and, at the same time, suffer as few casualties as possible. As the defender, on the other hand, you ideally need to stop the attacker crossing the bridge at all. But if you can't do this (and nine times out of ten you can't), you need to inflict as much damage on the enemy ranks as possible. Should the attacker actually cross the bridge in sufficient numbers, you will then need to retreat to a nearby hill to begin the next phase of your rear-guard action.

MUTSU

VALUE: 600 KOKU
FEATURES: NONE
BONUS: NONE
HELD BY: CLAN UESUGI (DARK BLUE)

STRATEGIC IMPORTANCE

Just as Musashi and Hitachi are vital to the financial well-being of the Hojo clan, so Mutsu is crucial to the prosperity of the Uesugi. Bringing in a massive 600 Koku per year on average, Mutsu is the biggest single territory in Japan, a giant rolling landscape of hills and fertile valleys. More importantly, it's also the Uesugi capital and home to the basic buildings that a Daimyo needs to get started on the road to total domination. It's in a reasonably safe location too—neighbouring Hojo lands Hitachi and Shimotsuke will concentrate on their own defence rather than invasion, and can't muster enough troops early on to fight and win. The only problem a Uesugi Daimyo has is the fact that the clan's troop-producing facilities are at one end of the empire. A savvy general will build castles in Echigo and Shinano as soon as possible.

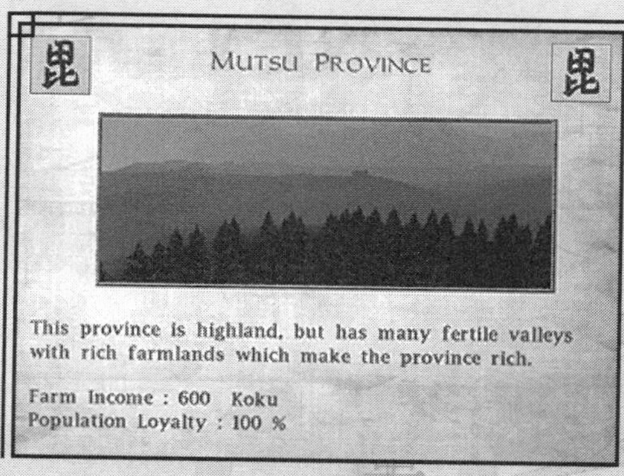

BATTLE NOTES

Bleak and almost featureless, Mutsu certainly lives up to its reputation of being a land of rolling hills and valleys. Provinces such as this are arguably much easier to fight on than the flatter lowland areas, where superior force counts for more than tactics. Sun Tzu suggested that a good general will manoeuvre his enemy into a losing position before the battle even starts. You can do this here by positioning your forces in such a way that the enemy must march down the shallow valley to get to you. Once again, you are taking advantage of the high ground while your opponent struggles below.

NAGATO

VALUE: 139 KOKU
FEATURES: IRON (ARMOURY)
BONUS: NONE
HELD BY: CLAN SHIMAZU (GREEN)

将軍

STRATEGIC IMPORTANCE

For Green and Light Blue, Nagato can acts as the gateway to the east, a beachhead in an expansionist push towards Red-held territory and beyond. As a coastal province with good Iron deposits, the clan that holds the Nagato lands will be able to benefit from their ability to host a Port and an Armoury. For Green, Nagato is a strong foothold on the mainland, a buffer against any attack from the Red Mori clan to the east. For Green and Light Blue clans, Nagato represents one of the only two routes off the isolated island of Kyushu—the other being via the Rebel-held isle to the south. For Red, conquering Nagato limits the vulnerability of the Daimyo's western border to one province rather than two (Suo and Iwami). Beware however, Green will not tolerate its loss.

将軍

BATTLE NOTES

With a low agricultural yield, Nagato is strategically rather than economically important. The landscape itself is a bowl valley—a wide, natural plain edged by steep, defensible hills. Any attacker will have to face the prospect of starting on the low plain and facing an enemy typically dug in on the high ground (usually taking advantage of the tree cover). The trick, as ever, is to march an attacking army onto the hills to either the left or right of their position, minimising the attack penalties and perhaps forcing the opposing general to abandon his initial starting position. Defending the Nagato province is somewhat easier; keep Archers and Footsoldiers in formation on the steepest incline that you can find and use the height to your advantage.

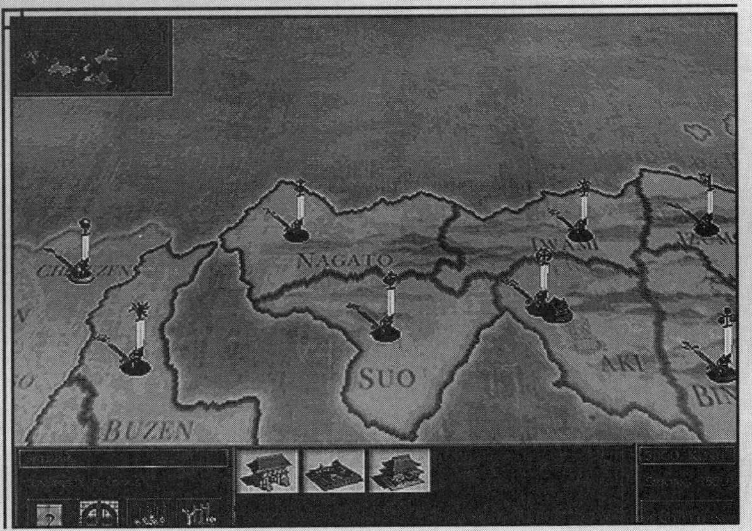

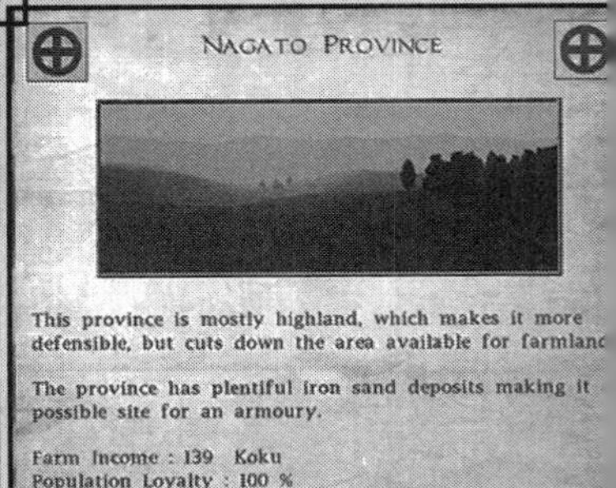

NOTO

VALUE: 100
FEATURES: NONE
BONUS: NONE
HELD BY: REBELS (SILVER)

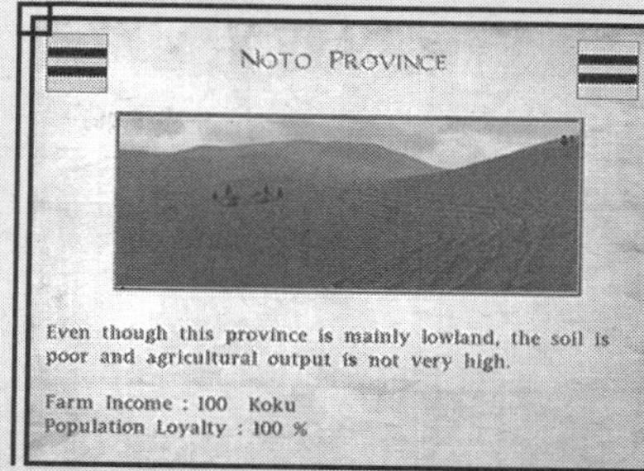

STRATEGIC IMPORTANCE

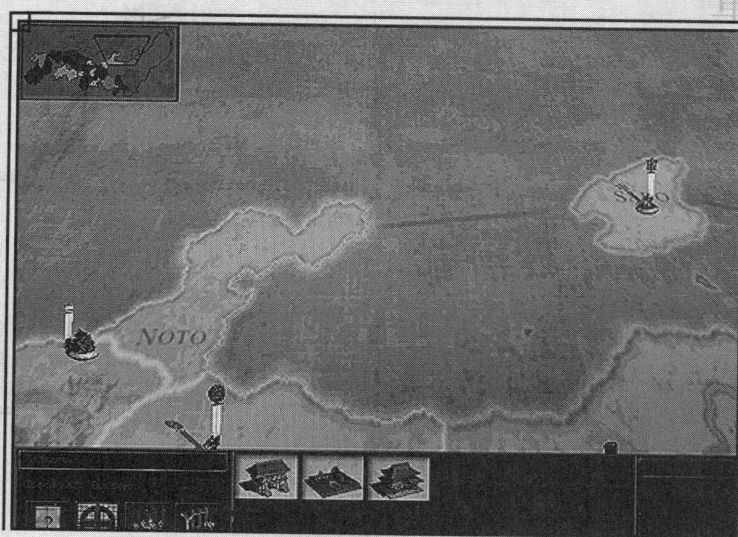

Situated in the far north of the Japanese mainland, Noto is one of four Rebel-held states that have formed their own independent mini-empire. Noto, like Echizen and Etchu nearby, seems to take its orders from Kaga, where the renegades have not only built a Castle, but constructed an Archery Dojo and founded a Buddhist Temple. Unless you happen to be attacking Noto from the Uesugi-held Dewa via the tiny island of Sado, potential conquerors need to conquer Etchu or Kaga before they can attempt to bring Noto to its knees. Because Noto offers a short cut to the Koku-rich Dewa, it's a strategic value is measured in geographical terms rather than the annual harvest. With no special features, no bonuses and only 100 Koku of resources per year, you spend more invading it than you'll get in return when you actually own it.

BATTLE NOTES

Conflict in Noto takes place in and around a giant, shallow valley. On one side, the ground gently slopes upward to the edge of the map. But on the other, the landscape becomes more mountainous, providing tacticians with numerous opportunities to gain a height advantage over the enemy. Most importantly, the type of forces that you choose to employ on a Noto campaign will go some way to determining the course of battle. The land here is perfect for Cavalry units, while the distinct lack of trees and wooded areas means that vulnerable units (Warrior Monks, No-Dachi) should be used with care. It's worth remembering that although the Arquebus and the Musket will eventually supersede the bow and arrow, the samurai Archer remains one of the most useful units you can have on the battlefield.

OMI

VALUE: 235 KOKU
FEATURES: IRON AND SAND DEPOSITS (ARMOURY)
BONUS: NONE
HELD BY: CLAN ODA (GOLD)

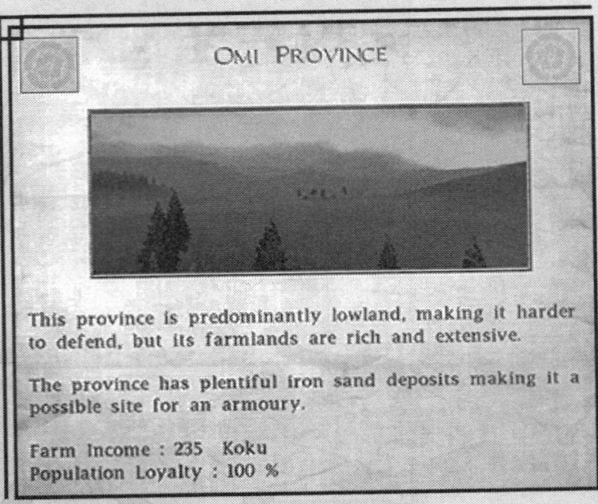

STRATEGIC IMPORTANCE

Situated to the west of the Oda's most productive and most strategically important province, Owari, Omi represents the centre of the Gold empire. To establish a Castle here, is to build a fortification which is protected by Owari and Mino to the east, by Iga to the south, by Kawachi and Tamba to the west, and by the lake and Wakasa to the north. Admittedly, Omi's rich, low-lying farmland is slightly harder to defend due to the lack of wildly undulating scenery. But, barring the close proximity of the Rebel-controlled Yamashiro, Omi has a one-province buffer zone in all directions. With an average yield of 235 Koku per year, the territory also boasts Iron and Sand deposits, enabling the Oda to construct an Armoury. The more you look at Omi, the more important it seems to become.

BATTLE NOTES

A large part of Omi is as flat as a pancake, but there are several strategic hills around the edges of the map that can be used to either defend the province or attack the defenders. The battlefield is a large one, so there's plenty of room to manoeuvre for position. Take care here, however: try not to march your troops too hard. If they are forced to chase the enemy units all over the battlefield, they'll be too tired to kill them by the time they make their final stand. Use your head, act wisely, and don't be afraid to retreat from the battlefield if the odds, the weather, or the landscape are not in your favour.

OSUMI

VALUE: 175 KOKU
FEATURES: NONE
BONUS: NONE
HELD BY: CLAN SHIMAZU (GREEN)

STRATEGIC IMPORTANCE

There's nothing particularly outstanding about the southern Kyushu province of Osumi. Its agricultural yield, 175 Koku per annum, is as unremarkable as the predominantly highland terrain that dominates this part of Japan. What makes Osumi interesting is the amount of protection that it has from the nearest enemy (in this case, the Imagawa-ruled Chikugo). Indicative, perhaps, of the easier route the Shimazu have to glory, it's unlikely that an enemy will be able to strike at the very heart of the clan. With the troop-production facilities based in neighbouring Satsuma, Osumi is the next logical location for Green to establish a Castle and further buildings. For the Cyan forces, it's only a consideration if they can bust out of the corner that the Shimazu have them contained in.

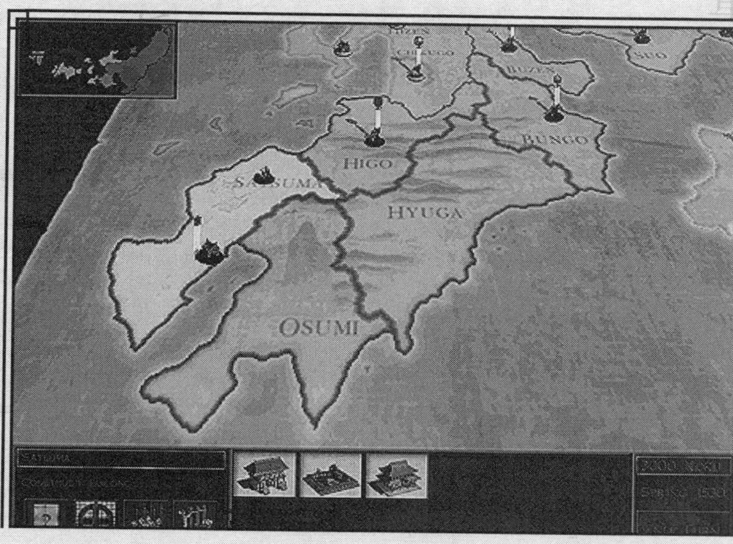

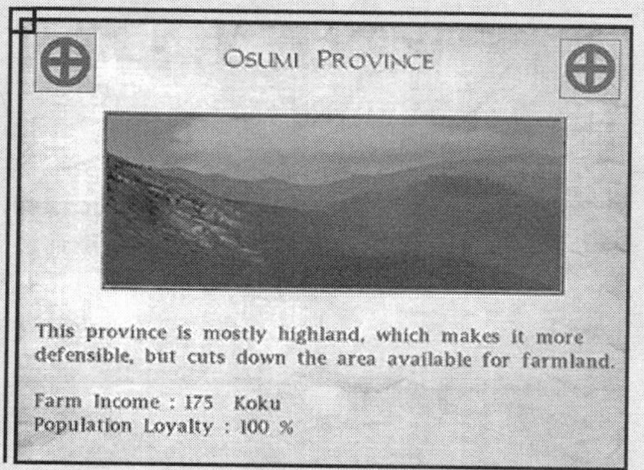

BATTLE NOTES

With so many hills and small valleys in the Osumi province, you should have no trouble finding a hill to defend the territory or bring it down. As the attacker, you have an initial advantage in that you start on much higher ground than the defending troops. This sort of area is perfect for Samurai Archers, who can be placed atop high hills to rain arrows down on poorly-armoured enemy forces. Even the more powerful units, such as Warrior Monks and No-Dachi, are vulnerable to bowfire.

OWARI

VALUE: 650 KOKU
FEATURES: NONE
BONUS: THIS PROVINCE IS FAMOUS FOR ITS ASHIGARU. ANY ASHIGARU TRAINED HERE RECEIVE +1 HONOUR.
HELD BY: CLAN ODA (GOLD)

STRATEGIC IMPORTANCE

Initially, Owari returns the biggest annual harvest of any of the 60 provinces in Japan. At 650 Koku, the resources of this small, Oda-ruled land exceed Musashi (Hojo) by 10 Koku and the Uesugi's giant Mutsu province by 50 Koku. Consequently, it's one of the most important territories in the sprawling golden empire, contributing over a quarter of the Oda's total annual harvest. And, just as every clan in the Campaign mode has a speciality, the followers of Lord Oda are the best at persuading peasant farmers to fight and die for their cause. Not only can the Oda recruit and maintain Yari Ashigaru units for 25 percent less than the other clans, but when they are trained in Owari they automatically receive +1 honour. Although bordered by the Imagawa province of Mikawa, it's unlikely that the Cyan generals will be able to match Oda's rapid troop development and mount a successful invasion.

BATTLE NOTES

The Owari scenario is not just another river crossing. The big difference here is that, instead of just one bridge over the river, there are *two*. If you're playing the attacker in the battle, then you'll find that each bridge is defended differently and thus you can choose which one to attack. As the defending player, you need to decide how you are going to split your troops to cover both bridges—perhaps using units of Cavalry Archers will allow you to remove men from one bridge and quickly reinforce another. Once you know the Owari battlefield has two bridges, you can plan a strategy that allows you to deploy enough troops to cover both of them.

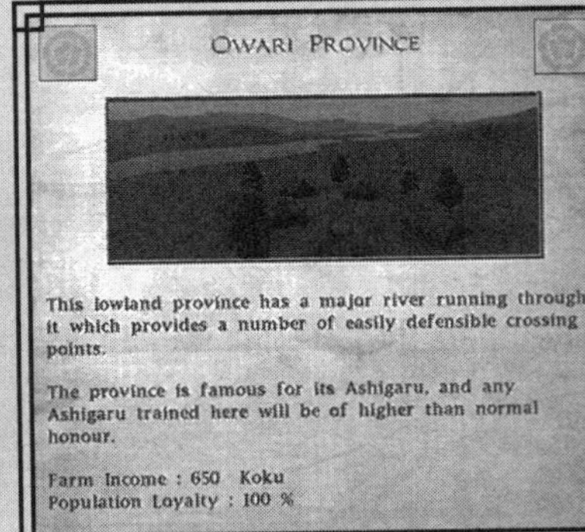

SADO

VALUE: 160 KOKU
FEATURES: IRON AND SAND DEPOSITS (ARMOURY)
BONUS: NONE
HELD BY: CLAN UESUGI (DARK BLUE)

STRATEGIC IMPORTANCE

It's easy to forget that Sado is actually a part of Japan. Lying off the coast of Echigo and Dewa, this small island contributes around 160 Koku to the Uesugi coffers, while initially guarding the vital Dewa province from Rebel attack. As a Campaign game develops, the role of Sado slowly changes—from a half-forgotten outpost to a front-line border fortification that blocks the route from Noto to Dewa. If the Uesugi empire has a weak link, it is here. While generals will obviously spend much time and resources fortifying Echigo, Mutsu, Shinano and Hida, Sado is often overlooked because the Rebels don't have an expansionist agenda. On the one hand, other clans could use it to attack the Uesugi from behind, while on the other the Uesugi could use the route to further their plans in the west. Note that rich Iron and Sand deposits here mean that an Armoury can be constructed.

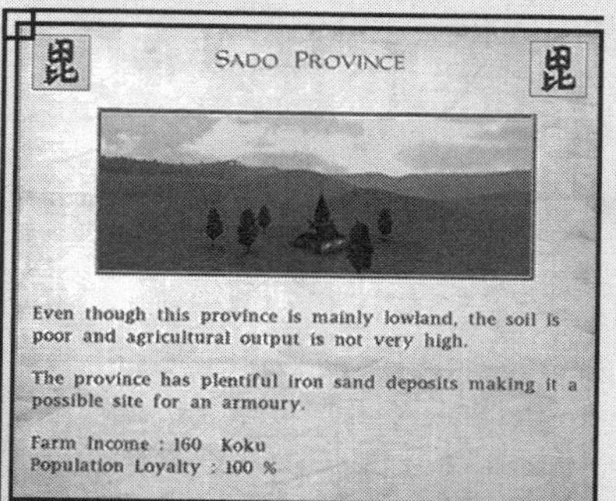

Troops in *Shogun: Total War may* suffer various penalties (and also gain bonuses) for the way in which they attack an enemy. For example, attacking from the side is more effective than attacking from the front. Take a look at the Battle Strategies section (page 42) for more information.

BATTLE NOTES

The Sado landscape is another example of a wide, bowl-like valley, edged by steep-sided hills. As an attacker, you can be certain that the enemy is waiting for you on one of these slopes. Having started the confrontation on the valley floor, march up the side of the nearest hill to gain some much needed height. If you can see the enemy forces in the distance, you need to make sure that you approach them on a level that is at a similar height to their own.

SAGAMI

VALUE: 460 KOKU
FEATURES: PORT (+200 KOKU FOR TAKEDA)
BONUS: NONE
HELD BY: CLAN TAKEDA (BLACK)

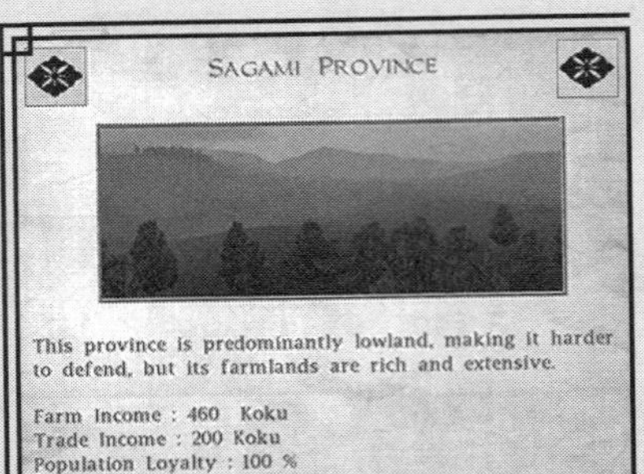

STRATEGIC IMPORTANCE

With such a high average yield (460 Koku), it should come as no surprise to learn that Sagami is mostly lowland, making it a little bit harder to defend. Yet, considering how the Takeda's great strength in the Campaign mode is cavalry, the flat nature of the landscape obviously suits the highly mobile strategies that the clan prefer. Bordered by the Koku-rich land of Musashi to the east, Sagami is vital to the Black war effort because it contains the Port which links these three states to Aki, Bingo and Bitchu on the western side of the map. If an enemy can mount a successful invasion, the Port (and the extra 200 Koku that come with it) will be lost, leaving the western states without a link to Kai's troop-production facilities.

BATTLE NOTES

Sagami province is another gently undulating landscape dominated by a large flat plain in the centre. If you're defending Sagami against aggression (and that means you've ousted the Rebels), there are some excellent areas of high ground surrounding the plain. If attacking, the enemy will attempt to try and draw you away from the hills and down into the valley itself where it will hope to attack you as you struggle to find a good position for your troops. Once again, long-range weapons will prove more than useful, as will fast-moving units such as Yari Cavalry and Cavalry Archers.

SANUKI

VALUE: 380 KOKU
FEATURES: NONE
BONUS: NONE
HELD BY: REBELS (SILVER)

STRATEGIC IMPORTANCE

Predominantly a lowland area, Sanuki is the richest Rebel state on the island of Shikoku. Consequently, its average annual yield of 380 Koku is not just coveted by the Mori to the north, but by the Shimazu to the west and the Oda to the east. The Mori armies are fortunate enough to have the most direct route, able to cross from Bizen to Sanuki in a single move. The golden legions of the Oda clan have to fight through Awaji before they can mount an attack, while Shimazu faces a bold march through Iyo to get to the Sanuki border. It's important not to forget that, the longer these Rebel states are left to their own devices, the more time Tosa has to supply them with extra Archers and Warrior Monks. Move in too quickly and you leave your clan exposed elsewhere. Move in too late and the battle for Sanuki will be a costly one.

BATTLE NOTES

Although Sanuki is dominated by farmland, there is ample scope for both defensive and offensive tactics in amongst this province's raised terraces. Controlling an army on level ground is possibly the biggest challenge you have to face during a Shogun battle. Suddenly, everything that you have learned about height no longer applies and the battles become a straightforward clash of numbers and troop types. You may want to practise controlling large armies on flat ground in the Custom Battles section of the game. For now, remember the words of your instructor in the Tutorial: Archers beat Spearmen, Spearmen beat Cavalry, Cavalry beat Archers.

SATSUMA

VALUE: 180 KOKU
FEATURES: NONE
BONUS: THIS PROVINCE IS FAMOUS FOR ITS NO-DACHI. ANY NO-DACHI TRAINED HERE RECEIVE +1 HONOUR.
HELD BY: CLAN SHIMAZU (GREEN)

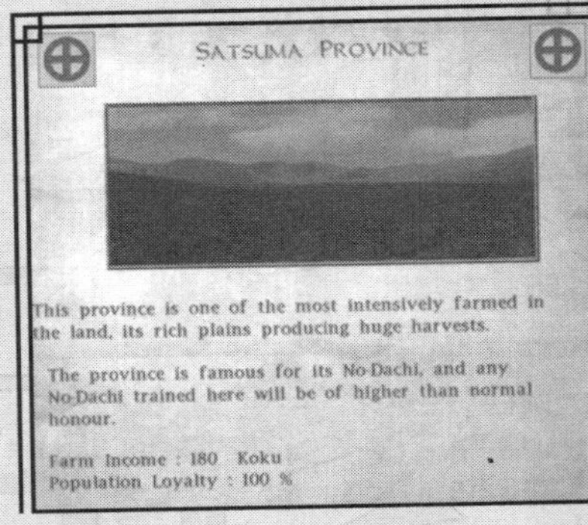

STRATEGIC IMPORTANCE

Safely isolated from danger by both Higo and Hyuga, Satsuma's protected position is the perfect place for the Shimazu capital. It's here that you'll find the Green Daimyo, and it's here that the Shimazu has established its Castle, Tranquil Garden, Spear Dojo and Archery Dojo. The gods have been a little stingy with the resources in this part of Japan, and Satsuma only has an average annual income of 180 Koku. But, as a coastal region, Green can boost this figure by adding a Port and Satsuma's defensive qualities more than outweigh the lack of financial gain. Best of all, this province is famous for its No-Dachi swordsmen, a unit that you can only get access to when your forces have won many battles. Any No-Dachi trained in Satsuma will automatically receive a boost to their honour rating.

BATTLE NOTES

When your forces appear on the Satsuma landscape, you'll notice a large, impressive hill that dominates the surroundings. Make a run for it! If you can claim the hilltop before the enemy force does, then you are in a perfect position to rain wooden- and gunpowder-related death down on your opponent. A word of warning: don't simply cram your army full of Archers or Arquebusiers and hope for the best. You'll still need some fearless spearmen or sword wielders to do the majority of the actual killing. For while the Archers and the riflemen can be effective, they cannot fell entire 60-man units in one volley of bow-fire. We wish...

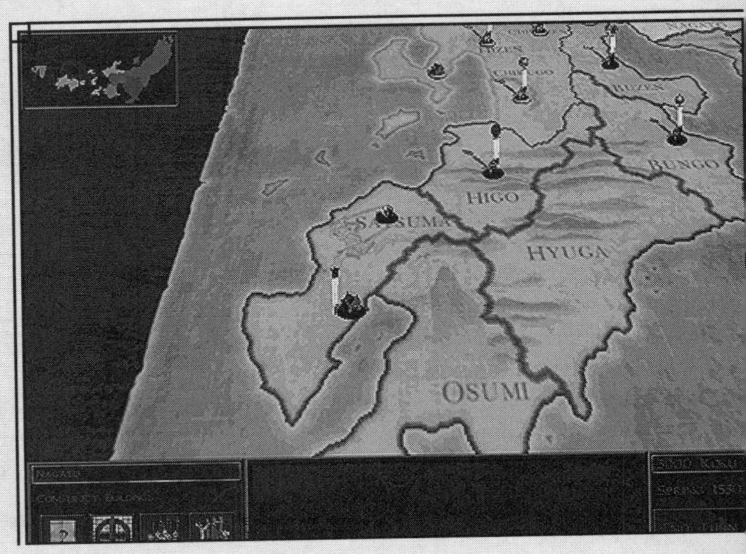

SHIMOSA

VALUE: 290 KOKU
FEATURES: NONE
BONUS: NONE
HELD BY: CLAN HOJO (PURPLE)

STRATEGIC IMPORTANCE

Protected from early invasion by four of its own lands (Musashi, Kozuke, Shimotsuke and Hitachi), Shimosa is the provisional capital of the Hojo empire. Not particularly Koku-rich in comparison to Musashi and Hitachi, Shimosa is the centre of operations for the Purple forces hosting the Daimyo's only Castle and the troop-production facilities that get the clan started. Sited on a lowland plain, cut in two by a river, Shimosa benefits from a good geographical location and a terrain that makes attacking this province fairly tricky. If an enemy manages to attack and conquer Shimosa, then the Hojo's days as a major Japanese clan are numbered.

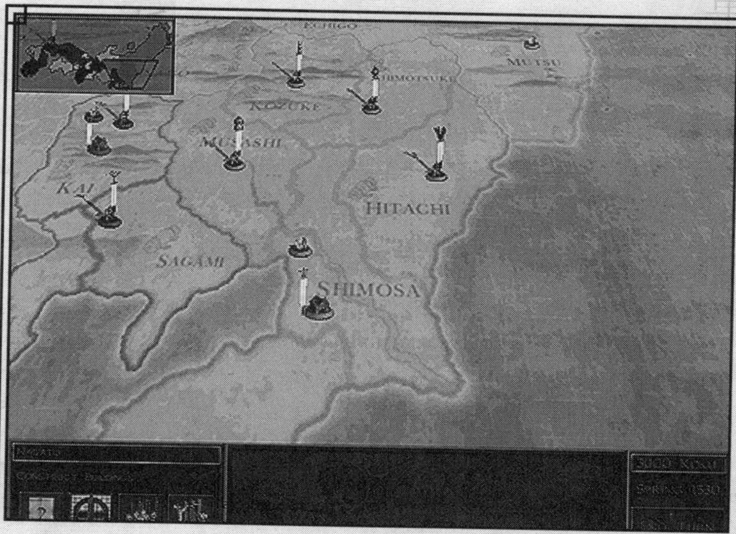

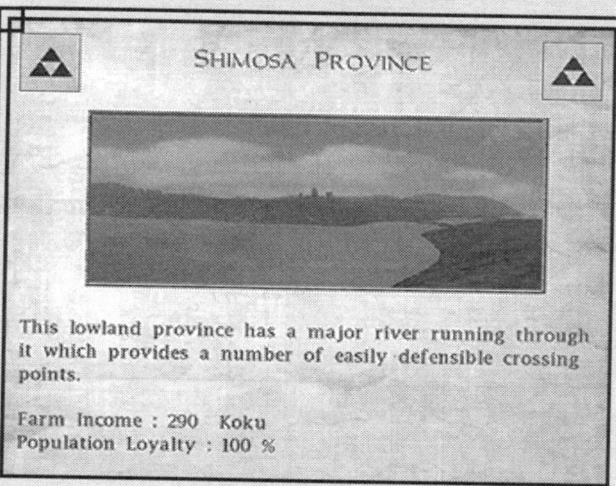

BATTLE NOTES

By watching how the computer defends as you attempt to force your way across a narrow bridge, you can mimic the strategy and use it. Here in Shimosa, for example, there is only one bridge to defend. Consequently, the game's AI will position the defending forces within bow/rifle range of the bridge, but just out of bow/rifle range of any troops you deploy on your side of the river. Then, the defenders simply sit there, waiting for you to make the first move. Send an Ashigaru unit across and the tactics quickly become clear—ranged weapon units hold a tight line and fire at the Ashigaru crossing the bridge. Behind the ranged weapon units hide either a unit of Cavalry or a unit of Footsoldiers who are ready to engage the invading soldiers before they can establish a foothold on the enemy side. It seems to work well. Why not give it a try?

SHIMOTSUKE

VALUE: 210 KOKU
FEATURES: COPPER DEPOSITS
(MINE: +200 KOKU PER YEAR)
BONUS: NONE
HELD BY: CLAN HOJO (PURPLE)

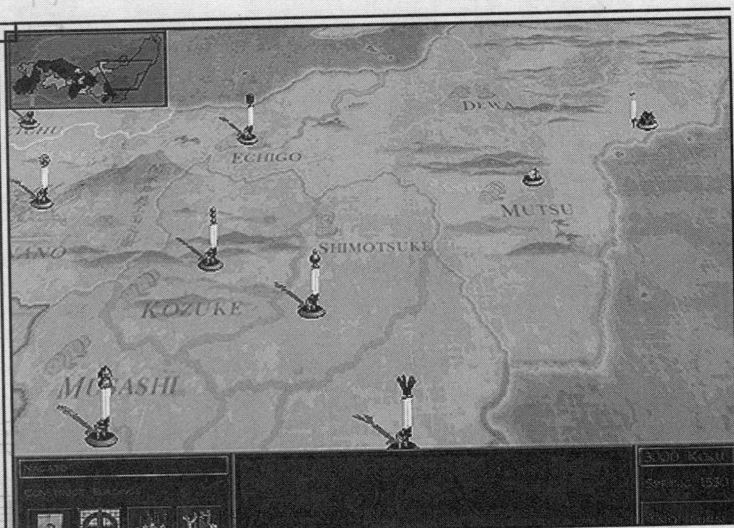

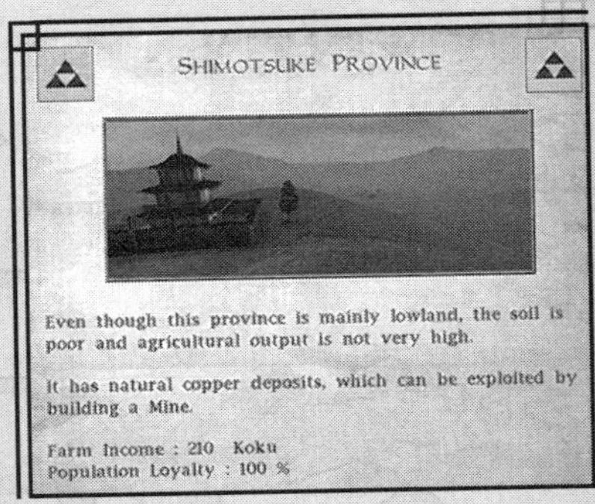

STRATEGIC IMPORTANCE

Nestling between friendly lands Kozuke and Hitachi, Shimotsuke completes the Hojo front line facing the might of the Uesugi to the northeast. It's a small province, contributing nothing like the resources that Hitachi and Musashi do to the Hojo war effort. Nevertheless, Shimotsuke is an important frontier state—less likely to be invaded by the Uesugi, and perfectly positioned to provide mobile support to any of the neighbouring lands who need it. To top things off, Shimotsuke also has a large vein of Copper in the hills, which can be mined to add an extra 200 Koku per month to the territory's initial 210 Koku total.

BATTLE NOTES

With its average agricultural yield, experienced generals should expect to fight on a terrain that offers areas of flat farmland bordered by high, steep-sided hills. On these types of battleground, there are few truly advantageous positions. So whether you're defending or attacking a province like Shimotsuke, it pays to follow the tactics suggested by Sun Tzu in *The Art of War*. "Generally," he proposed, "those who occupy the place of conflict early, can face their opponent in comfort. Those who occupy the place of conflict late, must hasten into conflict troubled." Unless you feel confident that you can defeat an opponent on level ground with superior numbers, seek the tactical advantages offered by the high ground available

SHINANO

VALUE: 340 KOKU
FEATURES: NONE
BONUS: THIS PROVINCE IS FAMOUS FOR ITS CAVALRY. ANY CAVALRY TRAINED HERE RECEIVE +1 HONOUR.
HELD BY: CLAN UESUGI (DARK BLUE)

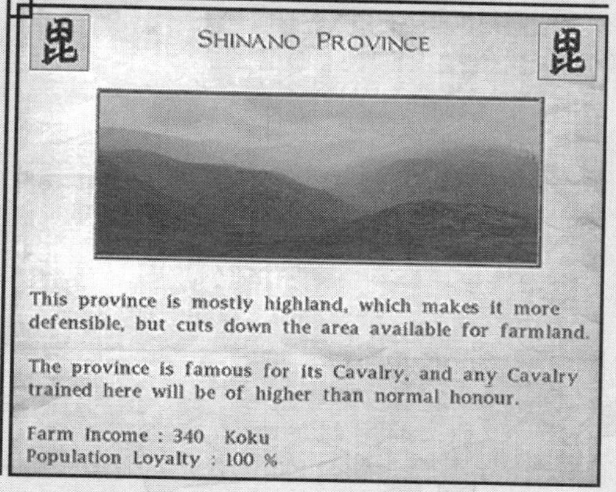

STRATEGIC IMPORTANCE

While the Uesugi empire is certainly large, it's very stretched, so much so that troops created in Mutsu have to pass via Echigo before they can reinforce the large Shinano district. As a result, Shinano is a tempting early target for the more untrustworthy, expansionist Daimyo and Black has its eye on the province from the word go. It's hardly surprising—Shinano's agricultural yield of 340 Koku is an above average one, while its location in the middle of the mainland means that any one of four clans can mount an attack at any time. Shinano's big draw, however, is the fact that whoever owns it can produce Cavalry units with +1 honour. Unless it's swiftly reinforced by the Dark Blue forces, it may not survive the first year as a Uesugi domain. The Cyan Imagawa clan certainly eyes it greedily.

BATTLE NOTES

Considering that Shinano is a province famed nationally for its Cavalry units, it might come as some surprise to discover that the province has very little horse-friendly terrain. Barring a large valley in the centre, Shinano is a land of sharply rising hills that make it difficult to successfully marshal a large army. Two large wooded areas dominate the east and west sides of the battlefield, but these will rarely be used as most of the action will take advantage of the hills and valleys so abundant in this area. Attackers will begin an invasion of this province at the north end of the valley—the lowest point of the battlefield. Generals are advised to seek higher ground quickly, knowing that the opposing forces are likely to be dug in on spectacularly high ground in the south.

SUO

VALUE: 139 KOKU
FEATURES: IRON AND SAND DEPOSITS (ARMOURY)
BONUS: NONE
HELD BY: CLAN MORI (RED)

STRATEGIC IMPORTANCE

Like the majority of the Mori lands, Suo is a bleak expanse of highland with very poor farmland. It's no wonder that the Red-clad Samurai of the Mori clan are so eager to conquer new land for themselves. Situated toward the western tip of the Japanese mainland, Suo borders the Green-held province of Nagato. Here, along with Iwami to the North, it acts as the frontier dividing the Mori empire from the Shimazu realm. While its average annual harvest (139 Koku) is nothing to get wildly excited about, Suo does boast considerable Iron and Sand deposits to enable the construction of an Armoury. For the Red forces, Suo is a very suitable staging point for an attack on Nagato—once this province has been conquered the Mori will only have to garrison one land instead of two. For the Green, meanwhile, Suo and Iwami are just the next states on their expansionist "things to do" list.

BATTLE NOTES

Located on the western tip of the Japanese mainland, Suo's landscape resembles much of the Red Mori empire. With relatively little flat ground, Suo is a province of steep hills and deep valleys, perfect perhaps for both the attacker and defender who wants to adhere to the "height advantage" tactic. When attacking this particular territory, the aggressor starts on the side of a long, low hill while the enemy is situated over the brow of the hill on a facing slope. The key here is obviously to move to the high ground as soon as possible, thereby limiting your exposure to a surprise attack should the enemy force have fast-moving Cavalry units. As ever, if you can get ranged weapon units (i.e. Archers) into a position where they can rain arrows down onto an opponent, the battle is yours for the winning.

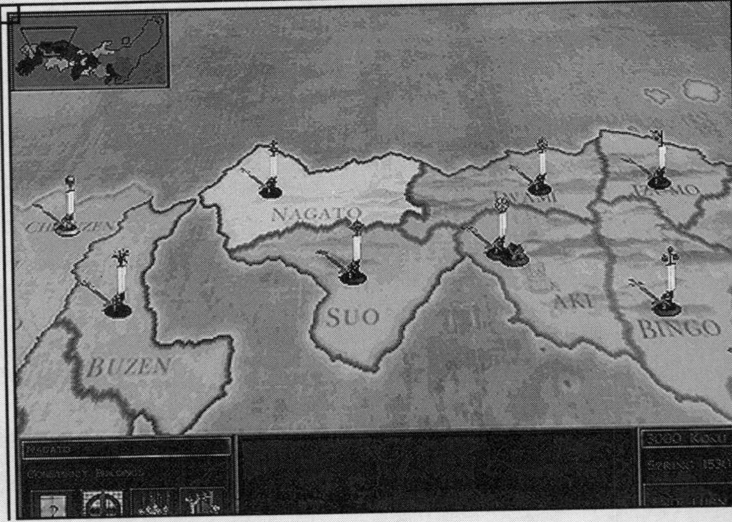

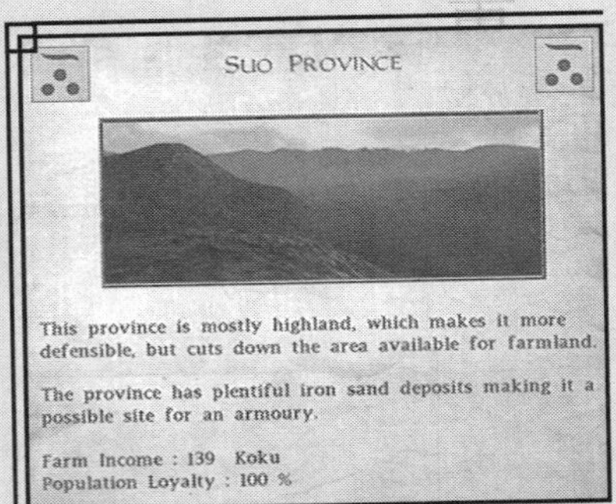

SURUGA

VALUE: 100 KOKU
FEATURES: NONE
BONUS: NONE
HELD BY: CLAN IMAGAWA (CYAN)

STRATEGIC IMPORTANCE

As you'll see if you read the details for any one of the Imagawa-owned lands, every territory is precious to the clan that rallies behind the Cyan banner. And yes, this even means Suruga, a poor lowland area with very little farmland. Simply put, the 100 Koku that Suruga contributes on average to the Imagawa war chest is better than nothing. With no special features or bonuses to speak of, Suruga's main role is to check the expansion of the Takeda clan based in Kai over the border. Unless the Imagawa commander leaves Suruga unguarded, the Black forces will tend to ignore this low-yield territory, turning their attention instead to Shinano in the north and the rich lands of Musashi to the east.

BATTLE NOTES

Edged by steep foothills to the south, Suruga's landscape gradually levels out as you look northward, giving way to areas of low-lying farmland. Unfortunately, while any attacking army starts on high ground to the north, they are forced to march across the low farmland to reach the defenders camped on the more impressive hillsides to the south. If there is an advantage to be had on this unremarkable expanse of land, it is that there is abundant tree cover in the southeast. Attacking armies are advised to march for the high hill directly in front of them, thereby gaining a position that can be used to defend against attack and to launch an attack downhill. Defending forces, meanwhile, have a good choice of steep-sided hills and the time to arrange troops to defend to maximum effect.

TAJIMA

VALUE: 95 KOKU
FEATURES: NONE
BONUS: THIS PROVINCE IS FAMOUS FOR ITS SHINOBI. ANY SHINOBI TRAINED HERE RECEIVE +1 HONOUR.
HELD BY: REBELS (SILVER)

STRATEGIC IMPORTANCE

Situated between the Mori-controlled province of Inaba and the Oda-ruled lands of Tamba and Wakasa, Tajima is a self-contained Rebel stronghold. As such, it has its own castle, plus a Spear Dojo and Archery Dojo. And despite the fact that it is a highland area and has a limited amount of farmland available, it will slowly amass a small army if left unchecked for several years. While there's no chance that a clan general will invade Tajima for its agricultural wealth (only 95 Koku can be sucked out of the soil). This region is also famed for the skill and daring of its Shinobi spies, and any such unit that is produced in Tajima automatically gains a +1 bonus to its honour rating. Like other Rebel-controlled states, the Tajima renegades won't actively seek to invade Mori or Oda lands.

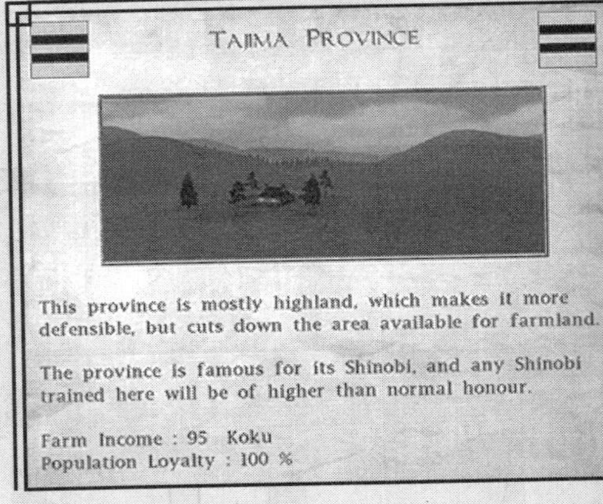

But it might think about it if defences are light or if it requires extra resources to support its growing army.

BATTLE NOTES

Yet another hilly territory with few areas of flat land suitable for cavalry units. Again, it's vitally important that, whether you are attacking or defending this poor province, you do not get caught napping in the lowlands. The high ground here isn't as impressive or as strategically enticing as some of the other provinces nearby, but there are a number of good locations from which to mount an effective defence. However, due to the undulating nature of the landscape, finding an area that has secure flanks may prove something of an impossibility.

TAMBA

VALUE: 220 KOKU
FEATURES: NONE
BONUS: NONE
HELD BY: CLAN ODA (GOLD)

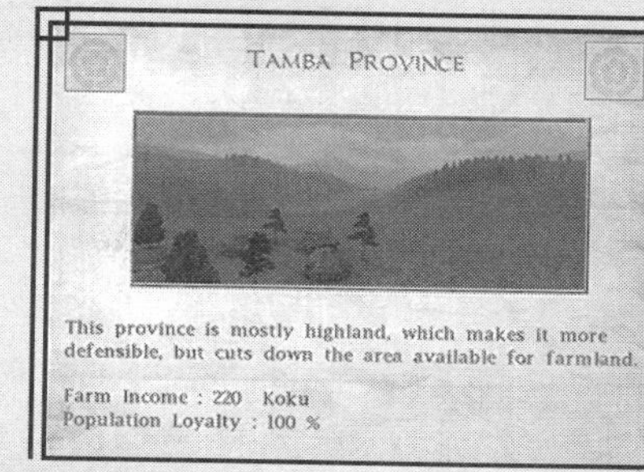

STRATEGIC IMPORTANCE

An important province situated on the Mori/Oda frontier, Tamba combines half-decent farmland with the sort of hilly terrain that makes the territory easier to defend. Although originally part of the Oda empire, Tamba will be one of the first provinces to swap hands when war eventually breaks out between the Red and Gold clans. Its survival is dependent on many factors. Have the Mori rid themselves of the three Takeda provinces? Do the Mori need to expand east or will they turn south for Awaji and Shikoku isle? Similarly, the Oda will only attack if they aren't actively fighting a conflict on their eastern border, and if they do they'll use both Tamba and Kawachi as bases to launch an invasion of Harima. Why Harima? A natural Port and Silver deposits are no doubt top of the list.

BATTLE NOTES

Despite the fact that attackers begin a Tamba offensive behind a small mountain, the majority of this province is a low, wide valley surrounded by hills. By moving scouts quickly to the top of the peak in the north, an attacking force can gain an almost unrivalled view over the battlefield (weather permitting, of course). There's a strong argument here for moving a large section of the attacking force up this large hill as quickly as possible. If the defender begins the battle camped on the valley floor, he will either retreat to find a more defensible position or make a run for the peak with the aim of capturing it before you do. As usual, he who gains the height advantage is in the best position for victory.

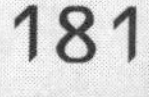

TOSA

VALUE: 242 KOKU
FEATURES: NONE
BONUS: THIS PROVINCE IS FAMOUS FOR ITS ASHIGARU. ANY ASHIGARU TRAINED HERE RECEIVE +1 HONOUR.
HELD BY: REBELS (SILVER)

STRATEGIC IMPORTANCE

This large, crescent-shaped province is part of the strategically desirable Shikoku island, a landmass located south of the Red Mori empire and east of the Green Shimazu realm. Boasting an average annual yield of 242 Koku, Tosa contributes almost a quarter of the total 1,000+ Koku that can be generated by the island. Most importantly, however, Tosa is the hub of the Shikoku-based rebellion, complete with its own castle, plus Archery and Spear Dojos. If any more proof were needed that Tosa is a prime clan target, any Ashigaru trained here also receive a +1 bonus to their honour rating. Ignore what's happening on Shikoku for a few years and you'll discover that the Rebels begin to build up a sizeable force that's difficult to dislodge.

BATTLE NOTES

Featureless apart from a few areas of woodland, Tosa presents an awkward tactical challenge thanks to its undulating landscape.

Because while Tosa has some hills and therefore some strategic high ground, most of it is not high enough and rival armies will doubtless clash across the bumps and hollows that make up the majority of the terrain. To make things just that little bit trickier, there's only really one suitable hill in the entire province and, if you're playing the attacking force, you'll discover that the enemy are stubbornly camped out on it. If you are playing the defender, however, you'll want to claim the same hillock—it's the one with the trees on top of it the southern half of the map.

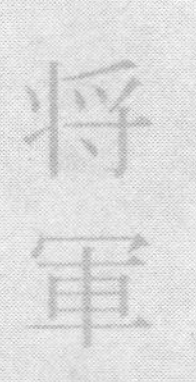

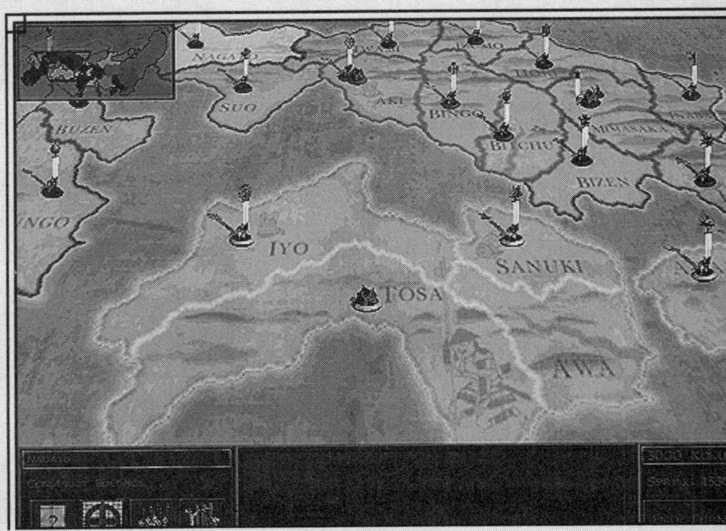

TOTOMI

VALUE: 155
FEATURES: PORT (+200 KOKU FOR IMAGAWA)
BONUS: THIS PROVINCE IS FAMOUS FOR ITS ARCHERS. ANY ARCHERS TRAINED HERE RECEIVE +1 HONOUR.
HELD BY: CLAN IMAGAWA (CYAN)

STRATEGIC IMPORTANCE

For the Imagawa clan, Totomi is the most important province that they own. Chikuzen, Hizen and Chikugo in the west may generate the bulk of the clan's resources. But without the castle, Archery Dojo and Spear Dojo that already exist in Totomi, the Imagawa would fall behind their rival clans in the race for supremacy. While Totomi is a lowland area, the soil is poor and farmers struggle to harvest more than 155 Koku from the land each year. As the provisional Imagawa capital, Totomi also has a Port, generating 200 extra Koku for the Cyan cause as well as providing a link to the three Imagawa lands on Kyushu. Best of all, the Totomi province is renowned for the skill and accuracy of its Samurai Archers. Any Samurai Archer units that are trained in the Archery Dojo here automatically receive +1 to their honour rating.

BATTLE NOTES

Practically flat as a pancake, Totomi needs to be conquered by sheer weight of numbers rather than a reliance on steep hills and a feisty band of Warrior Monks. Barring a few baby hillocks, there is no useful or strategically advantageous terrain at all in this province. Thus, whether you play the attacker or the defender, success lies in the type of troops that you have and how you deploy the troops in battle. Cavalry units are particularly well suited to this landscape, as are the gunpowder weapons carried by Arquebusiers and Musketeers. But if you can learn to fight on landscapes like this and triumph, then there isn't a province amongst the 60 that can challenge your tactical genius.

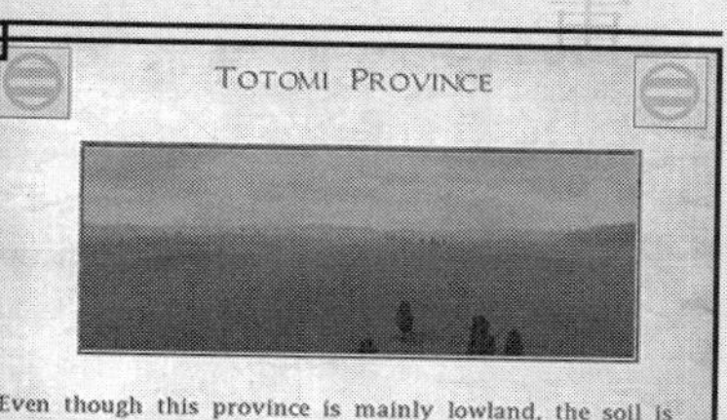

WAKASA

VALUE: 103 KOKU
FEATURES: NONE
BONUS: NONE
HELD BY: CLAN ODA (GOLD)

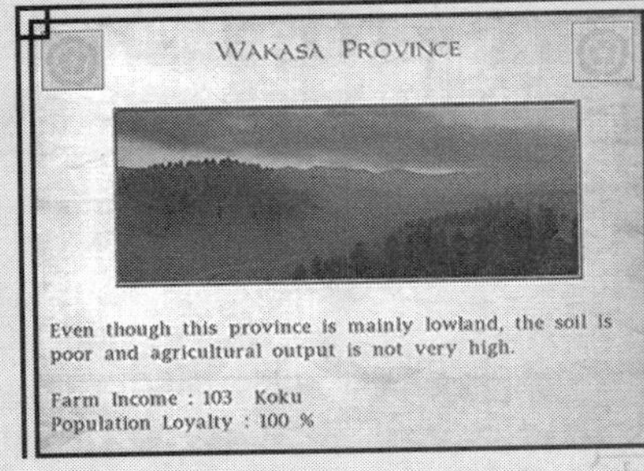

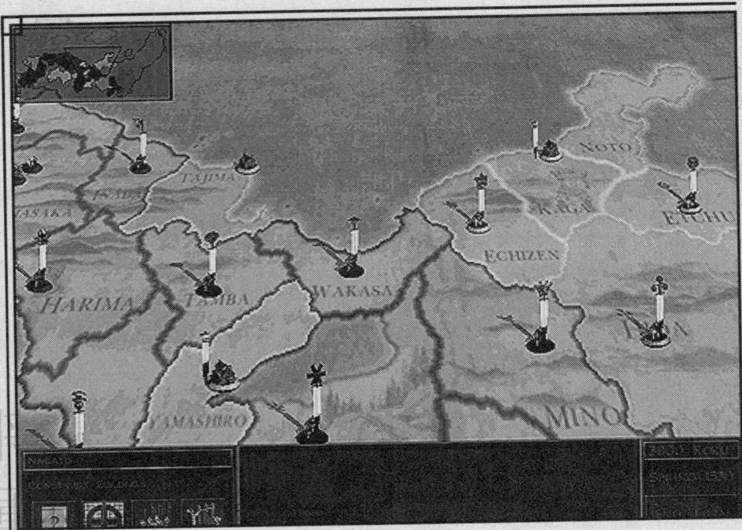

STRATEGIC IMPORTANCE

Wedged between the Rebel province of Tajima to the west and the renegades in Echizen to the east, Wakasa merely makes up the numbers in the Oda empire. Contributing very little in the way of resources to the Oda treasury, this is a lowland area with blighted farmland. As a result, the Koku returns are low, and without any special features (i.e. precious metals, materials for an Armoury, etc.) or bonuses, Wakasa is hardly a tempting target for invading armies.

BATTLE NOTES

The main feature of the Wakasa territory is its shallow east/west valley and rival armies will begin a battle here on either side of it. The strategy is clear: for the attacking force, it's imperative that they move quickly from the edge of the battlefield, across the valley to gain as much height before engaging the enemy. If this proves impossible, then a good plan B is for the attacking army to wait until the defender has made its initial move, before heading southeast in an outflanking manoeuvre designed to unsettle the defending army. What you must *not* do here is get caught on the valley floor as the hills here are roomy enough to accommodate armies of 800 men or more. Facing 800 soldiers, charging downhill, is not something that you want to see.

YAMASHIRO

VALUE: 150 KOKU
FEATURES: NONE
BONUS: EMPEROR'S PALACE
HELD BY: REBELS (SILVER)

STRATEGIC IMPORTANCE

Yamashiro, like Tajima and Ise, is another self-contained Rebel stronghold. Surrounded by Oda-ruled provinces, but hoping to hold out against them, Yamashiro boasts its own Castle, Archery Dojo and Buddhist Temple. Consequently, despite a low average yield of 150 Koku, the Yamashiro Rebels can recruit and train Samurai Archers and Warrior Monks almost immediately. Better than all of this, however, is the fact that the Emperor's Palace is located within the Yamashiro province. The advantage of capturing and holding this land is that the Palace boosts the honour rating of *all* troops produced here by +1. However, the Rebel forces will fight to the death to keep the Palace from an invading force.

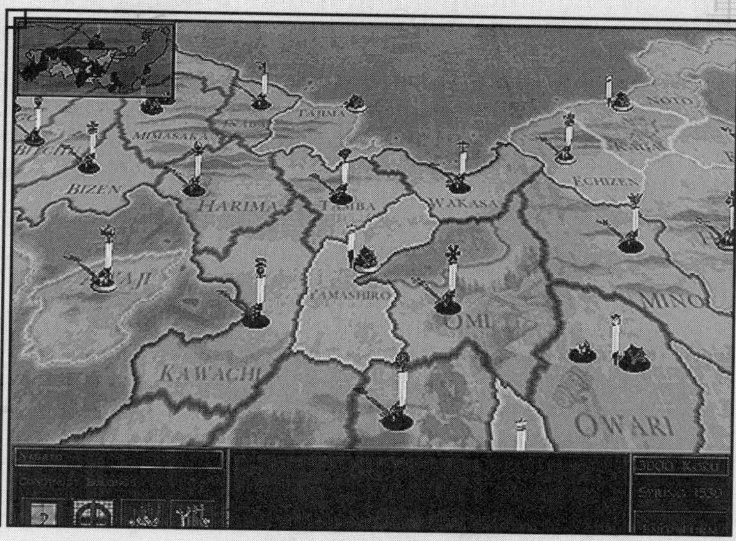

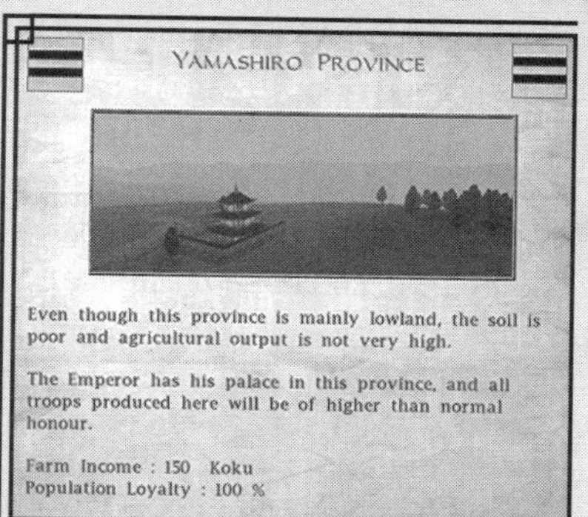

BATTLE NOTES

Yamashiro is one of the more interesting landscapes in the Campaign mode, neither heavily dominated by steep hills nor characterised by flat, sweeping plains. Yamashiro is a happy combination of the two, an undulating landscape dotted with small areas of woodland and broken up by jagged outcrops of rocky highland. Playing the attacking force, units will begin the battle in the north just in front of a ridge. It's this ridge that effectively divides the battlefield, slightly obscuring your view of the defenders who sit on the relatively flat ground beyond. If you can make it to the ridge (and entice the enemy forward), it's a good vantage point from which to conduct a missile attack. Defenders meanwhile should not get drawn into a hasty advance and are better off retreating to the high ground at the southern edge of the map.

YAMATO

VALUE: 202 KOKU
FEATURES: NONE
BONUS: NONE
HELD BY: CLAN ODA (GOLD)

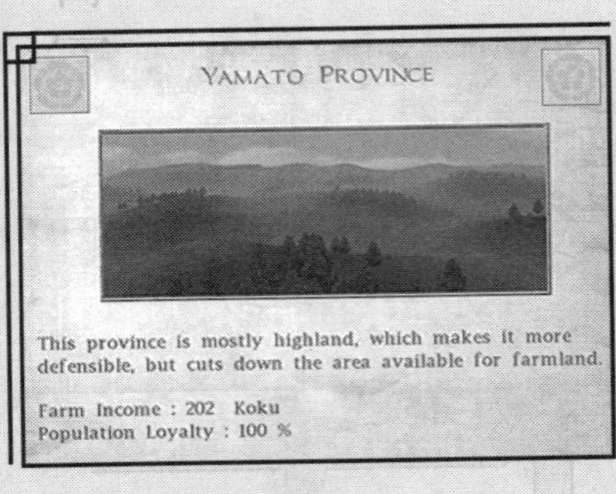

STRATEGIC IMPORTANCE

Located deep within the heart of the Oda empire, Yamato is a relatively unremarkable province with no special features. With an average agricultural yield of 202 Koku per annum, it's not the most productive territory in the game. But, located alongside the important Kii territory (famous for its Warrior Monks), plus the two self-contained Rebel states of Ise and Yamashiro, Yamato provides a handy staging point for troops marching west toward the Mori, or eastward from Kii to the Oda/Imagawa and Oda/Uesugi borders.

BATTLE NOTES

The Yamato landscape is essentially a wide vista of hills and valleys, all of a similar size. Each one of the many peaks in this area also has a small wood at its highest point, making them easy to defend but unsuitable for missile troops such as Archers who can't fire arrows through the branches. Whether you are attacking or defending this province, you'll need to work your way around and over the hills to engage the enemy in combat. Large armies may find the landscape hinders coordinated movement in large, ordered formations. While defenders who adopt a guerrilla offensive, hiding units in the woods atop the hills, may be able to cause havoc to a force which is unwilling to split and pursue its opponent in kind.

CAMPAIGN STRATEGIES

The *Shogun: Total War* Campaign mode not only requires a good, all-round knowledge of battlefield tactics, but an understanding and subsequently a mastery of the wider, geo-political picture. With seven family clans fighting for dominance of Japan, there is so much more to being a successful general than efficiently commanding 1,000 samurai in battle. Who do you make alliances with? And should you keep them? Which buildings are the most important? Is an aggressive expansionist policy preferable to a cautious, patient build-up? The Campaign mode creates a whole new set of strategic problems. A good general can solve some of them, but it takes a Daimyo to tackle them all.

Not only does the Campaign mode test your battlefield skills, it also demands a mix of diplomacy, resource management, politics and advance planning. By now you should be familiar with the troop types, terrain and weather conditions that you might encounter. If not, see the Analysis section starting on page 20. You should also have mastered the finer points of battlefield strategy and tested them in the Historical Battles part of the game. Again, if you haven't, see the Confrontation and Knowledge sections respectively. Finally, in this Intelligence section, you should have learned the strengths and weaknesses of the seven clans, which buildings produce what samurai units, and which of the 60 provinces in the game need to be held or invaded to further your ultimate aim—to become Shogun of all Japan. All that remains is to tie everything together, and to learn that there are paths that should not be taken and forces that should not be confronted.

In the Campaign mode, a mastery of battle tactics will only take you so far.

To become Shogun you must master resource juggling, battlefield strategy and geo-political thinking.

COMMANDING THE MORI CLAN (RED)

From their position near the western tip of the Japanese mainland, the Mori clan are in a position to instantly expand and invade. Although the Red empire consists of eight provinces, they only bring in average of 1163 Koku per annum. It's the lowest yield of any of the seven clans, and a big hindrance to the Mori's plans for internal expansion. Consequently, the Mori need to expand—they require new land and the income that comes from it to fund a building program and a sustainable period of troop recruitment. What's the use of being able to produce Warrior Monks for a lower cost, if you lack the infrastructure to build a Large Castle and then a Buddhist Temple to access them?

As with all the clans that dream of power, the Mori have several ways of pursuing their quest for land and riches:

- **Attack Aki, Bitchu and Bingo**—By ridding themselves of the Takeda threat early in the year, the Mori will gain three new territories and restrict the threat of invasion to two fronts: Shimazu to the west, Oda to the east. By striking within the first year, Aki's Port can be destroyed, cutting the lands off from the other Takeda provinces in the east. Without troop-producing facilities, the Mori have time to capture Bingo and Bitchu without compromising security.

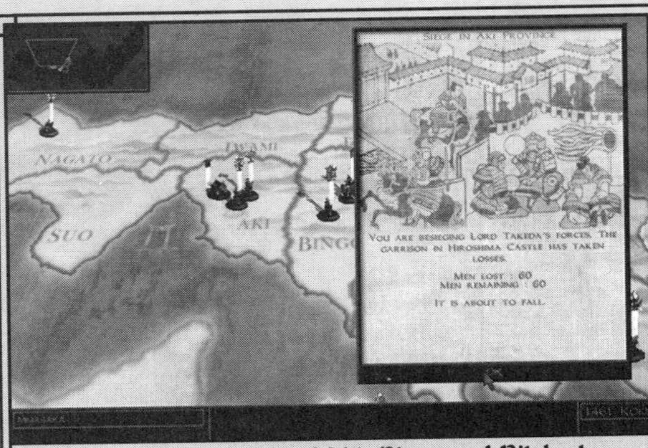

Attack the Takeda lands of Aki, Bingo and Bitchu to secure your borders.

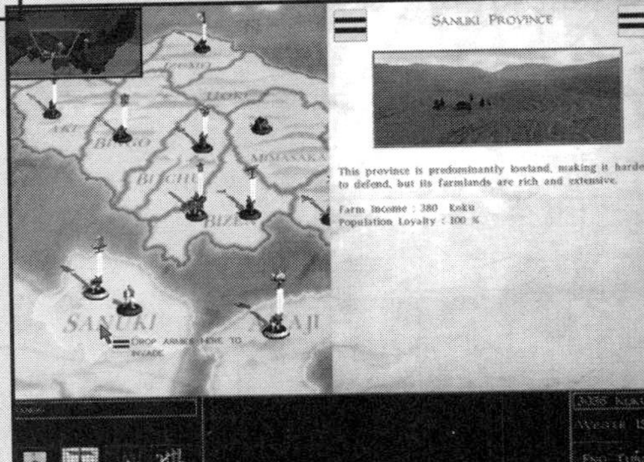

Push south to invade the rich land of Sanuki, initially held by the Rebels.

- **Ally with the Shimazu**—Of all the clans in the game, the Green Shimazu forces are more likely to keep any treaties that they sign. For the early part of the game, they will have their hands full dealing with the Imagawa. Don't bother them just yet.

- **Attack Sanuki**—With the Golden empire of the Oda blocking the way east, the most obvious target is the Rebel-held isle of Shikoku. Mass your troops and attack via Sanuki, taking care to remember that units are produced in nearby Tosa.

- **Push west**—By taking the Shikoku states you effectively cut the Shimazu off from the rest of the map. After they have dealt with the Imagawa, their own desire for expansion will lead them to conflict, but you will have time to prepare. Aim to invade Bungo and conquer the island of Kyushu before you turn your attentions towards the land in the east.

COMMANDING THE SHIMAZU CLAN (GREEN)

Isolated on Kyushu, the Shimazu clan are in the safest position on the map. The three Imagawa states—Chikugo, Chikuzen and Hizen—don't have the resources to threaten immediately, while the Mori haven't got the troop numbers to threaten Nagato and then Buzen on the eastern frontier. As a consequence perhaps of their highly defensible location, the Shimazu's lands are poor and farmers can barely bring in more than an average of 1194 Koku per year at the start of a new Campaign game. Like the Mori to the east, the Shimazu also need to expand to fund their building and troop recruitment programs. While other clans can bide their time, the Shimazu need to strike quickly and build wisely before they can break out of the island of Kyushu.

Like all the clans in the Campaign, the Shimazui have several ways of pursuing their quest for land and riches:

- **Attack the Imagawa**—The Shimazu's first aim should be to control the entire island and this means wiping out the Imagawa who hold three of the region's nine provinces. The only problem is that Hizen, linked to the Imagawa capital Totomi via its Port, is protected by Chikugo and Chikuzen.

Attack the Imagawa to the north to take control of the entire island.

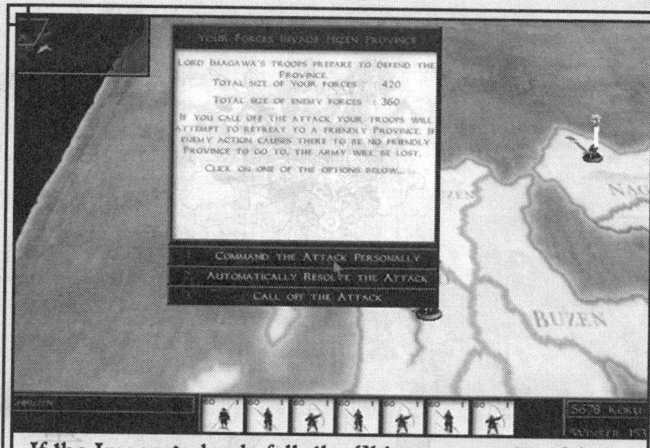

If the Imagawa lands fall, the Shimazu can sit safely in the borders, gathering strength.

To stand a chance of destroying the Imagawa, the Shimazu need to capture the Port quickly to stop reinforcements from arriving.

- **Reinforce Nagato**—protecting their eastern border, Nagato is a useful foothold on the Japanese mainland. It is also, however, a tempting target for the land-hungry Mori clan who want control of the whole peninsula.

- **Attack Iyo**—once the nine provinces that make up Kyushu have been conquered, the Shimazu can easily sit safe within their borders, developing their farmland, constructing Ports, etc. If the Imagawa lands have been captured, they boost the Shimazu treasury significantly, but the Green forces face the prospect of being boxed in to the western corner if they don't push into Iyo on Shikoku. For the Shimazu, Iyo is an alternative route to the Japanese mainland, an offensive against four states rather than the eleven that make up the Mori-held peninsula. Taking Shikoku is not just strategically vital, it also adds even more money to the Shimazu war chest. In addition, the more battles the Green forces fight, the more chance they have of activating the Legendary Swordsman event, the first step on the road to developing the clan's speciality unit, No-Dachi.

COMMANDING THE ODA CLAN (GOLD)

The Oda are in an unenviable position on the Japanese mainland, the ruthless rulers of a large, but sprawling empire. With an initial average income of 2020 Koku, they have more than enough to sit tight within their borders, using what resources they have to develop and expand the internal infrastructure. At the beginning of the game, the Oda face the under-strength Mori to the north, and the Imagawa and Uesugi to the east. The Golden empire also faces the dormant threat of four Rebel-held territories. While these renegade provinces won't immediately attack, if left unchecked they can grow into fortress states that are difficult to destroy.

When controlling the Oda, players should look to try the following strategies:

- **Attack Yamashiro**—If you have to attack one of the neighbouring Rebel states, then it might as well be Yamashiro. The bad news? This state is particularly well-garrisoned and, like Ise on the coast, it boasts a Buddhist Temple capable of producing Warrior Monk units. But the good news is that if you manage to conquer Yamashiro, the province is home to the Emperor's palace and all troops produced here gain +1 honour.

Invade Shikoku! Get there before the Mori do or face a costly battle to dig the Red troops out.

Yamashiro contains the Emperor's palace—any troops trained here receive +1 honour.

- **Invade Shikoku**—Like the Mori and the Shimazu, the Oda have access to the island of Shikoku via the smaller island of Awaji. By waging war against the Rebel-held lands, the Oda avoid a costly confrontation with any of the other clans, but do run the risk of antagonising the self-contained Rebel territories within its own empire.

- **Occupy Hida**—In the centre of Japan a fierce battle rages for control of Shinano. If this large state, famed for its cavalry, is taken from the Uesugi, then the land of Hida next to it is cut off and ripe for invasion.

- **Destroy the Imagawa**—As the game progresses, the Imagawa face an uphill battle to survive. Threatened by the Shimazu to the west and by the untrustworthy lord Takeda to the east, they pose a significant threat to Owari, the Oda capital. An Oda commander has several options: continually garrison a large army in Owari to deter an Imagawa invasion; invade Mikawa to secure Owari's borders; build troop-producing facilities elsewhere and turn Owari into a border post. If the Imagawa have already lost their lands in the west, they won't tolerate an invasion of Mikawa. An early strike, however, may just do the trick.

COMMANDING THE TAKEDA CLAN (BLACK)

Like the Imagawa, the Takeda empire is split between the lands of Aki, Bitchu and Bingo to the west, and Sagami, Kai and Izu in central Japan. Initially threatened on all sides, the Takeda nevertheless have access to a reasonable annual harvest of 1527 Koku which should be used to reinforce key areas of the Takeda domain. The Black armies are also famed for their cavalry units and the Takeda begin the campaign with a Horse Dojo already standing in Kai. With its lands in the west threatened by the Mori, Takeda commanders have to move quickly to secure their borders.

As Daimyo of the Takeda dynasty, players might like to try the following strategies:

- **Reinforce Aki**—A read-through of the Mori information will show you how easy it is to invade the Takeda's western lands, and Daimyo should use this knowledge to reinforce the troop levels in Aki. Not only does Aki's port generate an extra 200 Koku per year in trade, but it also has Silver deposits (which can add an extra 400 Koku). This alone is worth the loss of Bitchu and Bingo, so consider withdrawing troops from those lands to protect Aki's borders.

- **Attack Shinano**—With its reputation for Cavalry units (any produced here gain +1 honour), Shinano is a tempting target. As a clan, the Takeda can recruit and maintain Cavalry for a lower cost and the addition of a province with a cavalry bonus will add greatly to the Black empire. Be warned: the Imagawa clan also have their eyes on Shinano. Don't leave other lands unprotected at the expense of expansionist lust.

- **Attack Musashi**—While the Hojo clan to the east is certainly cash-rich, they initially lack a powerful standing army to match (only 491 men). Consequently, invading Musashi, with its basic annual yield of 640 Koku, would allow the Takeda to expand faster and also hit the Hojo's prospects. Taking Musashi, however, is one thing, holding onto it as the Hojo regain power is something else entirely.

- **Abandon central Japan**—It's a touch drastic, but another option open to Takeda commanders is to abandon the three central states in favour of a new empire based in Aki. From here, the lands of Iwami and Suo are vulnerable and the Takeda could use the tactics that apply to the Mori (see page 188).

STRATEGIES

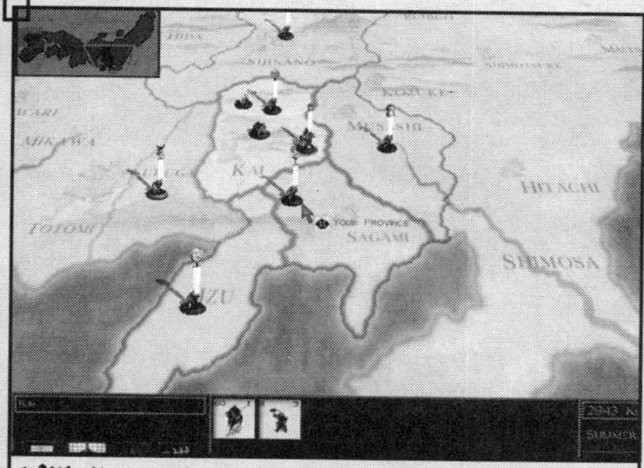

With its empire split in two, a Daimyo must keep an eye on events in both the west and the east.

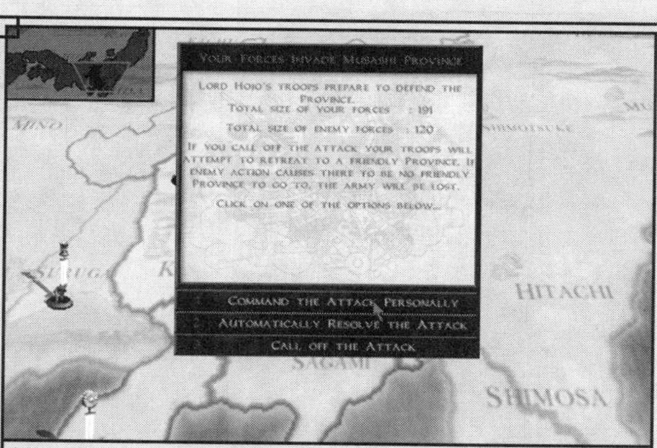

The Takeda need more land. See the poorly defended Hojo province of Musashi?

COMMANDING THE IMAGAWA CLAN (CYAN)

Like the Takeda clan on the previous page, the Imagawa's empire is split between three provinces in central Japan (Mikawa, Totomi, Suruga) and three on the island of Kyushu (Hizen, Chikugo, Chikuzen). From the very start, they face a fight to hold onto them — the Takeda desire new land to the east, while the Shimazu lust for control of the entire Kyushu region in the west. Their one saving grace is the fact that they start the Campaign game with an average income of 1947 Koku, allowing the Cyan forces to build quickly in the hope of reinforcing their fragile borders.

When controlling the Imagawa, players can try the following strategies:

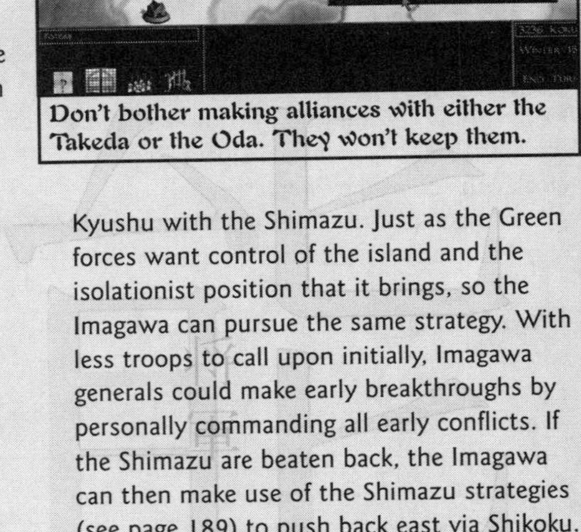

Don't bother making alliances with either the Takeda or the Oda. They won't keep them.

- **Abandon central Japan**—This tactic is less of a risk than the one suggested for the Takeda as the three lands on Kyushu contribute most of the Imagawa's wealth. Both Mikawa and Suruga could be lightly garrisoned, with a large standing army guarding the Port and troop-producing facilities in Totomi. The Imagawa can then transfer reinforcements to Hizen to protect the western empire from Shimazu attack.

- **Attack the Shimazu**—Continuing from the first strategy, the most obvious and perhaps safest strategy is to battle for control of Kyushu with the Shimazu. Just as the Green forces want control of the island and the isolationist position that it brings, so the Imagawa can pursue the same strategy. With less troops to call upon initially, Imagawa generals could make early breakthroughs by personally commanding all early conflicts. If the Shimazu are beaten back, the Imagawa can then make use of the Shimazu strategies (see page 189) to push back east via Shikoku. Or it can use the income generated by the nine Kyushu provinces to step up its presence in central Japan.

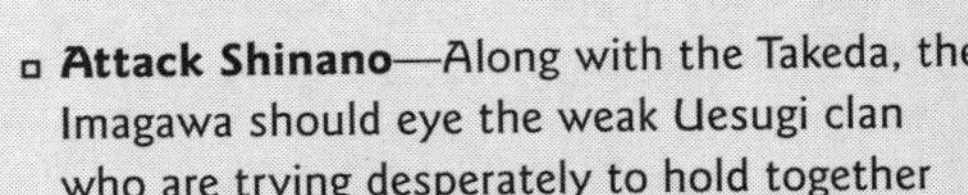

- **Attack Shinano**—Along with the Takeda, the Imagawa should eye the weak Uesugi clan who are trying desperately to hold together an empire that stretches from Mutsu in the east to Hida, north of Mikawa. By taking Shinano, not only do the Imagawa gain an extra 340 Koku per year, but they get the +1 honour Cavalry bonus when they have managed to build a Large Castle and a Horse Dojo.

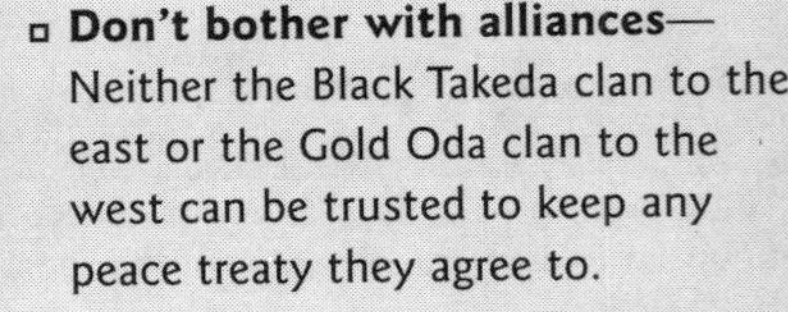

- **Don't bother with alliances**—Neither the Black Takeda clan to the east or the Gold Oda clan to the west can be trusted to keep any peace treaty they agree to.

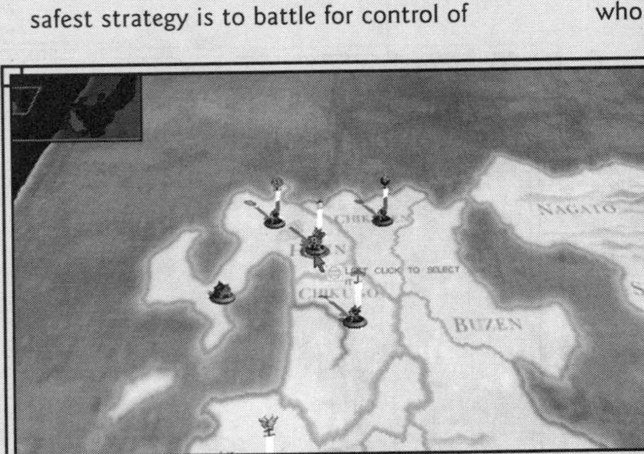

Abandon central Japan! Pack your bags and move your forces east to Hizen.

COMMANDING THE HOJO CLAN (PURPLE)

Despite the fact that the Hojo clan are the richest in Japan with an average annual income of 2360 Koku, they begin the campaign game with one of the smallest armies. As a result, the Hojo must be dedicated to consolidation rather than aggressive expansion in an attempt to retain what they have for now. As ruler of the six Hojo territories, the Purple Daimyo can sit safe within his borders for years, letting the other clans fight for land amongst themselves. At the start of the campaign, however, the Hojo will find it tricky just to hold onto their lands and some clever troop juggling is required to deter the Takeda from invading Musashi. To the north, the Uesugi have their own problems and, while they should not be ignored completely, Kozuke, Shimotsuke and Hitachi don't need to be guarded quite so fiercely.

When controlling the Hojo hordes, keep the following strategies in mind:

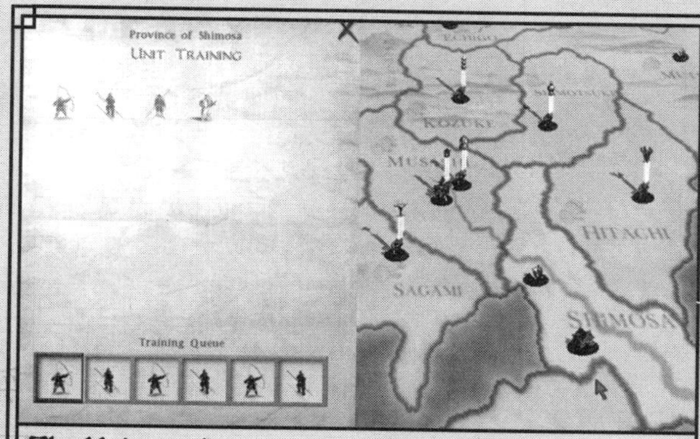

The Hojo need to consolidate their position to build up their forces before attacking their neighbours.

- **Consolidation**—While the other clans begin the merry-go-round of invasion, move as many troops as you can to garrison Musashi without leaving your other states vulnerable. Failure to do this will result in Lord Takeda charging across the border with his horse cavalry and the subsequent loss of 640 Koku per year. To replace the soldiers that you have moved, start a troop building program at the Castle in Shimosa. If possible, try to establish Castles in both Musashi and Hitachi.

- **Ally with the Uesugi**—While it may be tempting to gather your forces for an attack on the valuable Mutsu, this territory is the Uesugi capital and therefore well-defended at all times. By allying yourself with the Uesugi, you reduce the risk of an attack from the north, leaving you free to develop your empire's internal infrastructure.

- **Be a farmer!**—The Hojo need most of their forces just to hold onto the six provinces that they have, so it will take some time before there is enough of a surplus to challenge nearby states. During this period of intense consolidation, devote some of your annual harvest developing the farmland in both Hitachi and Musashi to boost the harvest. Even a 20 percent increase is a significant amount when applied to a province that already produces 640 Koku per year.

- **Develop Warrior Monks**—Along with No-Dachi samurai, Warrior Monks are one of the best units in the game. Unfortunately, they are expensive to access, requiring the construction of a Large Castle (1000 Koku) and a Buddhist Temple (1500 Koku). Of all the clans in the game, the Hojo are in the best position to develop Warrior Monks quickly. An army of Archers and Warrior Monks should finally allow the Hojo to break out of their borders. Sagami is a good first target.

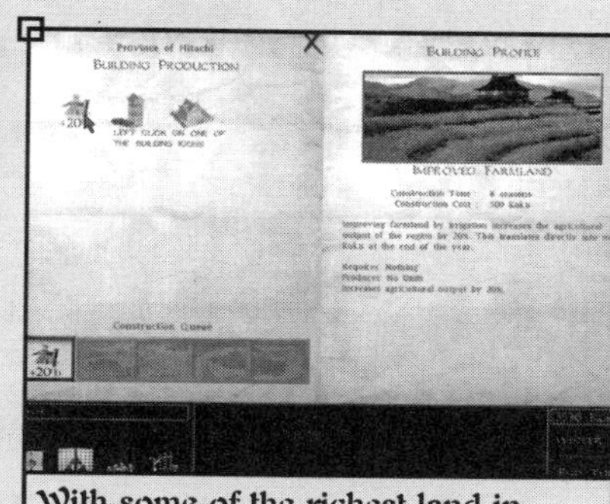

With some of the richest land in Japan, the Hojo provinces would benefit from farmland improvements.

COMMANDING THE UESUGI CLAN (DARK BLUE)

One of the biggest challenges in the game is taking command of the Uesugi empire. Admittedly they have the advantage of a large annual income—an average total of 2022 Koku. But they begin the game with a small standing army (551 men) and have to defend a sprawling empire that snakes halfway across the Japanese mainland from Dewa to Hida. It should come as no surprise to learn that, as the Uesugi Daimyo, you'll probably find yourself under fire at the end of the first season. Shinano, famed for its cavalry, is the likely battleground and if it falls, it cuts off the western province, Hida, from the Uesugi supply line.

When controlling the Uesugi, players might like to try the following:

- **Abandon Hida**—This province contributes barely 120 Koku on average to the Uesugi cause and any troops stationed here would be better off trying to defend Shinano from either Imagawa or Takeda attack. You don't need it now and you can always invade it again later.

- **Abandon Shinano and Hida**—Sometimes the best policy is one of consolidation and despite the loss of the 340 Koku that Shinano provides, the Uesugi can rely on an income of over 1500 Koku from Echigo, Dewa and Mutsu alone. By retreating from Shinano and Hida, the Uesugi can then pursue an isolationist policy of internal expansion, developing their high-yield farmland until they are powerful enough to expand westward.

- **Attack the Hojo**—The Hojo lands here are a tempting target, especially if the Hojo are being forced to stack up their forces in Musashi to deter a Takeda attack. Attacking and capturing Hitachi adds 620 Koku to the Uesugi coffers, while Shimotsuke or Kozuke can contribute 210 and 410 Koku respectively. Of course, with the Hojo's vast resources, the challenge is not to invade one of the Hojo's prized lands, but to keep hold of it.

- **Don't attack the Rebels!**—The Uesugi are hardly central Japan's favourite clan, so the last thing you need is a war with the Rebel states of Etchu, Noto, Kaga or Echizen. These states may seem like an easy option, but they are supplied from a Castle in Kaga that also has a Buddhist Temple. And a Buddhist Temple means Warrior Monks.

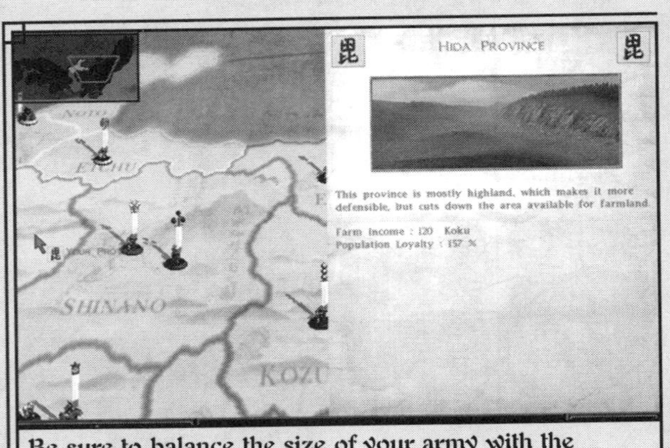

Be sure to balance the size of your army with the resources you have at your disposal.

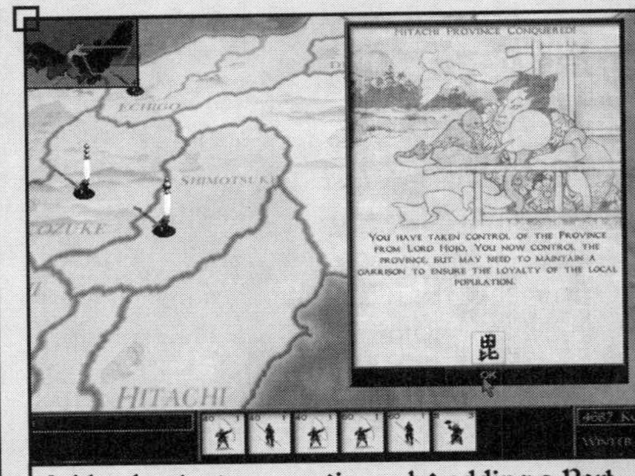

Add value to your provinces by adding a Port or an Mine (if applicable).

GENERAL CAMPAIGN STRATEGIES

- **Don't compromise your own security.** The key to playing the odds on the Strategy Map is balance, devoting time to both internal and external expansion. The worst mistake a Daimyo can make is to neglect his own security. This security aspect can take many forms, from the number of troops required to garrison a province to having an active Shinobi around to act as a counterspy.

- **An army marches on its stomach!** It's an old saying, but equally true of the tiny virtual, Samurai armies in *Shogun: Total War*. As Sun Tzu points out in *The Art of War*, the greater the size of the army, the greater the drain on your resources. If you allow your army to grow to such an extent that its maintenance costs are close to the average annual harvest, you will have no money left for new buildings or troops.

- **Keep adding value.** Extra money can be generated *without* continually invading new lands. Remember that Ports can add an extra 200 Koku per year, Mines up to 600 Koku and farmland improvements can boost a province's annual production by as much as 100 percent (which is still poor if it only produced 90 Koku per year to start off with).

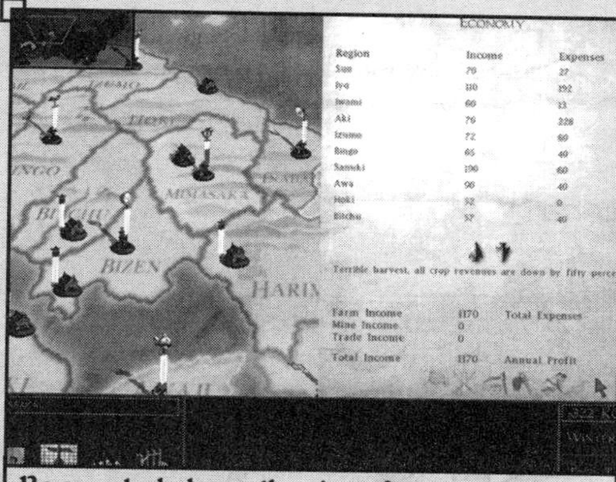

Be sure to balance the size of your army with the resources you have at your disposal.

- **Use your bonus.** Each one of the seven clans in the campaign game has been awarded its own bonus. The Green Shimazu clan, for example, can recruit and maintain No-Dachi Samurai for a lower cost, while the Oda clan can recruit and maintain Ashigaru in the same way.

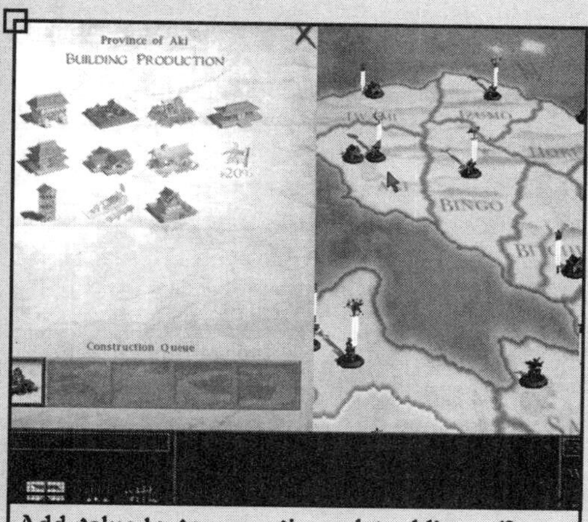

Add value to your provinces by adding a Port or an Mine (if applicable).

- **Learn the Five Advantages.** When planning your opening moves, remember that there will often be situations that should not be contested and areas that should not be attacked. Sun Tzu established what he called the Five Advantages. Through an understanding of these advantages, a cautious but effective strategy can be developed. The Five Advantages are:
  1. Knowing when you should and when you should not challenge.
  2. Recognising how to use the numerous and the few.
  3. Agreeing on superior and inferior objectives.
  4. Preparing to wait for the unprepared.
  5. Leading without influence from a ruler.

- **Know when to build and when *not* to build.** During the development of an empire, a certain degree of investment is required in infrastructure: new buildings, improvements to old buildings, extra troops, and special units. The key to maintaining growth in the campaign is knowing what to build and when. For example, it is well known that Warrior Monks are one of the most powerful units in the game, but they require an investment of 2500 Koku and 18 seasons of game time before you can access them. Naturally, while a province is undertaking one building project, it cannot build anything else until the current project is completed. What you build depends on your strategic situation, the clan you have chosen to command and how much money is available. As a general guide, Daimyo should look to invest in the following:

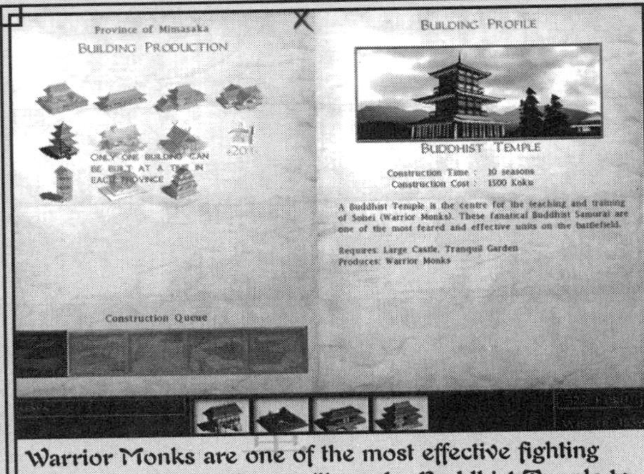

Warrior Monks are one of the most effective fighting units in the game. But you'll need a Buddhist Temple to train them.

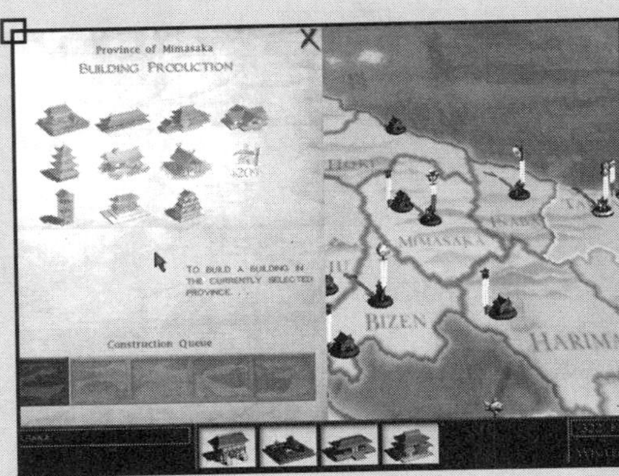

The harder the difficulty level, the less Koku you start with. But a Large Castle is essential.

Large Castle—this enables you to build the Buddhist Temple.
Buddhist Temple—this enables you to produce Warrior Monks.
Ninja House—this enables you to produce Ninja assassins who can also double as Shinobi-style security forces.
Border Watch Towers—decide where to mark your borders and build a Watch Tower there to keep an eye on enemy troop movements.

- **Make full use of Castles.** Costing only 500 Koku and built quickly within a year, a Castle is an excellent way of both protecting a province and ensuring population loyalty within it. Once a Castle is built, a Daimyo can add extra troop-producing facilities. Limiting yourself to the one Spear and Archery Dojo that you receive at the start of the game means that you can only build one unit at a time, either a Yari Samurai or a Samurai Archer. By adding extra Castles to your empire, you can add a number of extra Dojos, allowing armies to be raised much more quickly.

Building a Castle in a captured province helps ensure and maintain population loyalty.

- **Be aware of frontiers.** Even if you are planning to invade a neighbouring state, mentally mark out the provinces you consider your frontiers. A Shimazu Daimyo, for example, should reinforce Bungo (checking Rebel expansion) and Nagato (halting the Mori charge). This setup is based on the fact that any Shimazu Daimyo will plan the complete annihilation of the Imagawa clan who infest one corner of Kyushu island. While new Castles should be built, there is a strong argument for never adding any further buildings to an established frontier province. If an enemy invaded such a territory (i.e. with only a Castle in it), the Castle would be able to hold out until reinforcements arrived. A territory with a Castle and a Spear Dojo would see its second building destroyed upon a successful invasion. If you can't defend a frontier continually and strongly, it's money down the 16th Century Japanese equivalent of the drain.

- **Levy taxes.** Each year, a Daimyo, by clicking on the Koku button, can set the level of tax that he wishes his people to pay. The higher the tax, the faster a province's population loyalty percentage falls. Keep taxes set at the Normal level for the first few years, reducing them as your empire expands and you have more access to money. If you must raise taxes to fund emergency troop or building production, try not to keep them high for more than one year at a time. To access the Taxes menu, click the Koku button above the Season indicator and End Turn button.

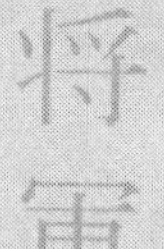

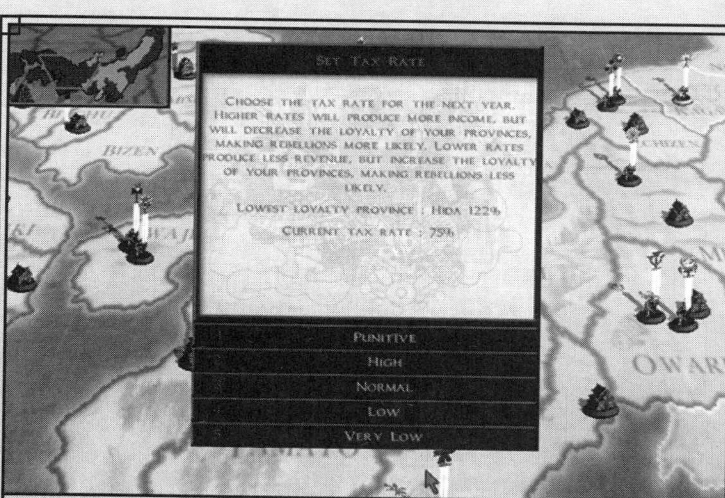

Tax your people intelligently—too high and they'll revolt, too low and your harvest will suffer.

STRATEGIES

Station a large army in the province with the Large Castle, ready to defend any of the outer Castles.

- **Follow the "satellite" system.** One of the most efficient ways to protect your provinces is to build a ring of small Castles around a much larger, base Castle. During the 16th Century, the Hojo clan reportedly employed a system where they developed a central castle and encircled it with small satellite fortifications.

There are a number of advantages of this satellite system. In the example shown here (see picture), the Mori have constructed a Large Castle in Mimaska and surrounded it with small Castles in Harima, Inaba, Bizen, Bitchu and Hoki. Each of these smaller forts is garrisoned by a skeleton force—typically a single Ashigaru unit. Manned in this way, by right-clicking on the Castle you can see how long the Ashigaru are likely to hold out if attacked (here, three seasons). Meanwhile, in the centre of the ring, the Mori maintain a single force of 440 men, perfectly positioned to reinforce whichever satellite Castle is attacked. In this way, six provinces are protected without the need for six giant and costly armies. By building Castles in frontier locations, the Mori can delay the invasion of a external force long enough for troops to be diverted to counter it. And lastly, by only having one unit standing guard in a frontier castle, the neighbouring clan doesn't build up a huge army of his own to counter the perceived threat of your defending force.

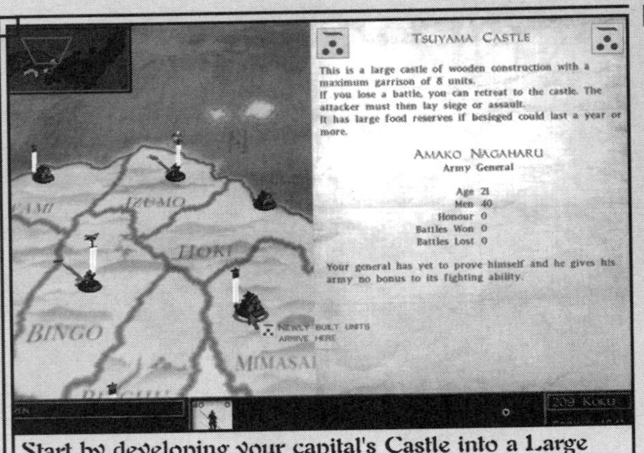

Start by developing your capital's Castle into a Large Castle (1000 Koku).

Build smaller Castles (500 Koku) in the provinces immediately surrounding the area around the Large Castle.

- **Forge alliances.** By reading the descriptions of the seven clans (see page 84), you'll be able to see which rival clans will keep to the peace treaties that they sign. Of the seven, the isolationist Shimazu are the most trustworthy, while at the other end of the scale, the Oda and particularly the Takeda value alliances as much as the parchment they are written on. In short, once you have signed a treaty with another clan, don't take it seriously. They break alliances as easily as they offer them.

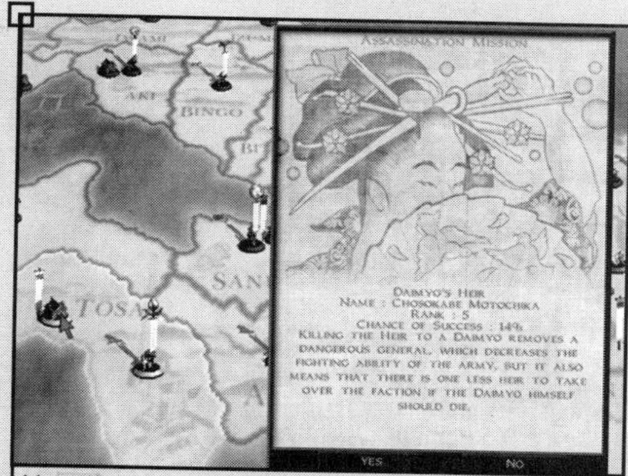

Use the "Special Units" (i.e. Shinobi, Ninja and Emissaries) to complement your military might.

- **Utilise special units.** One of the things that gives the Campaign extra depth is the availability of special units. These units, the Shinobi, Ninja, Emissary, Priest and the Legendary Geisha, can be vital to a general's success on the strategy map. Of all of them, make sure you have the facilities to build Shinobi, Ninja and Emissaries. Although Ninja can double as Shinobi, only by first developing the Tea House can you access the Geisha House to then produce the Legendary Geisha.

- **Continuously improve units.** If you have money to spare, invest in an Armoury (if Iron and Sand deposits exist) and a Swordsmith. Building and developing these two facilities enhances both the offensive and defensive prowess of your units by equipping them with superior armour and weaponry.

- **Be aware of the importance of honour.** The higher a unit's honour, the more experienced they are and the better they are in combat. If a general who has a high honour is leading an army, he will transfer some of that honour to the men that he commands. When one of your generals reaches an honour level of three or above, make sure that you assign Shinobi or Ninja units to him which can act as security against enemy Ninja (which are invisible to you on the strategy map). Once an army becomes large enough and powerful enough, it should always have its own Ninja and Shinobi escort (see The Perfect Army on page 200). Finally, should a general with high honour lead from the front or sit safely at the back of the battle on a folding stool? Tokugawa Ieysau is on record of having said, "No commander can conquer by gazing at men's backs..."

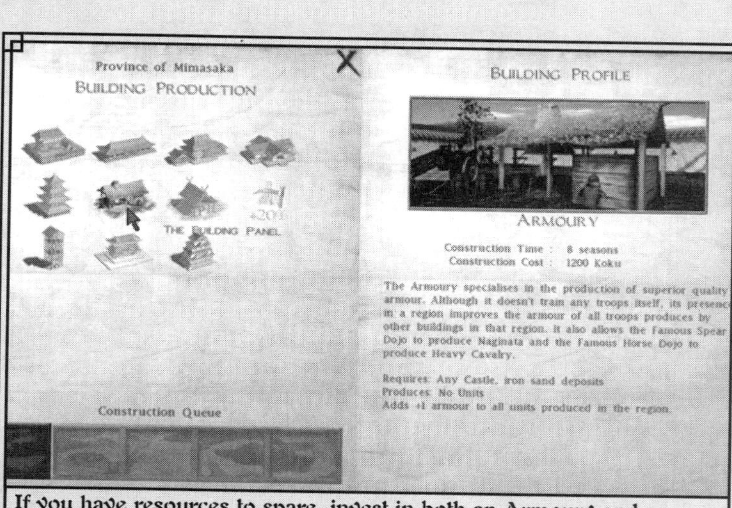

If you have resources to spare, invest in both an Armoury and a Swordsmith to improve the strength of your troops.

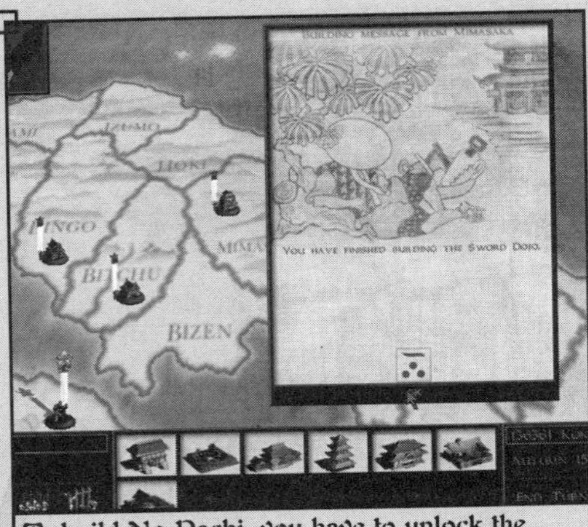

To build No-Dachi, you have to unlock the Legendary Swordsman Event.

- **Activate the Legendary Swordsman Event.** To access the No-Dachi unit, you first need to activate the Legendary Swordsman Event. Unlike Warrior Monks who can be built as soon as you have constructed a Buddhist Temple, or Cavalry units which require a Horse Dojo, you do not have the opportunity to build a Sword Dojo until one of your soldiers has proved himself repeatedly in battle. Thus, when you have a veteran unit that has won several major battles, one of the soldiers may decide to found a Sword Dojo. This event occurs when a Samurai has reached an Honour level of two or above, and once achieved the option to build a Sword Dojo (which allows you to produce No-Dachi units) appears on the Building Production menu. Note: a Large Castle is also required to access a Sword Dojo.

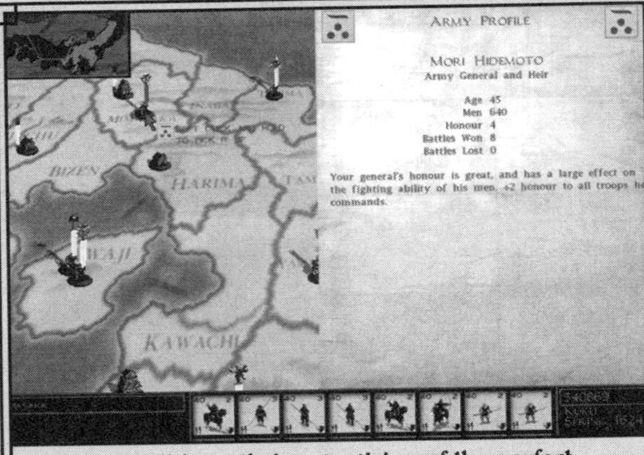

Everyone will have their own vision of the perfect army, but here's ours.

- **Creating the perfect army.** Is there really such a thing? Perhaps not, as everybody has their own way of playing *Shogun: Total War* and therefore relies on different units to get the job done. Our example of the perfect fighting force takes into account the simple fact that you need to use a combination of units. As each army counter on the strategy map can support up to 16 different units, our army would look something like this:

4X Samurai Archers
6X Warrior Monks
1X Ashigaru
2X Yari Samurai
2X Heavy Cavalry
1X Cavalry Archers

In addition to these 16 military units, the army would be accompanied by three Shinobi (for counter-intelligence), two Ninja (for assassination missions) and an Emissary (both to spy on enemy troops and to propose cease-fire treaties). There is a good balance to this army, featuring scouting units (Cavalry Archers), raw power (Warrior Monks, Heavy Cavalry), plus missile troops (samurai Archers), defensive Footsoldiers (Yari samurai) and an expendable unit (Yari Ashigaru). For provinces that feature a bridge, the armoured Naginata unit replaces the Yari samurai.

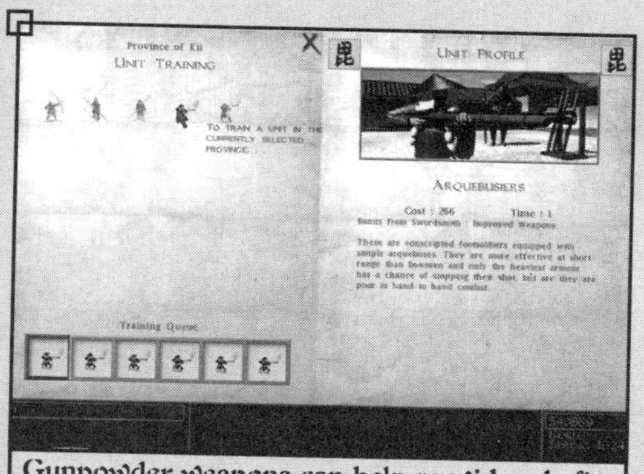

Gunpowder weapons can help provide a hefty battlefield advantage but beware: they don't work when it rains.

- **Go back to go forward.** As far as the expansionist strategy is concerned, it is important to analyse your overall situation before you attack. Sun Tzu was a great believer in focusing on the enemy as a whole rather than just a small part of it. With this in mind, a Mori Daimyo planning to attack the Rebel-held Sanuki on Shikoku needs take into account several factors. Are there enough troops in Sanuki to defeat me? Are there enough troops in the areas surrounding Sanuki to defeat me? What impact does the movement of these troops have on my own empire? Are any of my defences weakened as a result? Lastly, what sort of effect does this have on the neighbouring clans and are they in a position to do anything about it?

Sun Tzu said that no single part of a system can triumph at the expense of another part. Again, it is all about striking a balance. Sometimes it is even worth abandoning a province in order to ensure that another is suitably defended.

- **Make use of gunpowder weapons.** The arrival of Portuguese traders and the Arquebus forever changed the face of Japanese warfare. The big question that needs to be addressed in *Shogun: Total War* is this: are guns really worth the effort? Because this game is a simulation, the effect of the Arquebus (and later the Musket) on the battlefield is not as devastating as you might think. While massed gunfire (from four or more units) can be effective on flat landscapes, the guns in the game fail to work when it rains and take much longer to reload than the bow. Worse still, an Ashigaru who carries an Arquebus or Musket is considerably worse in hand-to-hand combat situations than the bowman of old, and so despite the introduction of guns, the bow still has a role to play on the battlefield. Still, because Arquebusier and Musketeer units are cheap, make up for their lack of accuracy by having lots of them.

Analyse your strategic situation *before* you attack a new province. See the whole picture, not just the local politics.

TRIUMPH

将軍 将軍 将軍 将軍

勝利

将軍 将軍 将軍

To lift an autumn leaf is not an act
of great strength.
To see the sun and moon is not an act
of sharp sight.
To hear a sudden thunderclap is not an
act of acute listening.

Those whom the Ancient Ones called
"Skilled in Conflict",
Are those who triumph because
triumph is easy.

Sun Tzu (translated by R.L. Wing in "The Art of Strategy")

CUSTOM BATTLES

Sun Tzu believed that for a skilled strategist, triumph was easy. To engage an opposing force without the knowledge that your planning and tactics will make you victorious is, he advised, a foolish strategy. But, to make triumph seem as effortless as the great generals that Sun Tzu describes, you must first put in the practice. Understanding how the battle system in *Shogun: Total War* works is but the first step. Understanding how to master it is a much bigger challenge, and nothing counts as much as experience.

If practice makes perfect, you can fight anywhere with anything in a Custom Battle.

Fortunately, there's an easy way to prepare yourself for the Historical and Campaign challenges that lie ahead. By choosing the New Game option and then Custom Battles you enter the *Shogun* "battle builder". This is a section of the simulation that lets you generate a battle on any of the featured landscapes (Historical, Campaign and Tutorial battlefields included), with any of the basic troop types and in any of the seasons. Thus, you can see how Warrior Monks match up to No-Dachi samurai; how Naginata cope against the ordered ranks of Arquebusiers; or what would happen if 1000 Heavy Cavalry faced 1000 Heavy Cavalry in the middle of a rainstorm. By playing around with the options available in the Custom Battles section, you can recreate any battle or scenario, honing your tactical skills so that when you face the situation for real in the Campaign mode, you'll know exactly what to do.

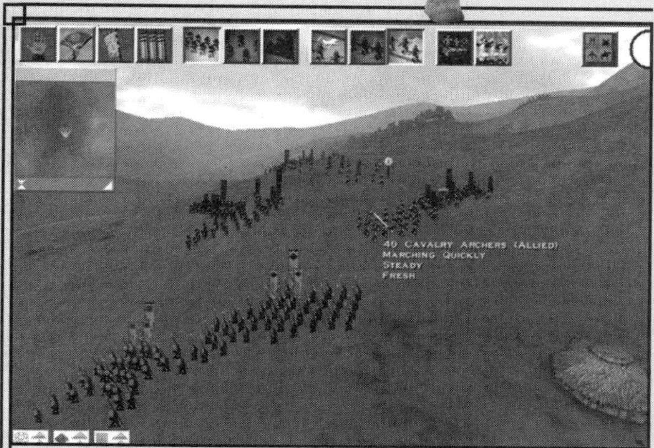

Prepare yourself for the Campaign and Historical Battles in the Custom Battle option.

CUSTOM BATTLE MENU

Creating a new Custom Battle in *Shogun: Total War* is a simple ten-step process. Follow the simple walkthrough below to generate a new battle scenario.

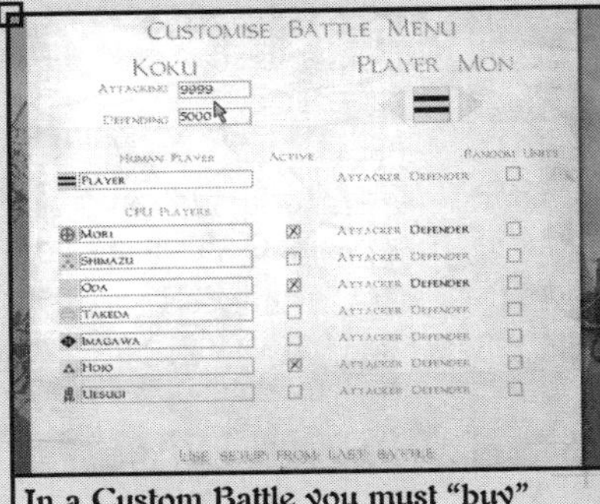

In a Custom Battle you must "buy" your units. Adjust the amount of Koku you want to use here.

1. CHOOSE THE NUMBER OF KOKU (MAX: 99,999)

In a Custom Battle, much like a mini-Campaign, you buy the units you want to use. In the two Koku boxes you can specify how many resources a commander has to spend on troops. For a straight fight, keep the 5,000 Koku default for both sides. Adjust this if you want to create an imbalance or like the idea of battling with more expensive soldiers.

2. CHOOSE A PLAYER MON

In this mode you can choose to command one of the seven clans featured in the Campaign, plus the rebellious forces of the Peasants and Ronin. Select an army banner from: Mori, Shimazu, Oda, Takeda, Imagawa, Hojo and Uesugi clans, plus the Peasants and Ronin.

3. ATTACKING AND DEFENDING

Once you've chosen which army you would like to control, you can then specify yourself as either the Attacker or the Defender. Similarly, you can also add extra CPU players to your battle, either as your allies or your enemies.

4. RANDOM UNITS

Just to make things interesting (and a real test of your tactical skills), by clicking on the Random Units option next to an army, you can let the computer randomly generate your forces spending up to the value of your specified Koku

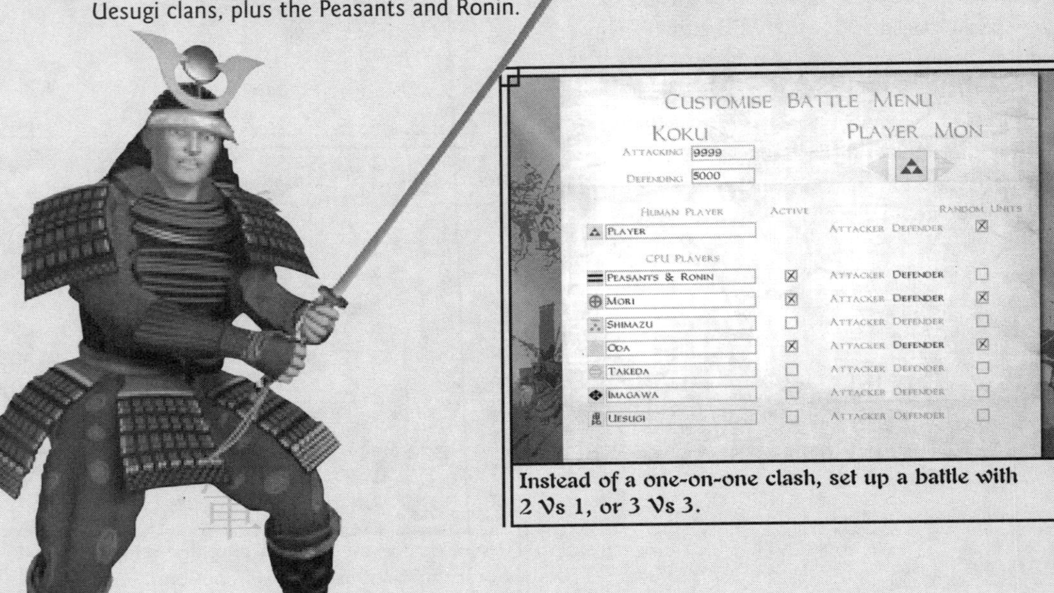

Instead of a one-on-one clash, set up a battle with 2 Vs 1, or 3 Vs 3.

5. WHERE TO FIGHT?

On the following screen, you can select not only where you fight, but at what time of year and on what difficulty level. To start with, choose a battleground from the scrollable list on the left-hand side of the screen. All of *Shogun's* featured landscapes are included here: the three tutorial maps, the six Historical Battle scenarios, the 60 Campaign provinces, plus 16 separate Castle locations.

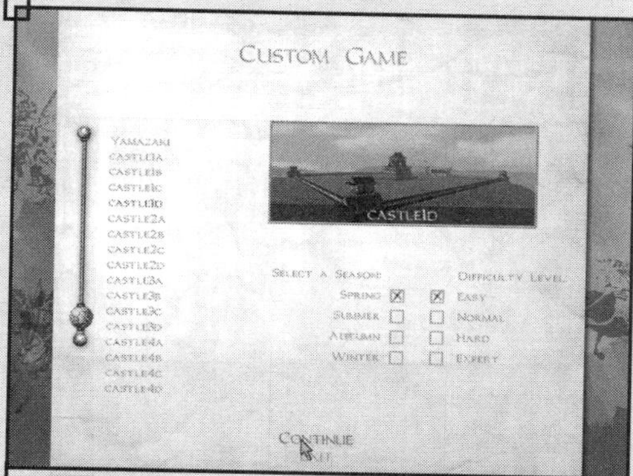

The Custom Battle option allows you to fight on any landscape featured in the game.

6. WHEN TO FIGHT?

Before you move onto the next screen by clicking on "Continue", you'll notice that you also have the option to specify what season you wish the Custom Battle to be fought in: spring, summer, autumn, winter. Each season has its own associated weather conditions (i.e. snow in winter, rain in the spring), all of which can affect the way that a battle is played out.

7. THE DIFFICULTY LEVEL

Lastly on this screen, you can select one of four difficulty levels: Easy, Normal, Hard and Expert.

8. CUSTOMISING YOUR ARMY

Unless you chose to use random units, the Custom Battle mode then lets you specify the types of troops you want to have in your army. All eleven basic units are available and can be purchased using money from the Koku store that you specified earlier. You can also purchase extra honour for your units to make them more effective in battle. The costs of the basic units are detailed on the next page. Note: the first unit displayed is designed as your command unit, or Taisho. Make certain that you spend some money giving it a high honour value which will help inspire the troops around it in battle.

Adjust the composition and the honour of your troops before entering into battle.

BASIC UNIT COSTS

Yari Ashigaru	100 Koku
Yari Samurai	200 Koku
Samurai Archers	300 Koku
Naginata	400 Koku
No-Dachi Samurai	300 Koku
Warrior Monks	500 Koku
Cavalry Archers	500 Koku
Heavy Cavalry	600 Koku
Yari Cavalry	500 Koku
Arquebusiers	100 Koku
Musketeers	175 Koku

The Arquebus is not too powerful so the units carrying it are cheap.

9. HONOUR RATING

Each unit is available with a default honour rating of 2. However, extra honour can be added (or removed) by clicking on the left/right arrows either side of the word "Honour" above the troop display. A custom army can feature a maximum of 16 different units, and the value of the army cannot exceed the amount of Koku defined on the opening Custom Battle screen.

10. FIGHT

Click "Ready" and play the battle as you would play a Historical Battle or Campaign confrontation. All the usual rules apply.

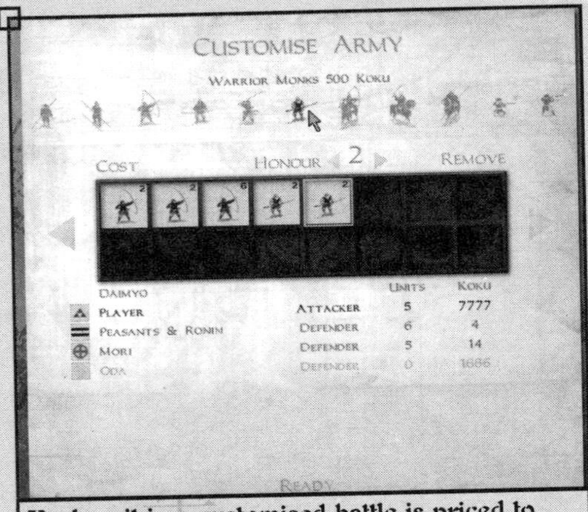

Each unit in a customised battle is priced to reflect its effectiveness (i.e. Warrior Monks, 500 Koku).

CUSTOM BATTLES

For a good, educational workout, there are several things that you can use the Custom Battles mode for to help you play both the Historical Battle and Campaign options. For example, you can test out your strategies on a variety of different landscapes, so that you're well prepared for any eventuality. Choose the Bitchu province to practise attacking or defending a single river crossing, or the Anegawa battlefield that features three separate bridges. Practise defending and attacking an army on relatively flat ground by selecting the Totomi province, while the Osumi territory provides a challenge with its undulating terrain and jutting peaks. Last, and by no means least, there are 16 Castle scenarios to try. Make sure you play as both defender and attacker so you can see what is required of a general in both situations.

To really test your skills, pit yourself against a computer opponent with *random* armies.

Most importantly, the Custom Battles section allows you to test out formations and troop types and to discover which units best suit your strategic approach. A sample 10-unit force, for example, might consist of four units of samurai Archers, two units of Warrior Monks, two of Yari samurai, plus a Cavalry Archer and Heavy Cavalry unit. As a basic army, this sort of unit combination works surprisingly well—the Archers provide ranged weapon support for the first wave of Warrior Monks, followed by Yari samurai. Cavalry Archers harass the flanks of the opposing force, while the Heavy Cavalry are either kept in reserve or sent around the back of the opponent to mount a devastating rear attack. Should some Naginata be included in case you need to invade via a bridge? Should the Monks be replaced with No-Dachi? The Custom Battles option allows you to experiment.

Build yourself a bridge-based scenario to test out your tactics in simulated safety.

MULTIPLAYER

As if the three varieties of single player weren't entertainment enough, you can also play *Shogun: Total War* over the Internet or via a Local Area Network (LAN). Consequently, you can log on and pit your strategies and tactics against other human players—commanders who aren't as easily bamboozled by the fog as the computer AI, or place their faith in the Arquebus during rainstorm. When playing via a LAN you can compete in single battles that can feature up to eight players. On the Internet, the dedicated EA Net server hosts a persistent on-line game, where players take on a family name and compete for total dominance through total warfare.

To access this Multiplayer world, click the Multiplayer option on the Main Menu screen where you will be given a choice of the following:

Play on EA Net
Log onto the dedicated EA server and join other players in a massive on-line version of the game. Play on EA Net to see how you rank against other human players and to compete for additional honour and cool prizes. Note: you must enter your CD serial code to access EA Net.

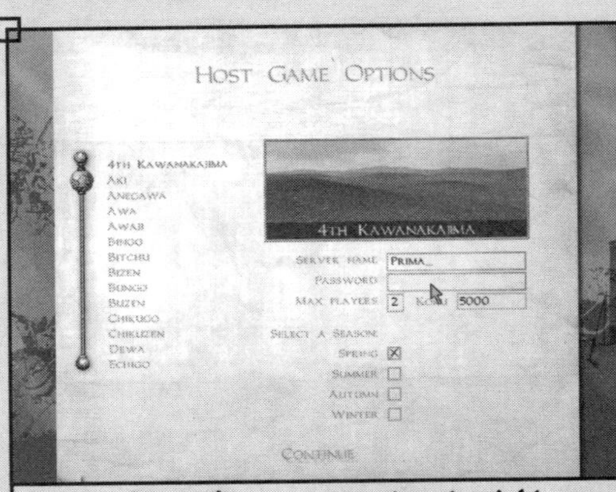

Shogun: Total War **can support up to eight players simultaneously for LAN-based gaming.**

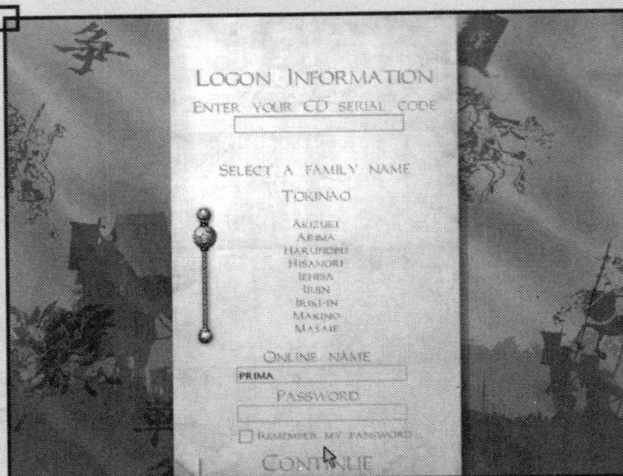

Select a clan name and enter your CD's serial code to access multiplayer on EA Net.

LAN Game
Join or host a Local Area Network game for up to eight players. Fight using any of the eleven basic troop types on any of the game's featured battlescapes.

Shogun **Website**
Click here for a direct link to the official *Shogun: Total War* website at http://www.totalwar.com

Shogun News Server
Click here to receive the latest bulletins about the game, EA Net and anything else relevant to the game.

Dial-Up Adapter
Before you can connect to the Internet to play *Shogun: Total War* on EA Net, you will need to specify your computer's modem connection. This option will automatically detect your PC's dial-up settings, so simply select the one that you wish to use.